ACCORDING TO SOLEDAD

Memories of a Mexican childhood

ACCORDING TO SOLEDAD

Memories of a Mexican childhood

KATIE GOODRIDGE INGRAM

SB

SOMBRERO BOOKS, B.C., CANADA

Cataloguing in Publication

Ingram, Katie Goodridge, author
    According to Soledad: memories of a Mexican childhood
/ Katie Goodridge Ingram

Issued in print and electronic formats.
ISBN 978-1-7770381-0-6 (paperback).--ISBN 978-1-7770381-1-3 (ebook)

1. Mexico--Memoir. 2. Mexico--Jalisco--Lake Chapala
3. Mexico--Mexico City.
4. Mexico--Artists and Authors.   I. Title.

Cover photo of girl on Ajijic pier (photographer unknown) is a family photo in possession of the author.

ISBN 978-1-7770381-0-6
First edition 2020
Text © 2020 by Katie Goodridge Ingram / Sombrero Books

With gratitude to my children and to my husband for their loving support

PART ONE ~ MEXICO CITY

PART TWO ~ LAKE CHAPALA

Soledad. Girl's name.
Nicknames: Sol, Sole,
Solcito, Sol, Chole,
Choli.

so·le·dad f. = 1. solitude, solitariness,
loneliness. 2. solitary or lonely place.
3. grieving, bereavement, mourning.

ACCORDING TO SOLEDAD

Memories of a Mexican childhood

PART ONE ~ MEXICO CITY

1

Who We Are

Ni fu, ni fa
Neither fish nor fowl
—Mexican expression

My father is a Book Man. He specializes in old books. The earliest books printed with moveable type are one of his specialties. His other specialty, and my mother's passion, are the *codices,* books from before Columbus that Aztecs and Mixtecs painted on fig bark, describing everything in their lives.

He is a hunter. I have postcards from Guatemala, Chiapas, Salt Lake City, St. Louis, New York City and more—the places he goes to hunt for the oldest of books, for books he loves and for the books he needs for his clients. He is a treasure hunter. He says all his friends are bibliophiles. But it's not just a love for books. He says they all have "a gentle madness." From his hunting spots he sends my mother packages and letters about his finds, even saying who would love them, who might buy them, and sometimes how much they are worth so my mother won't sell them for too little.

He is also a writer, so he always takes a small typewriter with him. Even the postcards he sends are typed. At the top are names like Tegucigalpa and Tuxtla Gutiérrez that tell where he is. The lines are tight together to say what bad luck he has had, and even to give the date but for some reason never the year. On the other side he types my name and my address:

```
Soledad Paz
Malinche #19
Coyoacán
México D.F., México
```

He is an adventurer. He was in Guatemala when there were shootings right in the plaza for a revolution, in Honduras when there were dozens of mysterious murders, and even in the hospital in Utah when his blood got too thick because he was addicted to salt.

He hunts and searches and travels. He goes away so much that I dislike his suitcases and even the reasons he gives for leaving, which are that if we want new shoes he has to buy books, find books, sell books, bring books home and bring strangers into the house to peck at his shelves—the shelves he built because he is a carpenter.

He also writes for newspapers, sometimes in English and sometimes in Spanish. Although he was born in New York City of Spanish and Southern roots, he and my mother make their life in Mexico. He has professors to teach him the best Mexican Spanish, and he himself works at learning Spanish so well it can be read by people whose whole education is in Spanish. He writes his own catalogs and letters, but he and my mother still speak with an accent and I think they sound funny.

My mother is a Dress Designer. That is what she was in New York City. It is not what she is now. She learns about books and customers, but she can still design anything from a gown to a house. Because thieves break into our house, she goes to the Club de Tiro to practice shooting pistols with Helen O'Gorman and Annette Stephens. My father calls them The Three Flames because they all have wild crowns of red hair. She drives so she takes me to ballet and my brother to Scouts and she takes turns with other parents driving us to school. Mechanics are not honest with her because she's a woman, so she takes classes with Anita Brenner and other friends. They learn to take engines apart, Mama says, and to figure out why cars don't start. She also writes for a newspaper to earn a little money for when my father is hunting and nothing sells. She does more than all of that, with three children and clothes to mend. People always think she is rich or famous. She makes friends from ambassadors to refugees because she has her own gentle madness to know and to be known. She is a magnet. In my parents' house, there are always artists, painters or writers. You see both the famous and the unknown. They seem to land here from all over the world.

My skin is white but my soul is brown. I know I am neither this nor that—*ni fu ni fa*. "Not fish nor fowl," my father says. At first, it's hard to tell about the solitude of how I feel different and alone, but people make choices about me. People choose you because they think they see you. They don't choose you because they know you. If they think your parents are white, then they treat you as if all of you is white. They don't understand how brown comes into the soul. Some hear brown in your laugh and choose all of you as brown. Some can't make up their minds, and their parents can't make up their minds and you become invisible. I like magic, but not that kind.

My parents are not really Mexican nor really American. Probably they have to be *gringos* because, whether I like it or not, they were not born in Mexico.

I was born in Mexico, but it does not make me a real *mexicana*. My father's black hair might be partly from Spain, but my mother reminds him that, who knows?, he might be Black Irish from an old family immigrant to New York. My mother's red hair and green eyes might be from the French, but she looks like Irish portraits. My father says she comes from Vikings. My older brother's hair is white—white like the *viejita's,* who never leaves her house. Some mornings we see her white head as she opens a second-story window to empty her chamber pot of night waters. For his white

hair they call my brother "*El Viejito.*" My little brother Amado is
just amado—beloved. He doesn't have nicknames. I don't know if
I have a nickname. Sometimes you are the last to know and that's
probably a good thing.

At first, it is hard to tell about *ni fu ni fa*. People might have
no marks, no special names, no clear labels. I collect the times that
feel like *fu* the way I collect coins, hidden in a velvet cloth and kept
in a shoebox. I keep the times that feel like *fa* between mental
cellophane sheets, the way I collect stamps. Sometimes, you look
at yourself and you are a blank. Then people's eyes start to decide
who you are. Some see a *gringa*. Others see another side of you, and
they guess *mexicana*. Neither word is your real self or your name.
Your REAL name is *gringicana*. Of course, you never say it. Who
will tell you if you are *fu* or *fa*? Who will let you claim a true place
between *fu* and *fa*? No one. Only I can. Because I include what
cannot be seen. I know I am *gringicana*.

I don't say it, and I won't tell about it. It will hide who I am
right in front of me, and it will keep inside me everything I love.

From my father I have the taste, the flavor of words, words that
have a sting, that have the caress of magical powers. Of course,
he always insists that we speak and write well in Spanish and in
English, even when we don't yet know how to say everything. *Gracias a Dios* I can at least spell better than my older brother Primo.
Otherwise he is the favorite in all things. I hide what I take from
my mother. From her I have the pain of hanging between grace
and the danger of what people might think, even though she is so
brave, so outrageous and surprising. The danger never stops her.
And all the time, even when she is her most amazing, she still
wants us to live properly in places where we use Spanish and even
more properly in places where we use English.

Because of my nurse Pilar, my soul is brown. I am *pilareña*
because of her ways, her cactus fruit and the secrets of corn mold
melting in a handmade tortilla. Because I was born in Mexico
City, I am *chilanga* but the city is indifferent to us who are *ni*

fu ni fa. Because of my time on the shores of Lake Chapala I am *ribereña*. I have soaked in the waves and sunk deep into the mud of the south shore to bring up with my toes the molars of mammoths and mastodons even though they died in different times. As a girl child I bear the curse of not being completed, not sewn up, of being flawed and vulnerable. Words are everywhere for how females are different. There are names for man and boy parts, and boys think it's funny to say them. But they love to whisper or shout the words for girl parts and it is not funny for girls to hear them. Everywhere you go, instead of a whistle, instead of your name, you hear the words. You turn the corner and someone asks for your taco. Or boys yell to each other, *"Ay, mamacita!"* as if they had the power to make you a little mother. *Taco, pan, pucha, panocha, mamey.* Sometimes I feel naked walking down a village street or in a crowded barrio, as if every boy or man can see through my clothes, as if I cannot even look at the fruit vendor's stand or wait in front of a bakery trying to make up my mind what to buy. Suddenly the rolls and pastries are private parts. If my little brother is with me they call him *cuñado* and ask him when he is going to give me to them in marriage. You are what "they" want you to be—female. And in those times I hate words and wish fruits and breads had no names and had no shapes and that our bodies did not live so loud in the outside world.

They say some men blame Malinche, saying that her woman-wound made men love war and blood and death—as if without her flaw they would have had a new Cortés, no greed for gold, no sacrifices to scream to the thousand gods, and no endless hungers of the new church.

We live on Avenida Malintzin, the street bearing Malinche's Indian name, in Coyoacán, the place named by the Aztecs for hungry coyotes, at the edge of Mexico City.

We write Malinche or Malintzin as our address on envelopes and letters. The *"tzin"* part says her father was royal. We say the word to the telephone man, the mailman, our teachers, the garbage man and to the men who collect broken glass. The dot where I am on the face of the world is that word, her name, both loathed and honored. Maybe even Huitzilopochtli, the God of War, fed from her hand.

To some, Malintzin was The Mother of Mexico After the Conquest. Others called her a traitor and also all the worst words they used for women. Sometimes I am sure she is my sad guide and in dreams it seems I carry her inside. At other times I think she is the Goddess of Things That Fall Apart. She had the skin I wanted. She traded it to be the connection between Tenochtitlan and Spain—Moctezuma and Cortés. Above all, she was The Queen of Words. She learned Spanish and she knew the languages from the kingdoms around Tenochtitlan. For Cortés she was the ambassador of conciliation and defeat. With both hands, with all of her gifts, she ate the still-beating heart of my Mexico.

Because we live on a street called Malinche and not on a street named for flowers leading to the market in Coyoacán, and not on a street named for water leading to the floating gardens of Xochimilco, life will be what it will be for my family and with the men in white.

2

Adventures of a Treasure Hunter

El libro es la voz del pensamiento
A book is the voice of the mind

—Mexican saying

Primo and I can't wait to hear the stories of Daddy the Treasure Hunter. Every time Daddy comes home he tells us about his adventures. Mama says he lives for close calls, a road falling away, a bus on a precipice, soldiers holding him up in Guatemala, highwaymen stealing from everyone in the train car. Mama has her stories too, and she writes parts of them down, but mostly she herself is a story. When Daddy tells his tales it's our job to remember them. It's important because although he seems to be telling them to us he's really practicing. He's going to write them all down some day, he says, and send them to a publisher because my grandmother says he has the gift. He has a list of titles: "Adventures of a Bookman," "Señor, My Books are Your Books," "Pigs Need Coffee Too," and "Books? What for?" His eyes look at us, twinkle and turn away, searching for the next words. He laughs here and there in his story. I don't know why. When he says, "Wasn't that funny?" Primo seems to know. As my father speaks he holds his older son by the shoulder, his little man, the boy to whom he is really telling the tales. We sit wedged into Daddy's wide velvet chair of gold and brown needle-thin stripes. It is his favorite place for stories. I am there, listening, though I feel extra, *de pilón,* not really needed. It doesn't matter. I get to hear his voice. It's soft and low. He sounds like an Englishman because of his southern accent. He says "fathah" and "mothah" and tries to get us to do the same. "Not firrrst," he says, correcting us. "Say 'fuhst'."

"When are you going to tell us more about hunting for books?" Primo says.

"Right now. I came to a clutch of huts after I left my hotel," Daddy says. "Everyone wore hats, even the women. They had hats on and babies on their backs. Don't you think that's funny?"

Primo thinks that's funny.

"Daddy, Daddy," I interrupt. "Tell us about the first book."

"You mean the first ever printed?"

"No, your first book. The first one that was yours."

"I love to tell about that one. Well, when I was six or seven years old I worked for an old bookseller. I earned a little each day for dusting his books and straightening them up on the shelves to keep the bindings from bending. But he let me borrow books. Every day after school I went to work, and every day I came home with a different book. One day I finally had enough money to buy a book for myself, to keep. I asked the old man if I could buy the two books that were stuck under the cash register to raise it. He told me I could have them. I could barely carry them, but I took them home and put them in my room. It was enough reading for a whole year, maybe a whole life! Do you remember what they were?"

Primo and I both said, "Yeah."

"Don't say "yeah." Say "yes." They were the first edition of the First Folio of Samuel Johnson's *Dictionary of the English Language.* So there it was—my days as a treasure hunter had begun."

"Go back to the women in hats," says Primo.

"All right, here we go. This story starts right in the middle of the village. I stood in the square and smoked a cigarette with the men. Little by little I told them what I was looking for. Then a small boy took me by the hand and said, '*Señor,* come with me. Come see what we have in our house." So I looked at the men and they nodded and shrugged and pointed with their heads for me to go where I was led. The boy, just about the same size as you," he said, rubbing Primo's head, "took me through the streets. People looked at the boy and asked, '¿Adónde llevas al gringo?' He told them, 'A mi casa pa' ver la caja.' He had a box at home he wanted me to see.

"My heart was beating hard but I knew I had to look calm. The cobbles ended and the boy took me down a dirt street. He let go of my hand and ran down to the last house on what was now a very narrow path. He ran in yelling for his mother and his granny. 'Mamá, Abuelita. Traje al gringo pa' ver la caja.'

"Two women came out of the house rubbing wet hands on their aprons. I didn't know if I should shake hands with them or not. What do you think, Son? Should I have been polite and shaken hands with them?"

My brother shrugs but he smiles. He likes being asked. He knows he doesn't have to answer. The velvet chair is silky soft on my cheek. I like the tobacco smell when my father moves his hands. I like the book smell all around us and the fireplace without a fire. I like the Picasso drawing of a woman with a baby on her lap.

"Well, I put out my hand," Daddy says, "but they giggled and touched my palm just for a second with their hands stiff as seal fins and then they laughed and I asked them if I could see the box. They lifted the curtain that covered the entry to another little room and asked me to come in. The boy and his mother reached under the bed and brought out a small trunk. A leather suitcase like the monks used to take when they went from town to town to say mass. It was so old I thought it would fall apart in their hands."

"Did it?" asks Primo.

"No. It had a wide leather strap on it like a belt."

"You have one of those," says Primo. "You have one like that for bringing home books."

"That's true. I do. Had it for years. But this one was older."

"What was inside?" asks Primo.

"That's what I wanted to know," Daddy says. "But I didn't even dare ask them to open it. I touched the edge of the trunk with my fingers."

"So you could guess?" I ask.

"So I could imagine! So I could imagine my dream coming true!"

"What dream, Daddy?" I ask. Dreams are important. I like dreams, and some of them have come true even though I don't always like it when they do.

"I have a dream every time I come to one of these villages that I will find a trunk just like this, left by someone who came over after Christopher Columbus or after Cortés. In the trunk will be books a man, or maybe a monk, brought from Spain to keep him company—poems, stories, histories, maybe books to turn the Indians into Christians."

"How do they do that?" asks Primo.

"With words—with words in books written 500 years ago."

"So what was in the trunk?" says Primo.

"Can you guess?"

"Gold coins and treasure?"

"Well, not exactly."

"Old bones from the monk?" I ask.

"No, not bones. They took the belt off slowly. Then one woman cleaned the top of the box with her apron. I could hardly wait, but I had to. Finally, the boy opened the box."

"What did you see?" asks Primo.

"I saw a white cloth, rough, hand woven. The woman unfolded the first layer. I thought, What if inside this trunk were *La Carcel del Amor* from Spain."

"The jail of love?" Primo repeats, making a sour face.

"Exactly, but remember. It was made in 1492. What does that year mean?"

"Columbus sailing to the Indies."

"Excellent. So think how old that book would be. I would send it straight to the Library of Congress."

"Is it about adventures?" asks Primo.

"No. It is a book of love poems."

"That's dumb."

"The woman opened another fold. I could see there were some loose leaves from a book, and then the edge of a cedar box. My God, a boxed *incunabulum*."

"Now did they know you were excited?"

"No. I stood back and acted as if the box might not have what I was looking for after all. At the same time I was thinking, What if? What if?"

Primo is not impressed.

"But, Son, what if it were *Aesop's Fables?*"

"I have that one," Primo says.

"That's true, but not the one printed in 1489 in Zaragoza."

I say, "That's *before* Columbus!"

"Exactly. So now all of the cloth was folded out over the four edges of the trunk. What I saw.... I could hardly breathe. There they were. Neatly stacked. A little dusty, but dry and safe."

"What?"

"Some of the oldest books I'd ever seen."

"Just books?" says Primo.

"Just books!" Daddy says. "Books that came over with the conquistadors, and books from the birth time of printed books. *Incunabula*. Books from 1460, 1490, 1503. The companions of some Spaniard—probably a monk or a missionary—traveling through Mexico, around people who did not even speak Spanish. Books. The old friends some man carried with him wherever he went.

"Right in front of me were books so precious and rare I thought my heart would stop. I bought them. I brought them home. You can touch them and smell them. There they are, right there on the dining room table. Nine beautiful examples of *incunabula*."

We get up and go to the table while he keeps talking. Each word of the titles he reads to us presses into me like a carved stamp on damp parchment. Later I will see them in the pages he types for his

catalog. I will see them on the printed catalogs we fold and stack
for the mail. Aesop, Esopo. *Carcel de amor.* Madrid, Barcelona,
Zaragoza. *El arte de morir.* Facsimile, Catalán, the only one, one
missing, one lost.

Except for the one loose in the cedar box, the books are covered
in leather. On their backs are words stamped in gold, the special
sign that they are my father's treasure. The word *incunabula* sits in
my heart. It is one of the words my parents say every day. It feels
like the first word I ever learned. I know what it is. The Cuna. The
crib. The baby time of books. Books bound in swaddling cloth of
leather. I chant it over and over in my mind:

Incunabula. Incunabula.

Incunabulum for one.

Incunabula for many.

Books made from moveable type. That's what he says. They
could carve hundreds of letters to lay out hundreds of words. They
could make more than one copy of a book. They did not have to
make copies page by page with quill pens and ink.

I feel the intensity. Daddy's body becomes fuller, straighter as
he talks. He seems electrified. *Incunabula* is shot into me on his
rapture, filling and swelling my body with the idea of something
miraculous, words, a book wrapped in cloth and laid down in its
cradle of time. My father's hand caresses one of his new books, his
fingers near my face. All around is the smell of dust, ink, nicotine,
paste, typewriter ribbon. He looks over at Amado in the playpen
on the floor and he leans in for a moment, resting a hand on the
white painted post. I want him to lift Amado up as if he were taking him out of an old Spanish trunk.

But he already has a treasure. An incunabulum—brought
across the sea, protected by many men before him. He holds it
tenderly in both hands. I wait for him to find me, as if I were a
book written just for him.

3

Our House is a Book House

Al buen entendedor, pocas palabras
For those who understand, few words are needed

—Mexican proverb

I want what my parents want. To read and write and to know books.

The most important things in our life beside the Old Books are the Codices—real ones and printed copies that Mama carefully colors where the printer left out the tint. The painting she does is more beautiful, the clouds fuller in skies of more blues than the colored parts that were done on other pages by the printer. When she finishes coloring all of the incomplete volumes she says they have to sell them. She says that, before Columbus, and before Cortés, the Mexica and others—though people just say "the Aztecs"—recorded everything in their drawings. Everything. Victory, birth, sacrifice, costumes, prisoners, cooking, medicine, weapons, herbs, and what Mama calls tribute: platters of peacocks' tongues and trays of hundreds of hummingbird hearts. She shows me the priests speaking with commas floating in the air near their mouths. "Not everyone has speech marks, or volutes," she says. "But interpreters do, speaking Spanish and Náhuatl, Mexica and Maya—and all the dialects and languages that needed translation."

Interpreter. That's what SHE was—Malintzin. After her mother gave her away, she spoke Náhuatl. From her new owners she learned Maya. Maybe more tongues. There were so many languages everywhere. They say that Malintzin, hidden in a group of slave women, was given to Hernán Cortés, so then she had to learn Spanish because also she became like a wife. Mama says Cortés found out how many languages she could interpret and that is how, with all of her voices, she became His Voice. Mama says Malintzin's father was important near Tenochtitlan but when he died her mother got another husband who didn't want Malintzin. He wanted his own children. They say Malinche was eight or six when her mother sold her or sent her away. No one knows for sure, but I think she was eight. Still, eventually she came to Cortés. There are drawings of Malintzin standing with Cortés. She is speaking for him with the ambassadors. But in the drawings, how did they know which curls to draw for the word-air coming from their mouths—was it Spanish or Náhuatl or Maya or another dialect? Some volutes go straight up to the gods like smoke. How did they know? Was there a curl for "I think"? Did the volutes turn this way for "maybe," and that way for lies? When the god Tláloc made the first words, did he tell which way to paint them?

My mother shows me the pictures of plants from the copy of the codex of Sahagún, how the *tlacuilos* drew and painted and wrote the records of everything in their world on fig-tree paper, the *ámatl*. Gods wearing enormous hats and carrying tools were painted in pale watercolors made from the blood of plants. Inside the dark outlines of ink from the mesquite tree are men in suits of jaguar skin. Mama says they put on the skin to be the bravery of the whole spotted cat. The paws look like cuffs at their wrists and at their ankles. There are men from another land in striped cloth with dark blue skin and men with pale yellow skin in the cloth of foreign tribes. The *tlacuilos* drew plants, deaths, hearts carved out with knifes of volcanic glass. Some books they made were supposed to be read from back to front, and they opened up like accordions. Daddy says that, much later, people in Spain copied them and printed them like books, like the one collected and protected by the monk Sahagún. Those are the codices Mama colors, but they are not big treasures like the original ones. She says the Spaniards—well, The Church—burned almost all the original beautiful codices. They were afraid of them so they burned the painted stories of whole worlds that were not in the Bible. She says hundreds of years of knowledge went up in smoke. And the codices that survived are in places like the Vatican and the British Museum. Not all died. That's what Mama says. Mama's beloved missionary Sahagún went to New Spain in 1529. The book she colors is copied from what he spent 50 years collecting because he believed in how the Indians recorded their food and their lives. Mama says, "He was from the Church but he was no burner. He even wrote the Bible for the natives in their own language. In Náhuatl!" Two huge volumes of the drawings are always part of Mama's work. Adding the color. Being a *tlacuilo* too, maybe.

Mama found the glyph for Cuautla in one of her other favorite books. Mama says the name in Náhuatl means the place of the eagles, the cuauhtli. But in another book it means the place for rivers. I like that one because Cuautla is where we go for the hot water that comes from the rocks.

Mama opens the red leather book she calls Peñafiel because that is the man who wrote it. The gold letters on the back are about the place names of Aztec towns. Mama shows me the picture, the ancient glyph for where we live, Coyohuacan. It is a sign like a sitting dog, but it is a wild-haired yellow coyote. "Cóyotl," Mama says, and then she shows me the perfect circle, an empty white hole, drawn as his stomach. His mouth is open and his tongue is hanging out. "Huaqui means thin," says Mama. "Maybe starving. The whole name, Coyohuacan, meant the place of hungry coyotes."

It is the picture for where our house is—exactly for my Coyo-acán, but where are the coyotes? Out on the lava bed—around our house—inside my head. The glyph for Mexico City, which was

Tenochtitlan, has red spines on the green cactus of the gods. The half sign of the sun is red and green and yellow. There are three cactus leaves like the *nopales* my nurse Pilar makes with eggs for breakfast. They come from the cactus that makes *tunas*, my father's favorite fruit. The red Peñafiel is always on the table. Sometimes customers want to buy it. Mama can't sell it. She and Daddy are married to it. She uses it for her drawings and to decorate Daddy's catalogs.

There is that other place that sounds like Coyoacán. It is Xocoyocan where the xócotl apple tree lives. I want it because the sign for the place is a footprint, the mark of a path. I want to live where my foot feels the earth, where my eyes see the black imprints of step after step, like a map, like the marks of how to go home through the land of *tejocotes*, the freckled crabapples that I nibble for their dry fruit and that Pilar makes into a jelly of sugar and perfume.

The catalogs that Daddy makes teach me the names in the letters and invoices that I copy letter by letter when I stand at the typewriter and help my father, even though I can barely write. The names are in the ceiling voices above my head, my parents talking about an elephant folio—the giant grey folios of the friar Sahagún, where he recorded how to kill head lice with goose fat and a ground-up toasted mouse head, and how to swim across a river with the eyes of a large fish pursed in your mouth to guide you. Every day they say the music words of Tláloc, Huitzilopochtli Tezcatlipoca, Quetzalcóatl made from the serpent cóatl and the quetzal bird, and the stories of lovers turned into the volcanoes of Popocatépetl and Ixtaccíhuatl—the young brave warrior and his sleeping beauty.

My mother says, "Tell me what to read. I want to learn more. Tell me what to read." She says that to my father Leo Paz whose first name means "I read" in Spanish. He teaches her everything. He shows her all the special books she should use to check names. There are even catalogs to check prices. And he shows her the records that tell him how rare, how scarce, how impossible to find a book is. He says, "We're making a nice little book business," and she says it too, sometimes, because they are partners.

I stand under them, near them, catching words and names, Spanish, English, Náhuatl. Mama has drawn the same coyote as in the glyph. The printer made the drawing in metal. On the cover of a new fat catalog, with pictures, big letters, small letters, and lists of hundreds of books, the hungry coyote is stamped in ink, the stamp of where we live. The coyote, with the full moon in him for his empty stomach, sits looking away into the distance, right above the line of my father's name.

Daddy is in the garden with Primo making more of the shelves he designed. Each one is like a ladder. Each board is narrower as he builds up the rows of shelves that then stand back to back in the middle of the book room. He says they can't fall, not even in a big earthquake. They lean on each other. The bookroom is full of those A's. His guests, the ones who really are buyers, love to walk around the stacks, pulling out one treasure after another. When they put them back wrong, we all have to look for them and put them back in their slot. Daddy can see anything that is changed. It's his nursery and he can tell if a baby is misplaced or missing.

Sometimes I read what Daddy leaves next to his typewriter. I read his dreams. One dream is about an unclimbable mountain. He calls it an unreachable breast, a powerful snowy crest that commands him to look straight up and lose his balance. I begin to dream his dreams. They start on the onionskin paper where he types them, always making a copy with carbon paper, as if dreams became letters waiting to be answered. I dream of paths in cities he visits. He is lost in the jungles of Salt Lake City. The Lake is supposed to hold him up because it's so thick with salt, but it doesn't. He can't float. Just as he is going under he looks right at me for the first time. The last things I see are his fingertips reaching for me or waving goodbye.

I dream that he is asking me to do something for him. Mother might do it, but she is mad at him. Primo won't do it, and Amado is too little. I watch for the pledge he wants to make. He shows me the ring that belonged to his mother. But the ring is only a talisman. He can't give the ring to his son because it has too many pretty stones. But I know that deep in each of the stones are the words of all of his women and of all His Men of Words—Mark Twain, Cervantes, Dickens, Joyce, alone like him. In the dream he gives me the ring. My father chooses me after all.

But at school, our teacher, Miss Salinas, says we are not ready for words. We are only ready for sounds. She makes us come to the board and repeat silly sounds—*ajo, uju, ojo.* I have to call her "Meess," not Señorita, and if I don't say the silly sounds just right, even though I am the youngest in the class, she sends me to face into a corner and whips into the backs of my knees with her long thin stick. I scratch my armpit when I am back in my seat. It is a secret sign with my friend Carlitos that we feel like monkeys. His brother Luisito scratches his head with both hands, and later, when She's not looking, he pretends to eat lice out of his nails. At home Primo and I are already reading books. And Daddy and Mama read to us all the time, mostly in English. But in the English primer Meess only let's us sing *see, say, saw.* At home, with Mama and with Daddy, I read over and over what I see on the catalog sheets, the bold black words, the ones I hear my father read, the ones my mother types, the ones I copy—De la Cruz-Badiano, AZTEC HERBAL OF 1522. Mama says the herbal is in the catalog, but she tells Daddy they can never sell it. It stays on the table with Sahagún and Peñafiel. They are like three brothers my mother protects from the buyers, even when we need money more than anything. My hands, my eyes know those names and hundreds of others because I hold them, book after book, up to the edge of the balcony to pat them and blow hard to get rid of the dust, and because I write them, following letter by letter on Daddy's Underwood. I like the bodies of books. They have spines. The top is the head and the bottom is the tail. And when you open them you are not supposed to bend them, and to turn pages you use the edge of the paper, not spit.

School is all right. The soft paper of the primers is the same as the paper of Daddy's catalogs. It is a small school in a little house. There are twelve grades and sixteen students. I am not the favorite and I am not the best. But two boys I love are there. They are the sons of Stevie, and since he is like another father to me, they are like brothers, but I love them too much. Sometimes after school Mama takes a whole group to her friend Annettet's house to make a play, which I hate because the smaller children get the parts of animals. They gave me the duck in "Peter and the Wolf" which meant I had to squat and waddle. I want a real part, where I am important between two people, and I can wave wands and have magic hands.

My favorite thing is to work with Daddy, standing next to him, learning how to type business letters for him. If I get a letter from his sister in the United States, he reads it to me. It is written in large, blue-black loops. At the end he looks up as if he were writing it himself and says, "Affectionately, your Aunt Soledad." "Affectionately" is a word longer than "love," but "Love" is what my grandmother says at the end of her letters and I know what she means. I can't tell if a longer word is better or if it only looks like more. He picks words from each of her letters and teaches them to me. He doesn't tell me about "affectionately." I don't care. I don't like it.

Later, I stand at his typewriter and slowly, letter by letter, find each word on the keys to copy what he wrote to the Library of Congress. He shows me where to put the new name of a book he's sending to them, and the new date. He comes back to check and correct me. He erases and I type over. His letters always end with BIBLIOPHILOS, and then his name. Many times the same words are typed on the paper. The same numbers. I memorize them. I type a letter to Yale University, to Purdue, to Mr. Sinese, changing the words my father changes. I copy letters to Redpath Library in Canada offering them the giant folios of Sahagún, of Fray Diego Durán who tells about the killings at Tenochtitlan, and about the tribes going from Aztlán to Texcoco, our Mexico City. About books and Codices, books and Codices.

4

Rabies in White

I dream of long-gone trees,
a monkey slung from memories.
I am dangerous with need.
Beware my rabid nails and teeth.

Soledad Paz

My mother's Airedales always kill my cats. Liffey is the worst. Mama says she named her dog for a real river in Ireland. In a book that she loves, the river is called Ana Livia Plurabelle. She says the name as if it is a song about crying, as if she misses it, as if the river carries her Irish blood.

· Mama knows I was born wanting a cat, but she won't accept kittens people give her and she won't buy me a cat because of Liffey. She buys me ballet lessons and boxing lessons for Primo, but not a cat. Still, once in a while I get strays because Mama and Daddy love exiles.

Exiles are special. They have such clear needs. They are always grateful for what she does for them. She knows how the soul of an exile aches for home. When she meets Catalans who left northern Spain, she cajoles stories and recipes out of them. She brings them to our house, listens to them, talks to them. She is their friend. She and my father welcome exiles from Hitler's Germany and gypsies from the Romany Rye, which is a book with gold letters in the living room. They know White Russians and Austrian counts without a country whose feelings are the same size as hers. She's an exile too, even though she and Daddy chose to leave New York and drive back to Mexico City along deserted roads where on telegraph pole after telegraph pole hung dead bodies of fighters in the Revolution.

Mama always has Airedales. She likes them. They are rare, so she raises them and sells them to help when there isn't enough money from books. They are boxy, wiry, with red, brown and black markings muddying into each other in dull, scratchy coats. Their straight legs hop and bounce with no bend to them. Mama thinks they look lovingly at her, but they have such furry faces I can't even see their eyes.

She has tried giving me tiny kittens hoping that Liffey, her breeding female, that nuzzles and nurses her puppies with such love, will accept them as her own. But Liffey has torn those kittens to pieces and looked up at Mama for more. Mama has tried old cats, experienced and used to dogs. Liffey has killed three cats like those. Mama thinks she can train her, but Liffey—who makes such beautiful, gleaming, tender, cuddly puppies with blue eyes and sour breath, that waddle into their shallow boats of oatmeal and eat whatever comes near their muzzles—Liffey isn't learning anything about cats from Mama.

I don't love Liffey, but her babies are mine to hug against my neck at least for a few weeks.

Then Rottenvaler comes. Mama shows him out to the grass under the eucalyptus tree. He sits on the stone bench. His large paunch is stuffed into a high-collar jacket barely letting him bend. His legs are packed into tight riding breeches and high black boots. I stand between him and the puppies playing in the grass, but it doesn't keep him from doing what Mama calls him for, to trim the Airedales in the official way before she puts the ad in the paper to sell them. He puts a leather rectangular case on the bench beside him. He takes out four long thin scissors, a small oval box for boiling needles for injections and then a long needle with a large glass base, scratched and frosty so you can't see through it. He fills it from four bottles in his box. He cleans each of the scissors with a wad of alcohol, rubbing the blade over and over as if deep in the metal there might be something that will never come out. One by one he picks up the glossy pups. One by one he injects them near their tails and sets them down. One by one he injects them right in the soft center of their petal ears. Then he cuts off their tails. After they drop onto the grass, the little black ends with red bleeding holes seem to turn and flinch. He trims their ears into points. The puppies are never the same after that, and they are not really my babies after that either. Something kills their senses as if their whole ears have been cut off. The hands of that Rottenvaler, who teaches Primo how to box, those hands take the puppy out of them, takes the gleam out of them, though they still eat and pile on each other for naps. I know he will take something out of them forever the moment he touches them. Rottenvaler may teach my brother man things, like boxing, and, in his thick German accent, the rules of what is so and what is not, but I smell more than puppy blood on him and I don't know why someone who smells of death is in our house. Mama says he is a refugee from the war in Europe, but he feels like the enemy.

After Rottenvaler's visits, Liffey's puppies are my mother's to sell. They are strange to Liffey and to me. They stink of gauze and alcohol. They keep their bellies close to the ground as if they have been blinded by their taped ears and bandaged tail stumps. One by one, new owners take them.

When they are gone, Liffey sniffs their oatmeal bowls and bedding. She sniffs under the stone bench where Rottenvaler cut them. For a day or two she whines. I can't help her and she can't help me.

I can't reach the large white cat on the stone wall of golden *tepetate*. But my brother Primo has shown me every day how to pile up bricks and how to climb up where the two walls meet at the corner. He has shown me how to get up on the round rocking horse of a wall, coated with the sun-softened black *chapopote,* where we can pick at the tar and chew it like gum.

The cat doesn't move, trapped by the long pine boughs of the neighbor's tree. She doesn't move but she puffs up and gets bigger. Her eyes are like green beans split in half with a black stripe.

This is my cat.

Inch by inch I come closer. She freezes into a growl that stretches out into a long elastic yowl on which I crawl toward her. She is stiff against the dark green pine, her own white needles rising sharp out of her. I fall forward onto her. Her teeth lock into my hand and together we fall off the wall into the garden. She growls and won't let go. I yell and won't let go. As we fall, I hug her tighter. I want to get her to my room and hide her from Liffey.

She screams and scratches, her claws cutting my chest through my dress, my neck, my arms, my chin. I won't let go, I won't let go. She's mine.

I hold her head against me hugging her into a kicking, biting ball, the two of us rolling. Liffey hears me, and Mama and Pilar. I yell. Liffey, like a hunting dog ready to bring a rat out of the hole, digs the cat out of my arms with her nose, tosses her, breaks her and starts the tearing she knows by heart. Pilar grabs me and runs toward the house. I turn and see Mama tell Liffey to Sit and Drop, then Mama takes off her sweater and wraps it over the torn cat and comes flying up beside us.

"I have the head," she yells.

Why does she want my cat's head?

"Quick, Pilar! Get Soledad into the car. *Run!*" Mama is the general, the commander. My cat is in pieces. But Mama knows what to do. Pilar cradles me.

"Don't touch her cuts," Mama says. "Cover her with your apron. What if the cat has rabies? They have to test. Run! We'll wash Soledad after we take them the head."

The white apron is cool. The car is cool and the cuts are be-ginning to burn. It is cool in the tall streets I watch through the window. It is cool in the white room where I lean against Pilar, in the room where the floor is large white tiles, and the walls are white tiles and the ceiling too, all white and shiny and bright, with chairs along the wall, chairs where Pilar holds me.

Where is my mother? I hear her voice. I see her speaking with the doctors, the hysterical anger from before is gone. She talks smoothly and softly to them in this white house, her voice musical as she looks up at them in the white room, handing them her sweater with the head of my cat. They look at it just the way Liffey did, as if Mama had brought them something good to eat. They say how smart Mama is. How good she is to bring the brain. Brains. That's what Pilar cooks for me—thin and soft, breaded, sprinkled with lemon. The men in white all bow around the head, then they take it away.

"And my daughter? What about my daughter? What about the injections?"

"We'll call you."

I don't like injections. It means the silver oval box with the hy-podermic set in water. The nurse, when she comes to give us shots, pours alcohol into a portable metal stove. Pilar calls it the spider stove. The nurse boils the oval box with the needles in it and the cloudy syringe. Blue flames dance around the silver box licking at each other over the top of the steam. A fresh smell comes from the burning alcohol. There are pincers for taking out the needle when it's cooked. There are bottles flicked with fingernails, a miniature razor blade that slices the bottle tops off, and the glass hypodermic, also flicked and squirted into the air. Then there is a slap on my bottom and the punch with the needle. It is like the butcher in his white apron. Out comes the meat, slap. He turns it, slap. He holds it up for us to see. Slap, he flaps it down on the board in a certain way and then the knife goes in.

"But what should I do now, for her, for my daughter?"

"Wash all the cuts and scratches with yellow soap and then put on alcohol. We'll do the tests on the cat's brain. Watch her. If there is any change, any, if she...." They have turned into another room. I can't hear them.

The telephone rings and my mother yells for Pilar.

"Pilar! The tests! The cat had the sickness, *el mal.* Quick! Come! Help me with Soledad. We have to take her."

We are back in the room of white tiles. Pilar is quiet with her eyes looking at something I can't see on the white floor.

Someone takes me away from Pilar. I hear their voices. Pilar and Mama.

The doctors put me on a cold table. One bright light shines in the ceiling and four men in white are bending over me. They are holding my hands and my feet. My back arches up and my stomach rises. I try to pull my head down to my chest. I can't get loose.

One man in white has his hands on my legs like straps, his hands brown and broken into fingers. My panties start to slip down from my trying to escape. Another white has his hands hard on my wrists, and I think he is looking where I don't want him to look. Or he's laughing. What does he say? He's not looking. His glasses are large and flat. In them is a picture of a little girl lying on a high metal table. Two girls, one in each glass, and all around her white —white in the corners and a splay of her, starred in the center of his lenses, spread to the whites who hold her at the corners:

holding   holding

holding   holding

In the frame of his glasses I see my head move and my belly twist, and how nothing, not even the scream that pops my hernia, makes them release me. Mama is back. She comes up behind me. She's going to take me home. No. She's there for the hernia. She's reaching into her purse for the pink truss she made for me, to tie it around me to push the egg back that pops out under my stomach when I scream.

"Not now," a white says, and she puts the truss back in her purse.

"How much will you give her?" asks a white.

"Half?"

"A quarter, I think."

What are they going to give me?

"How much does she weigh?"

"Maybe twenty kilos, Mama says.

"Have you done this before?" a white asks.

"Yes," a white answers.

The one with the glasses lets go of my leg and another holds it. Now the first one is holding up a needle. It's long. Long as my arm. Longer than the needle when my brother was sick. Longer than the needle when Rottenvaler did Liffey's puppies. Silver and white. He is holding it up in the air and staring at a drop on the end of it, a drop that starts to slide down. With his other hand he takes a handful of skin on my stomach. His head is black. There is a black ribbon in the throat of his coat. His glasses are curled in wires around his ears. A large gold watch is coming down to me. He pinches up the skin of my belly. Trapped, I arch my back like a cat and drop fast to the table, the metal hard on my back. I get out of an ankle hold and kick one foot right at his glasses. They slip down under his nose, twisted, one glass cracked into a star.

The needle comes back up into the air. He is angry. I think he wants to bite my head off. He looks at the four corners of the arms in white. "*¡Deténganla!*" One white presses harder on my knees. Another white presses harder on my chest.

They do not hold my mouth. Someone covers my eyes. It's not Pilar. I can't smell her. Who took her away? Whose cool skin covers my eyes, even though my head rolls and bounces on the table trying to pry loose my whole body? It's not my mother. I don't feel her there. Why doesn't she come with her pistol and shoot into the air so the whites let me go? Why won't they let Pilar come back? She will make them stop. She will fold me up into her apron and say, "*Ya, corazoncito, ya.*" After the sobs and hiccups, she will give me teas from the tall green sheaves that stand in the corner waiting to make a cure.

I turn my face from the hand. The white is taking my belly button up into the air again and pinching the skin. The silver is going to shine all the way in with a scream I can only hear in my bones and his silver gun is emptying into my stomach.

With a snap he pulls out the white needle as if I had burned him. His hand with the gold watch is rubbing circles of cotton, right there next to the belly button, and he is staring at nothing because I made him mad.

Now my mother comes back. But her fish mouth is blank. I can't understand what she is saying. She is talking to me in English. Maybe she's saying, "There, there. That's all. We can go home now." I am waiting for her to say, "*Ya, amorcito, ya.*" Mama has the pink truss and she slips it up my leg. Gently she pushes the egg back in, saying the word she always says, the word the doctor says. Strangulate. It could strangulate. Before she learned any of my words, she learned that one. Before she learned words like *mijita, cielito,* and *corazón,* she said the doctor's word so I would be afraid and call her when the egg came out. Pilar pulls my underwear back up to my waist because she says they shouldn't see you—with boys it's all right for people to see, but not with girls. The men in white roll me off the table into her arms and we walk to the car. She fills the back seat with herself and me. I curl up with my eyes open, so they don't take me away from her, from her brown flannel shoes and her starched sky-blue dress, from her glossy brown skin—so they won't take me from my mama in the front, ruffling papers in her purse and finally jangling her keys. My eyes stay open because if they close I'll see the silver needle in the white gun coming into my stomach or the hands of the whites holding me down. All the way home I don't close my eyes. After we get home, after I see Daddy, I'll close my eyes.

Pilar and Mama take me every day for twenty-one days. I think they are going to take me every day forever so I hide under the house, but hiding there alone is not the same as hiding with Primo when we crawl through the dirt looking for spoons or marbles or carrots that fell through the hole in the dining room floor. I flatten myself like a snake to hide under the couch. I squirm into dark corners where they won't find me. I hide behind the pile of dry manure next to the stable. I hide under the stacked wood where the spiders tiptoe over my face. Liffey barks and finds me. Primo finds me. My own heartbeat finds me under the house. Pilar has filled the blackness with such stories of dead men and ghosts, the *monje loco,* the mad monk in a long brown cassock, his peaked hood hiding a face so horrible even Pilar hasn't seen it. The rope around his waist whips and flies in the dark as he comes for me, and I run from him and crawl out to the light where they grab me and take me to the whites.

Between the trips to the needle something happens. I am not the same. It's like with the puppies. Maybe Rottenvaler came in the night and cut off my ears. I need to hit my head on the wall or on the floor. I need to fight the whites even when they are not in my house.

Sometimes I want to kick the house down, so they lock me up in a room by myself. I think Daddy will come get me and let me sit in the book room. But I only hear Mama tell him that I tear my hair out in handfuls.

In dreams, I am a baby small enough to fit in one of my father's hands. I have arrived and they do not want me. He tried to hold me but the little thing arched up, the beads of her spine stretched in the fear of his hands. I wore the pink hospital necklace spelling out his family name: P-A-Z.. He's afraid he'll drop me. Arm's length he holds me out. Mama rescues him. He lets go.

Clearly I call to them, but their minds are not tuned to a child. Mama is so tired.

Pilar's smell is the smell of the shepherd. I learn her smell because she feeds me. She scrapes apples and bananas with a silver spoon. I learn her smell of herbs and spices because her dark eyes of glazed ceramic look into me and feel no fear.

After the twenty-one days, everyone has a cure for my tantrums and they tell Mama. The old doctor next door says, "Bind her tight and leave her alone in her room." They do that, but I can bang my head anyway. The old lady down the street says, "Cold water stops them hitting their head. We do it in the village to children who won't stop screaming, to the children who won't stop hitting. We drop them in the cold water of a *lavadero*."

No. Our *lavadero* is the scrub-board of cement and the long tub of water where in the afternoons I watched Pilar scoop water out of the tub covered inside with glossy green moss. The water sloshed up and down the sides from the waves of the cup as she rinsed, washed and scrubbed. Her arms kneaded clothes with the yellow lump of Lirio soap. I watched her, my eyes at the edge of the tub. She rolled the mound of soapy white like corn on the *metate*, over and over. I knew to be thumped into peace by the heartbeat of her arms beating and stretching the clothes on the stone. In those afternoons, it was so calm seeing her with her head tipped, listening to her shoulder.

Pilar and Mama follow the water recipe of the old lady to make me stop pulling my hair and making fists they can't open. They carry me and stumble on the stairs down to the backyard. They turn to the laundry shed with the scrub-board of cement and the water tub.

This day the *lavadero* is different. Mama and Pilar hold me like a large wet blanket. I squeeze the sun out of my eyes and make fists that want to break everything. They carry me in that hold like when they take the garbage that's too heavy, with a quick solid walk—like when they took the dead dog down the stairs, afraid of dropping it, of not getting it to the street in time for the garbage truck, its bell in the distance warning them.

Are they going to throw me away?

They are saying everything together above the tub, spitting out the pieces of what the old *doña* said.

"She said like this up and down."

"Head first?"

"I don't know."

"Put her bottom in first. Put her *nalgas* in like that."

"And push the head under water?"

"Did she say put the head?"

"I don't know."

"Or all of her?"

"All of her."

There it is, the cold water of the *lavadero*. I drag in a hot breath as the water hits my back then I am on the bottom with the green moss. My eyes look through the waves made by their arms. My mother's face is white and surprised as if she had shot someone. Pilar's face is brown and secret, the silent face for cooking and stirring, the face of ironing, the face for shelling lima beans, stirring soup and turning tortillas, the face for pushing laundry down with the soap.

Then I am up and out of the water, coughing and spitting, their arms fat and close to me, their faces far away—the surprise of my mother and the secret eyes of Pilar because she's mad she obeyed the old *doña*.

The water opens my eyes. I see them. But it is not the water that stops the fists. It is not the water that stops the head from banging. It is that yesterday Mama was a light voice, songs and white skin.

Yesterday Pilar was gold skin, stories, and a lap. Yesterday Pilar rinsed the clothes, and the tin scoop scraped cup after silvery cup.

Now they have pushed me to the green moss on the bottom and I am washed away in the weight of their arms.

After this I don't eat. Even though I am really too big, they take me to a wet nurse. I am dry from tears and hunger. She can't come to my house because now she has her own new baby. She saves one breast for her child. Dark brown and wrinkled, the nipple enters my mouth like a small finger. I choke on it and want to spit it out, but the tongue and the throat work for the milk and I swallow *Colima, Puebla, the sand and cactus hills of Potosí, the bald mountain of Ajijic, its land too full of gold to grow even small things. Copper Canyon, the valleys deep with banana leaves as we move toward the ocean. Boughs of the tall Siranda Blanca blow out to the white strings on the waves, to the foam of Chamela and Veracruz. Their branches sway over the gray, brown sand, my land. Brown idols squat, hunchback, piping, singing, speaking, merely standing, a man and a woman, paired in ceramic, dressed in clay finery, their ear lobes hooped with riches in clay gold. These are the lands I have known. Huitzilopochtli showed them to me from the air and then taught me to walk on them. A god whose name I cannot say brought me here by birth. I have crested a thousand hills, crisscrossed over flat deserts sliced by rivers flowing to the palms and the ocean. These are the lands I have breathed thick in the parrot jungles where the air has to be swallowed whole with its dampness. These are the lands I have seen, waterless and cloudless, hot, flat, burned where the air has to be taken in small puffs so as not to singe the throat. These lands of sand, tamarind, mahogany, cactus fronds like hands, these I drink from her breast and then I sleep.*

If I were her child, she would sleep too. But I am not. She tells Pilar to take me home and feed me *atole* made with corn and milk.

5

Burning Heart

The healer boiled herbs,
mixed potions.
Through my sleep
his sucking mouth
opened my wound and
healed my heart.

Jungle Hut, Gustav Regler
Poet in exile, Mexico

Mama is sick. She told us the truth. She ate raw meat with a name—tartare—made with chives and raw egg. Mama loves chives. But now she needs to sleep and sleep. She is going to take us to that place in Cuernavaca where her friend takes her children. It's not that Pilar doesn't help, and Daddy too when he's home, but Mama is too sick to run the house. She can't drive us to school or take us to the doctor. I think Mama is going to die. No one says. Her friends tell her to take us to the children's home in Cuernavaca, just till Daddy gets back.

I don't want to go there again. Primo doesn't either. He calls it Cuernatoro and says, "I don't need that place. I can take care of myself."

I want to hear Gustav's German voice. He'll know what to say to Mama so she doesn't take us. She helps him with his poetry in English. He wrote a poem about her. He told me that he called it

"Mother on Guard!" I don't understand. She's sick. But I know she is calm with him, and he is happy with her fixing the English in his poems. When his wife died Mama knew how to talk to his sadness. Mama listens to him. I want to hear his voice because he'll tell her not to take us.

I look for Gustav's face in my head. Mama's friends call him "our poet." Stevie calls him Gustavo. His hands lie smooth and bent on his sheets of paper as if he were about to play a piano of letters. He says words like *buch* softly, when in English it's "book" and hard. A word like God that is soft, he says hard, "Mein Gott!" You think he's speaking two languages at once and you understand both.

I sense the hands of his worry around me even though he never holds me. He has a "burning heart," and I feel the heat of it on mine. When he speaks with my mother I know what he believes about the important things, that pain is sad, that separation is not good, that there is enough bad in the world. In my head I let the threads of his words weave a cocoon around me. I know he loves me, and our family. He is quiet and gentle even though he has killed people in the war. Also, he was wounded in the war by soldiers who tried to kill him. He lost a Nazi prisoner in France because Gustav tried to take care of him, give him first aid. He said they were both German but on opposite sides. But the Nazi called Gustav a traitor. The Nazi grabbed a thermometer, broke it and stabbed himself in the throat with the glass. He wanted to die rather than be saved by "the enemy." Gustav tried to save people in Spain and was wounded. He was thrown away by Germany because he voted against Hitler. France didn't want him because he was against something big that was already in Paris. Hemingway loved him, and Mama says Eleanor Roosevelt and Hemingway brought him to Mexico. Anyway, he is one of Mama's special people.

"Again?" Gustav says when he comes to check on Mama. "That's no *kinderheim*. You can't take them there. He's a *Nazi*. You can't do that, not to that, that... *kinderkennel!*"

"How do you know he's a Nazi? Anyway, I have to. Everyone uses him. I have to rest. I can't talk about it any more. Come back later."

My Mama thinks she takes us there to be safe. She takes us there when we can't stay with Stevie and his boys, when she has nowhere else to leave us. The man where we are going is a German. His white coat and fancy manners are the magic of *fu-man-chu* that makes Mama think she is doing something right. He gives her a tour of his little *kinderheim*, showing her the tidy kitchen, the perfect little garden and the green pool where frogs, which Mama doesn't see, sit in the drains and croak at you and burp bubbles when you reach for the edge. The tall man in the white coat shows her the cribs and beds, in neat white rows, bathed in sunshine, the windows open for plenty of fresh air. His sister, all in white and silent, walks behind.

Mama likes tall men and doctors. She loves white coats.

Mama knows Gustav is right. She trusts him for advice when Daddy is away. But she does not always do what he says. She does what she has to. She sleeps all day and all night. Then she takes us to Cuernavaca. Primo and I sit in the back seat. I want to throw up on every curve. There is nothing to hold on to, especially not Primo. He hates that.

The first time Mama took us to the *kinderheim* in Cuernavaca, Pilar said we were going to the house of the Animales. She was supposed to say Alemanes, but she only used this right word for Gustav because he was a German she loved. They did not put me in the same room with Primo.

i am in a house with children   there is a pool   there is a frog in the
side of the pool   the german man is very angry with the children
in the night   i don't want to make pipi in my bed   they have put
me in a high crib with gates on it even though at home i am in a bed
i want to go to the bathroom the way Pilar teaches me   but i am

afraid to climb out   i go back to sleep   in the black night   i wake
with the hands of the tall Animal in the white coat   his hands are
inside my clothes   i am wet   the bed is wet   he is very angry   he
picks me up and throws me onto my stomach in the crib   in the black
night he pulls off my wet clothes and spanks me   suddenly the room
is bright   his sister is standing in white by the door   he lifts me up
over the rails and out of the crib   fast   like a flying thing   the
sheet falls   he holds me up   high away from him   in the black of
the hall he spanks me again   his sister is watching

> *first i am in the sink   cold water then*
> *I am under   the   sink   he kicks the*
> *door   a lock clicks   my eyes open to*
> *black   and a black   wet   smell   my*
> *head is against the top   my knees are*
> *under my   mouth   if I cry it will hurt*
> *more   far away he says things   his*
> *sister answers   he is angry with her   I*
> *can't hear her I am too cold   she comes*
> *to the black box   and opens the*
> *lock   no words*

but pulls me out gently   takes me back to my bed with gates on it
and slips me over the bars onto the cold   a soft light is coming over
the black edge of the mountain
where is Primo?

This time at the *kinderheim*, I swim alone. Primo wants me in
the corner furthest away from him and the other children. I stare
at the frog that is staring at me.

In the night I dream of a pig in a car. The pig is thinking of
that house and that pool, wondering why a little girl would stand

in the far end of the pool alone, not talking to anyone, looking into the drain at the edge. The drain is green and mossy. It is dark and slimy. Green, fat, fearless frogs with scabby black craters on their backs live in there.

In the dream I look into a mossy drain and it is just the way it is when I am awake and in the water. The frogs jiggle their swollen throats and draw down their lips all the way to their shoulders. They hold those long sneers while they balance on their toed-in toes. I dream of it over and over. I think of Alice in Wonderland, even in my dream, wondering if something better is going to happen, something different. I feel the water in my armpits and notice that the horror of seeing the frogs is gone. I have changed places. I am inside the black drain with them, looking out at the pool and at the children far away. The eyes of the frogs talk. They say I have been left for a bad reason even though Mama said it was because she was sick, and because the doctor said she couldn't walk around and would have to lie for more weeks trying the medicines to kill the tapeworm growing in her again.

I remember the crib, the frogs and the water at the "kinderkennel." I don't remember food or games, walks, books, or toys. No tables, no chairs, no drinks. Around the memories of the angry man in the night and the black drain around the pool, there are only blanks. When one of Mama's friends brings us home, I am empty. Pilar tempts me with crispy, fried maguey worms. We both eat out of one piece of oily brown paper. We share sliced figs with fresh cream. Her cooking counter is too high for me to see, but I smell jar after jar of crabapple jelly before she pours the hot wax on it.

Some afternoons Gustav and his new wife take me out of Malintzin Number 19 to their apartment smelling of vanilla. Gustav writes in his study with books all around him and paper rolling out of his typewriter. He leaves the door open, so I can see him—as if he were my father and he wants to glance up and see me too. His wife doesn't have children. She teaches me to make lace cookies with almonds and oatmeal. I begin to get full again. These things cover the blanks of Cuernavaca and the man in white. At least Mama did not give us to him forever. Malintzin—she was given away when she was six, and it was forever.

Mama is still sick when we come home from the kinderkennel. The raw meat with raw eggs had a worm in it and she can't get well from it. I watch blue veins wriggle on her hands as she sleeps. When she moves, small blue serpents slip from the tendons on her fingers, grow thin and drain away under the bones. Soon she is so weak she can't get up. Nothing the doctors give her works. The tapeworm is inside her to stay. And if it stays she will die. The worm eats more than she does. She takes pills, liquids, poisons—all the newest treatments from the United States, from France, from Spain, and nothing works.

After Mama has tried everything, she asks Pilar for help. Pilar gives her the real *remedio*, the cure from hundreds of years ago. Kneeling at the stone *metate*, Pilar grinds half a kilo of whole, unshelled pumpkin seeds. She makes a rough paste of the seeds and shells then mixes part of it with water and pours it into a tall glass. Mama has to drink it all. Then Pilar mixes some more till Mama has two liters inside her.

Pilar knows her *remedio*. She watches Mama's stomach twist and turn. Quickly, Pilar helps Mama get out of bed to sit on the blue potty at the side of the bed. The tapeworm shoots out, meters and meters of it, long flat white noodles, folded over and over, with tiny gray breaks on its long fluid ruler. It piles up in water, curled up and dead, or alive, or sleeping, waiting to be shown to the doctor, because, finally, this time, it has come out and is still wearing its head. Last time the head stayed inside to grow new meters.

My mother drank the pumpkin-seed milk and pushed all of it out.

She gave birth to her own snake.

6

Flying over Father

We fold sheets of the codex,
records of ancient lives.
We learn to press a binder's bone
for a sharp crease.
Inside thin outlines
dances birthing death.
My father holds the codex
wrapped with leather cords—
children's voices dim,
night closes down.

Soledad Paz

Malintzin Nº 19. Daddy leaves for downtown at dusk. I can wait all night. Asleep or awake. I think sometimes my mother doesn't know where Daddy is. Maybe sometimes she doesn't care. I stand against the French window made of small frames. My white nightgown makes gray shadows on the panes. I am too small to look over the balcony into the garden, but through one glass I see him go out the front gate into the silent danger of the night. Next time I won't wait. I will go with him and not be afraid.

Some nights Daddy doesn't leave for downtown until we're in bed. I lie flat on top of the bed with my eyes closed. A foggy breath comes from the ceiling and cools my heart and stops all thoughts. Finally, I float to the ceiling. I am ready to go with my father as he leaves the front door and descends the difficult stairs to the "S" of the stone path before the gate. He puts his packages down to undo the lock. I float above him and turn and wait. One package is books to The Library of Congress. Up in the corner is the label with my father's name and under it the sharp capitals he taught me to type: BIBLIOPHILOS.

The other package holds catalogs to be mailed. The packages are tied with rope. His hand is like a claw that grips and releases the knot at the top. He closes the lock on the other side of the wrought iron gate. He walks down the dirt street between the plane trees painted white up to their waists to keep away the ants. My feet know the feel of the soft dirt. But this time I fly above him.

I get on the trolley car with Daddy. My body hitches up the step, copying his crooked way to spare his sore leg. I copy him to be his limp. Pilar says the body wounds itself to match the pain in the spirit where something is missing. That way the spirit is not alone in its limp, its *cojera,* its lack. In my mama's mirror I have seen how it is happening. I stood there with my dark bangs cut the way Mama wants them, my eyes the eyes of another, looking out from a stranger's life. My right leg was shorter than the other. So, it's true. My spirit is eating a piece of the father, nibbling at the crest of the bone.

A limp is the sign of the house of my father, the house of Leo Paz. Whether he sees me or not, I am marked as his daughter.

He gets off the trolley. I follow, weightless above him.

The box of catalogs pulls him down harder on one side. Catalogs list the rare books he sells. Sometimes they even show engravings on their pages. Plates, Daddy calls them. His books are the words we hear at breakfast and lunch, spoken just like the names of friends, relatives, politicians. The catalog sheets are folded the way he taught us, first with our fingers, then with the bookbinder's ivory, flattening the crease sharp as a knife blade. In catalog after catalog, I see the names my father talks about each day as they appear at the edge of the ivory and disappear under my thumb.

I fly higher than a tree above Daddy, on his way to downtown Mexico City. I am with him, like on the nights when he took Primo and me to the night bookbinders, the night printer, the all-night post office. He is in his dark three-piece suit, in a yellowed white shirt, his black mustache neatly trimmed. He smells of oatmeal soap from his afternoon bath. That's when he starts his day. When he sits in the dark of the trolley, looking up at the metal roof with a globe covered by a wire cage, I float above him. After we pass San Juan de Letrán, I know he will get off. I follow. He likes to walk the nightstreets in the heart of the city, walking, left, right, through the alleys lit by the yellow umbrella of one small bulb, and past the street he calls Bucareli. Daddy's black felt hat is down low on his face. Daddy speaks night.

On the black and silver sidewalk, he is drawn to the clack of the night printer, called by the sound of the press, led to the soft yellow rectangle of the open door. The metal corrugated shutter is down, but they have left a narrow slot and he has to turn sideways to step in with the packages we will mail at the next stop, the brass castle of the night Post Office. I follow him, just as I did when he took me with him alone, when my brother Primo went camping with Boy Scouts, and my mother visited her mother.

I think he's getting ready for another trip north or south. He's making a new catalog that Mama will mail to him in El Salvador or Boston. He seems lighter, ready to pull out his old metal suitcase filled with smaller and smaller cases so he can buy books and send them home for Mama to catalog and sell. He steps lightly around the presses, as if lifted by anticipation. He laughs. I can't hear why, but he laughs, a big rare laugh with his head thrown back, showing gold teeth at the back. On his desk at home I saw him write *domingo, lunes, martes, miércoles, jueves* with 4, 3, 2, 1, 0 after the days of the week as if at 0 he will shoot from the house like a bullet from Mama's gun.

Maybe this time Mama is too upset. Daddy did something again when he was supposed to stop. The fight was bad. What if this time Daddy is not coming home? No. I don't want that. The best time of all is when Daddy comes back from a trip with his stories.

My father puts his packages deep into a corner, leaves his hat on top of a tall file, and pulls his horn-rim glasses out of his chest pocket. Then he disappears with his galleys into another room.

My body rocks to the whirl and turn of the press. The roller drops down to a bath of ink, rises up on a shiny elbow. Coming to meet it, the flat moon face receives the roll, the caress. With a small sucking sound the ink covers her face and the disk lowers slowly again to the blocks. Something clacks and moves forward and back in the entrails. A white paper the size of a newspaper slides in just before the face falls, and out of her belly comes a sheet covered with black words.

A man turns to greet Daddy. At the same time the man's arms receive the sheet like a live birth, raising it up in the air and waving it down onto a long wooden rack. The face has come up empty. The roller has emerged from below, long and black, covered with wet. It covers her face again and she falls to the type. The hush and clack and hiss of it, over and over, while the legs and the insides move, in and out of each other. Again and again, the man turns and sweeps up the white sheets, with his arms held high, and lowers them onto the wooden bed. I watch, lost in the loudness, where I am unseen and unheard, lulled by the large noise of it filling me, filling the room, calling out into the street its rhythm and beat.

Moving above the roar of the machines is like flowing through water. No one can call me. I don't have to answer anyone. Far away across the room two men speak through the depths. Their mouths move large and slowly. Their eyes emphasize the words and their heads nod hard. I float to the linotype. The setter moves his fingers over the white keys. He wears glasses like a welder, with thick lenses shielding him from the glare of the keys. He reads a page hung on a wire near his face. I watch the molten lead shiver in the small square tub near my chest, the silver of it catching in its liquid all the lights in the room, smearing pinks and blues on its gray face. I think the lino man reaches for me, as he always does, hardly looking, reaching out a large old hand, inked deeply in the cracks, without touching me, placing his hand in the air for a moment between me and the hot lead, in the roar reminding me of the heat, checking the distance of my heart from the box of gray liquid that pours down the chute, gets a message from the fingers, and drops out in lines, lines, lines, lines, lines, into a page of silver words stacked up in order, first in the heart molten, then typed, tapped and pecked according to the white order on the sheet, then slid out metallic into the wooden frame ready for the press.

The heat writes on me how it is done.

The silver writes on me how it becomes.

The frame stamps on me how it is held.

I think about the shapes and how they will glide, slide up under the face of ink, how they will be caressed and pressed, how they will fly up in his arms on the white sheet and then—how someone will cut them and fold them and bind them and I will hold them in my hands close to my heart.

It is the book that I want to smell. It is the book I want to hold so close that my eyes can see the rivulets in the grain laid in the paper, so close I can have my face near the words as my father does. I want to hunch over the bound, open prayer of it as my father does, lift and turn a leaf without harming it, as my father does, and which I do, but which he never sees.

After the printer my father goes to the *zócalo* for hot chicken soup. If he stands at a bus-stop that does not go home, I pull away toward the yellow glow of the streetcar to Coyoacán. He looks like a black cardboard shadow of a man in a dark hat. I ride the light of the car to our house. I ride the pale blue of the porch light up the stairs and into my room. Already asleep, I lie on my bed, uncovered and cool.

May 12

Malintzin # 19
Mexico, D.F. Mexico

Dear Daddy,
Mama read me your letter to me from Tlapehuala.
When you are gone, who teaches English to your stu-
dents?
I tell Mama my letter to you and she types. Next day
she lets me type like you with two fingers but she
will fix it. When I am bigger I will write my whole
letter by my self!
Mama is working hard on your work with your books.
She says Primo and I can typewrite on your machine if
we write to you in English.
I want to write to you in Spanish.
I type every day like you. One day I will learn to
type without looking. I will copy more letters for you
when you come home with your books.
Matemática. (Mama let me type the numbers)

$$235$$
$$6785$$
$$(7020)$$

I did a problem so you know I do Arithmetic.

Love, Soledad
Soledad Paz
tu Choli

7

Ixtapalapa

La nana, la nena, Nina, Nora y Nuria
van y ven al bobo bebé.

Nanny, Nena, Nina, Nora, and Nuria
bend and blink at the boo-boo baby.

—Mexican tongue twister

For her day off, Pilar likes to go home to Ixtapalapa and sometimes we go with her for the day. Mama usually drives us there, but this time she has to stay home with her feet higher than her head. She has to be like that for most of the day because a little brother or a little sister, maybe Amado, if it is a boy, or maybe Milagros if it is a girl, pushes at Mama and doesn't know it is not yet time to be born. The bed is raised at the foot with three bricks so the baby won't fall out. Daddy is home. He's going to work in the dining room. He knows that Mama needs a lot of help to move or to eat or to drink and he helps her when she has to walk to the bathroom. He's going to take care of Mama and wait with her for their baby. It has already been months, so her time out of her tilted bed is shorter and shorter every day. She doesn't like it. She says it will make her weak for the birth, but the doctor tells her what to do to keep the baby.

So Primo and Pilar and I take the bus to Ixtapalapa. I love the bus. It is like another country with people coming and going from villages and *el centro* of Mexico City.

In Ixtapalapa one day feels like two or three. Nothing is like life at our house. Especially, we don't have to have ten drops of iodine in our milk because Mama says we live too far from the sea. Sometimes we go for a birthday Sunday. Once we went for Good Friday and once for Palm Sunday. We walked along the streets. Christ rode to the church on a donkey. The whole street was covered in green alfalfa. People wore crosses woven from palm fronds. There were miniature woven donkeys carrying two baskets filled with candy. Over most of the windows two palm fronds were crossed for decoration. Pilar took us to the church where palms, woven into scenes, plates, even crowns, were all over the stone steps. Pilar said they are not going to sweep up the palms like garbage. They were going to burn them and save the ashes to paint them in crosses on everyone's forehead on Ash Wednesday. On that day Pilar always has ashes on her forehead, sometimes in the shape of a cross. But we don't. Mama doesn't take us to church on that day. We only go to church on some Sundays.

Droopy palm leaves covered the giant glass jars filled with flavored waters—tamarind, rice and melon water. My favorite drink is the *raspado*. They scrape ice from a huge block until your glass is full. Then you pick a syrup to pour over it. I pick *jamaica* made from hibiscus flowers and sugar.

There were actors in plays in front of the church door. In one, Christ washed the feet of his people who were wearing long robes and turbans. In another play, Pontius Pilate tied Christ to a pillar and made men beat him. The guards, wearing red costumes and helmets of shiny silver paper, whipped Christ. Then Pilate pushed a cactus crown on Christ's head and shoved a palm frond into his hand. Pilar got her name because she was born on Good Friday, the day of Christ tied to the Pillar. Even though it was a play, when Pontius Pilate laughed and called Christ a king, the laughter was real. Pilar told me the man who acted Christ was a *penitente*. He chose this way to be punished because he killed the man he found with his wife. So the crown of thorns was real, and the whipping and the blood were real. Pilar said God and the police would forgive him now, and he would not have to run away and hide in the hills.

In the afternoon a different man was chosen for Christ. He carried a giant cross of wood beams. Veins came out on his neck in bumps and sweat fell like water from his face. They tied him to the cross as if he were nailed to it and left him there until sunset. Pilar didn't tell me what he did, but he wanted this pain for something bad, and, because he was sorry, they let him be a Christ.

This time we are here for a special Sunday with turkey in *mole* because Lent is finished.

There is a big room, so tall that even with both windows open to the street, and both courtyard doors open, there is still only a smoky light up high in the beams where I see the ghosts. Each bed is made and the bedspreads are each a different color, yellow, white, green and peach. One is for Epifanía, Pilar's sister, one is for Rosario who might be Pilar's secret daughter, one is for Pilar if she should ever run away from our house and come home to Ixtapalapa, and I think the white one is for the shadow woman. But I can see from the absolute tightness of the bedspreads and the hard flatness of the beds that each is like a trampoline for the ghosts to come down and leap back up to the ceiling, over and over, and then hide, barely moving in the fuzzy light above. The ghosts don't frighten me. I am even sure they know how to take turns sleeping on the perfect beds during the day. Maybe at night they pile like folded sheets on Pilar's bed since she is hardly ever there. Maybe they don't need beds and rest on the brick floor when they get tired of the ceiling.

The kitchen is under a tile roof and is open to the courtyard. The counter is covered in red floor tiles. Cut into it are the holes to fan the charcoal fires. On the back wall, brown painted mugs hang from nails in a half circle—the big mugs up at the top of the arch, and the tiny ones down at the ends. From the beams hang buckets and bean pots, long ladles and short whisks. In the corner is a dark red pot with a broken spout. It holds a bouquet of chocolate mixers, spoons and sticks. At one end is a sink that is really just a cement slab with a hole in it so the water can run out along a thin ditch to the street. Inside the sink is a white enamel tub with royal blue edges. Next to it is a big ball of *estropajo,* the white coil of hemp for scrubbing dishes. It looks as if it was pulled from an old lady's hairbrush. On top of it is a bar of yellow Lirio soap. Towels for drying the dishes hang on nails. Nails are everywhere. Nails for the big flat ear of a clay tortilla pan, for the woven *sopladores* to fan the flames, nails for string.

I look behind and around everything. I am looking for the pink top of the glass bottle with *Agüita de San Ignacio* that one of the *doñas* in the market gave to Pilar. The *doña* said it was for *pena,* which is everything—pain, sorrow, grief and shame. I want to find it and take it home and put drops of it in Daddy's coffee. In Mama's juice.

There are nails for a broom with its hempy head standing up, its handle pointed at the floor. A nail for the broom of red thistles for sweeping the street. Rope to tie turkey feet. Leather straps for carrying a heavy pot on your back. Spurs for a horse that does not exist. A man's hat, though there are no men here anymore, and maybe there never were. Enamel cups for heating Pilar's herbs. Iron tongs. Baskets with nails through one edge. Nails along the kitchen beam. Everything is out. Everything is up. No shelves, no cupboards. No drawers. But lots of hiding places. The kitchen is like Pilar. She does not have to carry a purse to know where her money is. There is a place for Epifanía's rat poison, but only she knows in which narrow basket. There is a place for Rosario's ground powders, and for the tightly wrapped bunches of herbs that Pilar collects in different seasons and in certain fields for headache, earache, bone-ache and heartache. All of their secrets are put away, but on which nail, in which old aspirin box, in which knotted handkerchief, in which ball of beeswax, under what pincushion, in which cracked cup, only they know.

At the back of the courtyard is a beehive oven slathered with dry, cracked clay. Its small door is open and inside are the ashes from baking bread. Next to it is a pile of mesquite wood and resin chips for when they bake again.

The bathroom is a fenced square of weedy ground with a three-sided wall of split cane. I know how to walk around the leaves and the fresh little piles to find a new place to squat. In the rain it is all the same, all mixed with mud. I don't like it when it rains and I have to find a broken tile or a flat stone to balance on. I like it when it is dry and I can tell where to step.

Epifanía is Pilar's older sister, but she could be her mother, a nun or her grandmother. Pilar is round and short and soft. Epifanía is tall and thin. She might be a tree, with a trunk of gray, softly folding cloth. Instead of a head of leaves, she wears a tranquil face, smooth cheekbones and eyes so peaceful you think she is praying even when she looks at you. Her hands are as gentle as water. She is where you see her and she is also somewhere else. She has died and come back for a visit. Or she has stayed alive, vowing to protect her family with her roots and branches until they let her go. She moves like a willow in the long space under her gown that goes all the way to the ground even though it is not the fashion. I have to be fast in my mind to be with her in the kitchen and at the same time in the big room with the shapes in the smoky ceiling. But I am not quick enough. I am never sure if the house ghosts are hiding in her clothes so they can walk around with her in their old world and not be seen, or if they are in the sleeping room waiting for her while she does her chores, slices onions, picks pebbles out of the rice, kills chickens, makes tortillas peacefully—as if she were a saint from a niche in the church.

The turkey is Epifanía's—her *guajolote*. In the early morning she holds him under her arm and pulls his ugly head against her breast. His head is covered with blue and red bubbles of skin. Gray growths almost cover his eyes. His eyes blink up but don't really seem to see anything. She scratches his chest and his head falls over her wrist. A lump of loose purple flesh flops over one side of his beak. Epifanía closes her eyes too and rocks him gently. She raised him from a chick, talking to him for the full year of his growth. He follows her to the street gate like a dog and waits for her to return.

I barely see how fast she does it, neck over the rock, machete down, the head falls off, the flapping body wants to run from her but she holds him and drains the blood into a bowl. Near her feet is a huge bucket of boiling water. She plunges him in and holds his body down with a stick. Over on the laundry tub Pilar spreads out newspapers. The ink is brown because these are the papers with gossip and detective stories. Then Pilar and Rosario and Epifanía haul the steaming bird onto the laundry slab. They all bend over him, yanking out feathers in handfuls, in a hurry, as if any moment the plumes might refuse to leave the skin they grew in.

Then there are the sudden slits at the throat. His craw is pulled out and Primo and I get it to see what's in it, how many stones and how many pieces of corn that are still whole. With a tiny knife Pilar takes out the gall. Nobody moves. If she punctures it, the bile will spoil the whole bird. Then they slit another hole in his bottom and take out his guts. Pilar throws the intestines to the chickens. They caw and fight over them like buzzards. She keeps the gizzard, the liver and his large strong heart and puts them in a pot to cook by themselves with garlic, lemon skin and thyme.

Epifanía carries him into the kitchen. The shadow woman has fanned the charcoal fire into a blaze of flames and sparks. She and Epifanía sizzle off the last stray feathers around his neck and feet and tail. Then Epifanía hugs him tight, all shiny from his own oil, and slips him into the giant clay pot boiling on the stove.

Outside, behind the oven, is a square of nine red tiles just like the floor tiles on the kitchen counter. A metal hoop bigger than a bicycle tire has clothespins on it to hang a sheet. They hide behind it when they stand in a round metal tub to pour water on themselves for a bath. Afterwards, they hang the tub on a nail so long it looks like the nail in the Coyoacán church that goes right through the feet of Jesus with still enough to stick out behind the cross. Next to the tree is a laundry slab with a scrubber made of ripples of cement. It's like the one at our house, but it does not have the extra cement tub of water for rinses, and there is no faucet. In the sun and in the shade laundry hangs from branches and from short lines of rope.

Everyone smells of soap. Their hair shines. They smell of the perfume of Palmolive and Colgate, which is not what we use at home because to save money my mother buys big cartons of oatmeal soap. The round bars have deep letters printed into them—AVENA—and each bar is wrapped in creamy tissue. I wonder if it really saves money. They look expensive, and it's special when Mama gives us a fresh one for our bath.

The shadow woman moves back and forth along the back wall of the kitchen. Sometimes her hair is hanging wet down to her waist. Some Sundays it's up in a ball at the back of her neck, like Epifanía's, and white strands fall around her face. She is short and round like Pilar. I can hug and lean on Pilar, but I would never touch this one. I don't know if my hand would pass through her or hit bone. Anyway, I know she does not want to be touched. She doesn't speak. She doesn't eat when we eat. She is always busy, back and forth, on her path along the charcoal burners, along the line of dark shadow the roof makes before the light of the courtyard cuts in. I think she is like that Bartolo we see in the streets. They kept him inside his house until he was a large man then they let him wander in overalls with his fly open and his sausage hanging out. They found out he could walk the streets all day and come home like a dog to sleep. So they didn't keep him inside any more. Or, she is like little Aparicio, who only left his house twice—once as a baby with his mother and against his father's orders, and once when he was seven. They had moved to a house near the river. Aparicio's mother took him for a walk on the sandy edge. After that her husband punished her by hanging her by her feet down the open well in their garden. His children screamed behind him and all the neighbors looked in through the iron gate. Finally, he pulled her up and then he left the house. When he came home he was drunk. Once I saw Aparicio sitting on his bed watching nothing, his face peaceful and beautiful, his fingers endlessly knitting the air between his knees. He was locked up in the house so no one could see what his father had made, or, if someone had paid for a curse, then so no one could see the fruit of the curse. Or, if his wife had held the baby outside in the night air, then, for fear of the sin of letting night spirits crawl into her child, emptying out those black eyes, leaving him with a face of white and perfect stone. That's why they said the father drank and hid his only son.

The shadow woman is like Maia, the daughter of Mama's friend the architect who lives in the monastery near the house that Juan O'Gorman painted Diego Rivera blue.

The architect's wife made almost all perfect and beautiful children, with hair so blond it made you squint. Like my brother Primo's. But one baby they had to keep inside. Maia never went with us to the circus. She never went with us to the *feria*. She never went into San Angel to the plaza. When I stayed overnight with them, I watched her *nana* wrap soft strips of sheets around her legs and around her chest and tie them under the mattress. Maia lay calm as an angel with her arms spread out in a white gown. She stared up at the ceiling, opening and closing her mouth like a fish breathing air, taking in and releasing one mysterious and inaudible word. Her bed was lined up with the others, each covered in white, set up under the high windows in a room where monks once slept, later nuns, afterwards prisoners, and then no one until the architect bought it for his family.

Every door in the house was a large stone arch. The only arches with wooden doors in them were the architect's bedroom and the front door. I liked his room best. Easels held plans, drawings, sketches. There were piles of transparent parchments and enormous rolls of paper with blue ink. Clothes and embroidery and woven cloth were draped everywhere. Ancient statues were on the dressers and drawings of them in pencil on an easel. Old benches from the monastery were against every wall, piled with birdcages, stone heads, an old clay couple sitting on one ceramic stool, both of them with small clay rings through their noses and clay hoops through their ears. The bedclothes flowed off one side of the bed, white sheets mixed with weavings, rebozos. Shirts and gowns hung on the walls on flat wooden hangers made all in one piece including the hook. A huge monastery desk had ceramic jars filled with brushes, pens, and a ruler bent into a perfect "L." There was an enormous briefcase with another bent ruler. On one easel was the drawing of a house he was building for Stevie, the friend of Mama and Daddy. On it he already showed where their tower would be and where each tree. Some were pepper trees dripping down to the ground. Some were eucalyptus like the one at my house, and there was a fir like ours too. In faint lines were two more groups of cottages, one behind the tower and one near the enormous gate. The stones of the wall were drawn in pencil in hundreds of pale "0's".

Everywhere in the house the air smelled of wax, incense, and the burnt string of candles. The rooms held something. Sometimes I stood still because prayers came out of the corners, whispered up to the ceilings of arched brick *bóvedas,* turned into mist and settled in my head. Sometimes something like a cloth leaving the room blew against my legs.

On the days I stayed at this house, we jumped out of bed in the morning and ran down to the kitchen for hot chocolate. The open kitchen was arches covered with green vines and yellow flowers they called goblets of gold, which, the architect said, could not grow in Mexico City, but they did at his house because it captured the sun. When they brought Maia down, they fed her bite-sized chunks of bread soaked in chocolate and pieces of chopped egg. Her jaw moved up and down like the jaws of puppets. When breakfast was

over they picked her up in a long hug and carried her to a huge
rain barrel in a corner of the patio. They sat her down inside, her
shoes tied, her clothes and her embroidered Austrian sweater
with silver buttons all closed up and neat. After a few minutes she
would stand up. She had taken off one of her shoes and held it by
the lace draped over the side of the barrel. Behind her were more
stone arches. Sun was on her blonde hair and she smiled like an
angel as she turned the white shoe at the end of the lace, twirling
it one way and another, staring at her fingers, at the lace and the
endless blur of her red and white shoe.

In the house next to Frida and Diego's, I sometimes saw a little
boy like Maia. Mama would go into Frida's house to leave a book
or an invitation, but I would stay in the car with Primo. With a
big double door open in front of him, the boy sat in the middle of
a square of sun staring at nothing. I called him Mono. Mama said
that was not nice because it means monkey, but I used it because
it also means cute. Ropes held his thighs onto the straw seat of his
woven chair. Loose ropes held his shoulders against the painted
flowers on the back of his chair. It was magic. He could rock for
hours in that chair. The front feet came off the ground one or two
centimeters and then the back feet. It was like a clock the way he
rocked perfectly back and forth and never fell.

Here in Ixtapalapa, Epifanía does not tie down the shadow
woman—her mother, or her godmother, aunt, sister, or cousin. She
lets her find her own path on the dirt floor of the kitchen where she
can mind the charcoal and clean the tiles, where all day she does
things you can't completely see. She turns the *tejolote,* the pear-
shaped pestle, inside the three-legged stone bowl of the *molcajete,*
making green, yellow and red salsas. On the special Sunday when
we eat the turkey, she kneels for hours on the straw mat in front
of the stone *metate,* her whole body swooping down and back,
while with both hands she pushes and rolls the long grinder of
black stone, an old, good *metlapil,* made of black rock and pitted

with a harder river stone, a *pedernal* that she hammered into the surface to make the holes that catch and tear at meat, grind down spices and turn pumpkin seeds to paste.

Pilar knows how to pick a new *molcajete* or a new *metate*, checking for how they have been chiseled out of lava rock, how they have been struck with the stone *pedernales* for good grinding. Then for days she works rock salt into them till she likes the surface. She knows how to do this, but she tells me, "One *metate* for life, if you are lucky. But there is always someone...."

"Someone what?"

"Someone who breaks the stone you spent your whole life smoothing."

Like Epifanía, we have two floor *metates* in our house and two round *molcajetes* because one is for sweet sauce with chocolate and one is for dishes with salt.

The sauce we are having today for the turkey is the most special *mole* that Epifanía knows. Even Pilar does not know everything that is in it. But the shadow woman does, because she grinds one by one the piles of pumpkin seed and almonds. She shells peanuts. She reaches up to nails on the beams and brings down small bags where Pilar has written *ajonjolí* for raw sesame seed. She takes cloves, peppercorns and cinnamon out of boxes and cups. On the counter she churns *chile ancho*, blood red *chile pasilla,* and *chile mulato* in the *molcajete*. When she has finished with the wet chile pastes, she burns the skin off garlic and green tomatoes and grinds them too. In the *molcajete* for sweets, she mixes raw sugar, and chile seeds with toasted sesame. Back on her knees, she turns three old tortillas and rock salt into flour. Over the charcoal fire she fries beans in lard then pours them into her round *molcajete* and stirs stone against stone till the beans are smooth. In a small enamel bowl she sizzles lard all by itself till it is burned brown. She pours it over a pile of stale *tamales* and drizzles them with vinegar before she makes them into a paste. Little by little she adds all of her grindings to a giant pottery pot on one of the charcoal fires.

She steals broth from the turkey pot. The only job left is to stir the *mole,* to stir and stir until it is time to eat. That is when she adds the dark bitter chocolate to the *mole* and the sauce shines.

While the turkey is boiling we go to the plaza. Even though Christ died, everyone is happy because they say that now he is alive and sitting next to his father. We go to the church with Pilar. Her apron pockets look silly carrying seven bitter oranges that bounce on her legs. When we get to church she puts the oranges under the painting of the mother of Jesus. "*Una para cada pena,*" she says and then she tells us the seven sorrows of Mary from before her son was born till after he died. Then Pilar walks with us to each station of the cross, and tells us the story painted in each of the pictures lining the walls of the church. By the time he is taken down from the cross and laid on Mary's lap, by the time the stone is rolled away and Mary talks with the Angel and Mary Magdalene sees Christ and he tells her not to touch him, by the time he disappears into the sky, Pilar is crying so hard we can hardly understand what she's saying. I am crying too because I never wanted anyone to hurt Him.

On the way back to eat we go into a house that has a store in the corridor and Pilar buys a thin pulp book of love stories. At the house we play marbles in the dirt by the clay oven until Pilar reminds us to help with the tables. She brings out two tin Pepsi Cola folding tables and two tablecloths with creases ironed into perfect squares. I put them on nice and even, but she turns them so the points fall over each edge. There is not room for everyone. The Shadow Woman eats in the kitchen from a plate near her face. Epifanía sits in a chair by herself where she can reach the *comal* and turn the tortillas. Pilar slices turkey for tacos, pours *mole* sauce on it, and serves us a little of everything. It is a feast of turkey with *mole,* soft hot tortillas in baskets with clean white cloths keeping in the heat, white rice with green herbs, black beans with *epazote.* We tear our tortillas in pieces and use them as spoons, and to wipe up all the *mole* from the plates. Afterwards, just because we love it, we have a giant *capirotada*. It is Pilar's best bread pudding made from her collection of old sourdough bread, pecans, eggs, cream, raisins, cinnamon and fresh crumbled cheese. When it comes out of the bread oven, she sprinkles it with drops of tequila mixed with vanilla. It has a perfume we can almost chew.

After we eat, Primo and I lie down carefully on the tight bedspreads on the bright beds. I feel Mama's baby curled tight against my chest. I wrap my arms around it as if it was already born. Primo and I try to sleep in front of our portraits painted by the woman with the screaming eyes.

8

Amado

This soul of many names
from tadpole to Blue
is still called Beloved.

Soledad Paz

If Daddy is talking on the telephone to his friend Harrington it must be important. Daddy looks terrible with green circles under his eyes, leaning his forehead on his hand. I don't like it that he is whispering. So it must be Mama. I hear the broken pieces. "...maybe in a few hours."

I didn't know my Mama was so ready, mostly because I was scared, and now Daddy is scared.

"She thinks this birth will be her death," he says.

So Mama is scared too.

"Thank you, dear friend. But... So worried. I can't bear.... Blessing what? Your prayers? That they both may live?" Tears fall on the phone table.

I slip back into the kitchen like a sheet of paper. But the baby doesn't come that day or that week.

It's still dark when Pilar wakes us up for breakfast before school.

"*Ándale, ándale,*" she says to pull Primo from his room. Your *avena* is ready and Don Alejandro will be honking for you to run to his car. You are all going early to school."

"Why?"

"The baby."

"It came in the night?"

"No, we have to get your Mami ready for the hospital."

I want to stay. "Pilar, I'll help you."

"Well, *doctorcita*, the only one who can help her now is the doctor. The taxi is coming to take your Papi and your Mami to the hospital. Hurry, get out of the way."

"I want to see Mama."

"Go then, and then right to the kitchen."

Mama is lying down, but she is ready. Her pale green night-jacket is tied at her neck. Her slippers and her suitcase are ready. A car toots, but it is not the taxi. It is the funny claxon of the Austrian count and his rumble-seat car.

Daddy surprises us, "Children. Quick, go off to school. I have to pick up Mama and carry her to the gate for the taxi. Ándale, ándale."

"Mama! Can I go with you?"

Primo says, "Don't be stupid. We can't go until the baby is already there."

I hear Mama say in a thin, stringy voice, "Leo, where's the taxi?"

"Don't worry, darling. It's coming. It's coming."

We run down the stairs. The taxi is there now too, tooting over and over as if he knows everything is urgent. We pile into the rumble-seat car. I don't get to see Mama carried down the stairs, or if the taxi is too late and the baby is already in her bed. I don't get to see anything or if she is too tired to have a baby. The *doña* next door told Pilar that women who have to lie down so many months are too weak to give birth and that usually both the baby and the mother die. Pilar said, "¡*Cállese, pues!*" Not the nice way to tell her to shut her mouth and stop scaring us.

Daddy is not home when we get back from school. Through the whole night he doesn't even call Pilar. I get up when it is still dark and ask Pilar please not to send us to school. She said, "No, no school. We'll wait for your Papi to call. It's fine. You and Primo stay here with me. Don't be scared."

"I am."

"I know."

Even Primo is hovering around us, to eat, to leave, to pet the dog, to ride his bicycle around the outside of the house. He knows Daddy is sad, too. He doesn't like that. He wants Daddy not to worry so then Primo doesn't have to worry.

It is still dark when Daddy calls Pilar.

"*Ay, Señor.*"

Ay, Señor, what? What? What? She is talking forever. She is crying and smiling and then crying again. But what happened? The baby died, so she cries? My Mama lived so she smiles? Both are gone so she cries? Both are here and coming home, so she smiles?

"*Sí, Señor. Gracias, Señor. Sí, a sus órdenes, Señor.*"

Primo and I are standing in front of her—two statues.

"*Ay, ay, ay,*" she says and gives us a big hug. Primo gets out of the hug first. I stay inside the hug to hear what she is going to tell us.

"Your Papi will tell you more. You have a new baby. He started to come last night, but he was not born until a little while ago this morning. Your Mami had a hard time. Your Papi will tell you. She's very delicate. The doctors were heroes. Her heart stopped many times last night and they gave her injections to make it work again."

"Where did they put the injections?" I want to know.

"Your Papi said some right in her heart and others, many others other places. And they gave her lots of blood. They kept saving her. Her heart stopped and they gave her another injection. They refused to let her die. Your Papi said the doctors were not going to just say, '*Si Dios quiere.*' He said they were going to do everything they had ever tried or learned or heard of and THEN if God wills, well, then…. He was so scared he would lose her. He told me. So scared he would lose both of them."

"How many injections?" I need to know.

"Fifty-two. He said fifty-two."

"That's even more than when I had twenty-one for the rabies."

"Oh, you and your rabies," Primo says. "Pilar, when can Papi come home?" Primo asks.

"He says he has to come home to sleep. He has to make sure it is all right to leave them. I'll go find you when he comes home or when he calls."

"Then when is he going to bring them home?"

"If he tells me, Primo, I'll go get you, ¿está bien?"

"Sí." And Primo is gone to be alone in his room. Maybe he had been thinking we would all die from broken hearts.

But they are alive. I will have my baby, and my Mami and my Papi.

"Soledad, when your Mami comes home, will you help a lot?"

"I'll do anything you want. Everything."

"Gracias, m'ija."

"Did he say my baby's name?"

"They wanted Esteban, but your Papi said that name was too sad. I think they are going to pick Amado.

```
                              Malintzin # 19
                              Mexico, D.F.
                              May 14
```

1
Dear Daddy,
Mama is writing my little
letter on small pages.
You said not
to waste. We are writing on
both sides.
You were gone for
your birthday when
there was a sandstorm
and no rain. It was
boiling hot.

2
Here is a pretend
chocolate for your birthday.
          O
Mama says you are 43.
You will come home with books
from there. from
Oaxaca and from Chiapas.
          X
                         un beso de
                              tu Choli

9

La Feria

Alone with bottled babies
I see something
I don't understand—
feel something
no one can see.

Soledad Paz

When the fair comes to Coyoacán, tubas and drums march over the cobbles in front of the church. The bird song of the flute juggles balls for clowns. The parade goes through the streets, passing our house. A miniature Chihuahua dog with a red collar studded with bells stands on his hind legs on a giant ball and walks it along the dirt lane between our plane trees. A fiddler steals the ball from the dog, leaps onto it and plays a miniature violin stuck under his chin as he rolls backwards down the street. I love the *feria*. Mama does not give permission. Pilar takes only me. Not Primo. Not Amado because he is too little, Pilar would have to carry him all day, Mama doesn't like him in the dust of the fair. Usually when we are out, going to church or to market, she holds my hand tight and scares me about the kidnappers. But this day, even though I am too young to walk alone, she does not make me hold her hand.

At the *feria*, Pilar meets her boyfriend, the one who is going
.o work in the fields of El Norte and then come back for her with
all his money. While we wait for him, she buys the best treat of
the whole *feria*. We get a square of waxed paper with a piece of
chicken breast covered with a hot paste of black *mole* from Oaxaca.
In a metal cup we get a thousand gold crickets deep-fried in lard.
When Pilar sees the man leaning against a tree waiting for her, she
gets up and gives me the first set of coins for me to stay as long as
I want in my favorite places.

First I go to the old tent leaking yellow light. It's not the tent
where you see the woman with a full beard we can pull and test.
It's not the one for the man with another man stuck to his side,
dressed in a double black suit, shiny and mended, with sleeves
that are too short. Their faces are painted with black lines
shooting up their temples to make them look Chinese. Black
lines, like the mouths of wood dummies, come down from their
noses. They don't have to move or do tricks. They have to stand
there receiving the arrows of stares while the manager collects
money. The tent I choose has one yellow bulb hanging in the
middle of the tent. Its pale light falls on dusty shelves filled with
large pickle jars. I push my nose against a bottle. I want to be
eye to eye with a baby, soft and doughy, settled in its juice. Its
two heads fill the top of the jar and the single pair of *nalgas* are
spread out flat on the bottom of the glass. The four eyes are sleepy,
like a cat's, with black oval slits that stare at me but do not follow
me when I move.

A baby with a hairy tail has its back to me. Others are stuffed
into jars with white metal lids, the paint scraped from many open-
ings. The babies have one hand, or one hand with one finger, or
three hands with no fingers. One girl baby wears her pastry legs
crossed over the place we don't show. One boy has his little *pajarilla*
for peeing, but it is coming out of his belly button. Another baby
boy has a sack like Chava's, but it goes halfway up his front and
halfway up his back.

This is the true room. There is nothing painted here. It makes me feel safe to see that almost nothing changes. No one is taken away and no one grows up. I like it that my memory is the same as the real forehead with one eye above a perfect face like any beautiful baby's. No one laughs in here the way they do outside at the clowns farting and spanking each other. Usually I am here alone. If there are others, they say nothing, as if they visited the babies, as if they remembered the children with no legs, noses without faces, hands like frogs growing out of sagging shoulders, the nails green through the old waters they sit in. No one makes fun. I think no one breathes.

Some people come in alone, like me, then run out to get a brother, a *nana,* a parent. I pay every year to look at the jars, as if I had never seen them before.

There is a salamander baby with lizard lumps down his spine. Another baby is a fish, his hands stuck to his ribs like fins ready to fan its pickled world and rise and fly. There is a two-baby baby like the living two-men in black suits that stand expressionless in the other tent. This baby is joined from the neck down. It is two perfect bodies, back to back, one facing one wall of the tent, one facing the other. They are a team, ready for anything, with perfect arms hanging straight at their sides and perfect thighs over four perfect feet. Both of them have long black eyelashes lying on their cheeks. Both of them have long lines of stitches on their stomachs.

When I come out, Pilar gives me more coins. I look for the man with pink spun sugar and then for the woman sitting on the ground. She wears a rebozo folded into a square on her head. In funnels of brown paper she sells *pinole,* corn ground with raw sugar and cinnamon. I lick up the powder till pieces of paper came off in my mouth.

The next coin I use for the bird in an open cage and the woman who reads fortunes. She wears a satin bandana and hoop earrings. I heard Mama call such earrings vulgar and told me I must never wear them. Bracelets go from the gypsy's ring-covered fingers all the way up to her elbows. Her breasts are like balloons trying to get out over the edge of her velvet blouse, and tier after tier of her gathered skirt fall around her on the dirt. She laughs for nothing, pushing the large circles of pink rouge up to her twinkling eyes. A blue parakeet perches on a swing until you come up. Then on a secret sign I never see, it hops down to a low velvet-covered table and picks a folded fortune out of a match-box. It flutters over to the gypsy and drops the paper into her hand. The gypsy leans one hand on her little table, looks at me and carefully reads to me. I will have jewels and sorrows. I will travel the world in the company of a dark man. I will sing like a bird but be quiet as a mouse. I will never tell anyone the desire of my heart or it will not come true. I stare into her green eyes and can't look away. Her hand drops my message onto the velvet table. She grabs my hand and pulls it open. There is a ring on each of her fingers, red stones, snakes entwined into a square, a large pearl. On her first finger is a gold coin. The two shiny crabs etched into it are fighting.

I look from her rings to her face. Long eyebrow hairs reach the edge of her satin bandana.

She gathers her fingers together and passes them in circles over the palm of my hand.

"They are waiting for you," she says. "*T'están esperando.*"

"Who?"

"*Los que necesitan cangrejos,*" she says. "People need us who were born under the sign of the crab. Crabs heal others—when they're not too busy defending themselves." I don't understand except that Pilar says sometimes, "You change your mind because you're a *cangrejo.* Primo says I'm crabby, but he doesn't really know about crabs.

Her eyes become slits hiding a green light. She laughs. Her tongue is enormous. She pats my hand hard, then leans far back in her chair and blows kisses to her little bird.

If Pilar could give me a hundred coins I would stand and watch the flutter and plucking, wait by the side of the gypsy every day to hear her read each *papelito* as if she had never seen it before, until the matchbox was emptied of all its wisdom, until everything that had already been and everything that was yet to be had been read to me. But I have to wait for the next *feria* to hear my fortune as it comes, one little paper at a time.

When Pilar is done with her *bracero,* who any day will disappear to Texas or California, she walks with me to the exit. Here she gives me one more coin, a silver *quinto,* a coin so beautiful I can hardly give it away. On one side it has a large 5, as beautiful as the lettering Mama does. On the other side are swords and lightning. Pilar and I stand in front of the organ and the monkey and listen to the uneven wail of the song the man grinds out. It ends. I ask the man to play another song. The monkey jumps on the organ, onto the man's head, over Pilar's shoulder, and onto my arm, as if he knew I was the one with the money. There, listening to the music, he twists his head up and down and around like a bird looking for seed, then suddenly, as the last note plays, he snatches my *quinto* from my fingers, hops onto the organ and drops the coin into the cigar box hanging from his master's neck. He never looks at me after that. He knows that the end of the song is the end of my time. He bobs his head and looks far away into the audience for the next coin, the next listener.

All the way home we sit on the hard seats of the trolley with its windows of yellowed glass. When we roll slowly around a corner, with the bell ringing for the next stop, people on the sidewalk turn and look. I think they are staring at us caught in our yellow glass box. All the way home Pilar and I sit without a word. I can see her reflected in the window. She can see me. When we are not looking at our reflections, we are not looking at other things, not even at the glass, but at the day that has passed.

                                    Malintzin No. 19
                                    Coyoacán, Mex., D. F.
                                    November 26

Dear Daddy,
I try to type my letter but Mama has to do it. Mama
says maybe next time I can spell by myself. But,
Daddy, I am the best speller at school. It is a secret
with Miss Galindo. I don't want her to tell anyone.
Primo will laugh. Miss Galindo does not have a stick
to hit us like Miss Salinas so I like my new little
school. We are only thirteen students. We each have
our own grade. I only am the third grade. Primo is
the only one in fourth. After lunch we do Spanish,
but outside in the shade.

I thought that you were coming home last month but
you did not come. Mama took me to have curls for permanent but someone didn't give me good curls. Mama
told them No frizzies. Now they are already gone.

Besos de tu Choli
x x x
a mi Papi solito en El Salvador y ?

buscando books books books

LIBROS LIBROS LIBROS
      Choli

10

My Mother the Hero

The half-moon bricks
held your foot in the wall.
You climbed over
when you lost the key.
Crescents made stairs
for the bandits to climb.
Cement flew as you opened
a hole in the wall with your car.
Memory dances
on shattered bricks.

Soledad Paz

The robbers are already on the roof when Mama wakes us up. She holds Amado tight in her arms and pushes Primo and me like chicks to go get Pilar out of bed. With hard, low whispers she tells us to wait in a corner of the living room, right near her room, in the center of the house. She hands Amado to Pilar. He falls asleep on her shoulder. Mama's hoarse voice makes us freeze. "Don't talk. Don't even whisper. Don't move or cry. Just stand there until I get back."

Primo whispers, "Mom, let's turn on the lights in the garden and the porch."

"I tried, Primo. They cut the electricity lines."

"Well, call the police, then."

"They cut the phone."

He seems to get smaller, and comes closer to us hiding in the corner.

Mama looks out through the French door. "There's a car with more men in front of the house. "Don't move! I'm going for help."

She's like a general, a policeman, like the soldier in the movies who holds up a flag and disappears over a hill of war and the next time you see him he's dead and the flag is running down the hill with someone else. But she's my mother, the one who makes my clothes and teaches Pilar to cook. Who drives a blue car and grows spinach and broccoli because they're good for you. She's the one who takes Amado to baby school at a place called The Pagoda because he's too young for kindergarten. Her husband my father travels to find rare books, travels in his mind, in the night, and to places he loves and hates. She stays home ready to shoot anyone who breaks into their house.

We stand in the corner near the fireplace, where the room is blackest—Pilar, Amado, and Primo. He's eight and stands straight, apart, with his head cocked to one side, his chin out aggressively, ready to take charge, maybe ready to shoot the men on the roof with his .22. I am only six but he's just as scared as I am.

We stare at the dark ceiling and hear the robber boots walking around on top of the house. They climbed up the red iron staircase that goes up to my father's apartment, now that he and Mama moved him out of the bookroom. Daddy is not home. Mama is the guardian of the house that sits in the middle of the gardens, inside the thick yellow walls of *tepetate* hung deep with honeysuckle and rose vines, and, on each side of the gate, tall walls of half-moon bricks that made arched steps the robbers climbed like stairs.

We had robbers before. Under my window. In the laundry room.

This is different. Not like the time I woke Mama up and she threw open my bedroom window and shot six times and then sat down on the floor with me as we heard the robber running away down the walk and over the fence.

Quickly she takes keys out of her purse, opens the front door just enough to slip out on her hands and knees, and crawls down the stairs to the separate garage. We hear her unlock the padlock to the side door. We hear the Chevrolet start up, then the shattering bang of wood as she rams through the locked garage doors, a squash of metal against the wall to the street, a tumble of bricks and then the screech of her tires as she speeds backwards to the corner and turns. The roar fades. She's gone.

With the men in front and the men on the roof, we huddle as small as we can into Pilar, making sure we are invisible and quiet even though Pilar is barely whispering *Diosito mío, Padre nuestro, Santa María, Madre de Dios.* We hear the robbers run down the metal stairs in back. At each step the iron clangs and echoes like a broken bell. My heart feels like a watermelon about to split open in my chest. We wait for them to bash in a door, shoot us, steal everything, and lie in wait to kill my mother. But they run around the house, clamber over the broken wall, and jump into their car. We hear it take off with its doors slamming.

In minutes, Mama is back with the police. She must have imagined that while she was gone her brood had been killed, and that even if she had found help, there would be machine guns pointed at her from the turrets of her house, from the eyes of the bedrooms, through the half-moon hollows of the brick wall.

The police shine flashlights at us and then at her and they all chatter with relief that we're alive and that the robbers are gone. In the flailing beams of light that rise and fall all over the walls, to her, to us. Mama's hair shines like a crown of red flames around her white face. Her huge blue eyes are wild, filled with tears of relief.

One of the policemen says to Primo, "*¡Tu mamá sí que tiene pantalones!*" I hear something special in his voice when he says my Mama sure has trousers. I know he means she's a hero.

In the morning the new gardener Francisco takes a ladder out onto the street and cuts off the branches of the plane tree the bandits used to reach the wall. A carpenter kneels by the garage and measures for new doors. A mason takes out the rest of the half-moon bricks and throws them on a pile. He mixes cement and starts a solid wall of flat brick. He tells Mama how on the top he's going to put a thick cap of cement, and then hundreds of pieces of broken glass. Pilar gives him our collection of empty bottles—bottles of every color, white long-necked ones of *Tehuacán* sparkling water, greenish for Coca-Cola, purple for *Leche de Magnesia,* red for *Jarabe de Codeína.* He pulls open a hemp sack. Pilar throws in the broken, hand-blown plates and cups she's saved for the recycle truck from the glass factory. The mason knots the neck of the sack and throws it down—a tan, headless torso with lumps like body parts sticking out through the cloth. With the side of the axe-head he pounds at the shape until all the elbows and knees are smashed. When he unties the sack he pours giant splinters into an old hub-cap and holds it up—a dish full of treasure.

He has completed enough of the wall to start mounding one end of it with thick cement. He climbs the ladder and mounts the end of his long new wall like a *jinete* at a rodeo. He starts at the end near the gate and works backwards. His helpers hold up square pans of cement and pans of broken glass. The cement slides off his trowel. He grabs handfuls of glass and punches their edges into the cement as if they were birthday candles. He leaves the sharp colors pointing up. As each of his cakes is finished, he slides back along the wall, slathers the cement, and punches in the glass, long pieces and short. "*Pa' que piensen primero,*" he says, as if the robbers might think twice the next time.

After the night of the men on the roof, Mama goes to the pawnshop at the Monte de Piedad and brings home a new gun, a small one that fits in her purse. The ways of her purse change. She doesn't leave it around on chairs and beds any more. It sits on top of the tall armoire, or is locked in the highest drawer of the mahogany chiffonier. Mama keeps her old pistol too, wrapped in a little blue flannel case that she made for a hot water bottle. When she goes to bed, it sleeps under her pillow.

She is not the same after that night. She is the woman of the purse. I still listen to the night and run through my dark room to her room when I hear noises. Sometimes she has to shoot into the air. Sometimes she says, "It's only *tlacuaches*." Their noisy possum fights seem like attacks on the house to me, but she can tell when it's real bandits and when it's animals coming over walls.

December 14
Malinche #19, Coyoacán

Dear Daddy,

Now the wall is different and you can't use it
like stairs anymore because of the robbers that
climbed in but don't worry. Mama drove through the
garage door and got the police.

I think you are coming home for Christmas. Or
maybe you are coming on Three Kings' Day.

The tree is so tall, I can't see the top. Mami got
on a ladder. Pilar held it and Dr. Romero from next
door. Primo held tight and said that Mami would not
fall. The doctor wouldn't let her.

Mami put a white dove on the top of the tree. The
dovetail is silver threads that fall like water. The
dove is shiny like the inside of a shell.

Mami says you like real candles on the tree. Primo
and I put white candles in all the holders.

Please come home before she lights them.

                    Your
                        Choli

11

The Child in the Hand

Quien sabe decir que sí, también sabe decir que no.
Anyone who says "Yes" can just as easily say "No."

—Mexican proverb

We are driving to Taxco for a holiday. Daddy is coming too. He has not gone on one of his book trips. We are not going to leave him at home. Usually, Mama takes us on trips with people who have children she says we'll like. Those times when Daddy didn't come I worried for him even when I rode horses, climbed the pyramids, floated in a *chalupa* on the gardens of Xochimilco, slept on the beach at Acapulco, where I felt lonely and strange. Primo and Chava went off to find caves. I practiced eating raw eggs, making a hole in each end of the egg and sucking out the yellow scramble.

When we came home from those trips it didn't really matter if Daddy did not jump up to hug us. He wasn't like that. I was happy to see that he was all right, that he was there so if he was home and he was all right, I could go to my room or I could watch Pilar cook. I didn't need anyone, or words, or touch. I didn't have to look out for the horse handler's hands sliding up my legs as he helped me mount the rental horses. I forgot the grabbing hands of the guide at the Pyramid of the Moon. He tried to help me. It was easy climbing up to the top. But going down it was so steep and the steps were each so high, I couldn't see the next step. He probably thought he was saving me from falling all the way down the face of the pyramid, but the guide held on to me too hard, bruising me, treating me like something he wanted to keep.

When we got home, I was glad to see that Daddy was fine. Ever since the worry of Salt Lake City when the hospital said that his blood was filled with salt, from putting too much salt on his food even after Mama said No. Mama said his blood was too thick to move. He almost died but they watered his blood and he got well and went to float in the lake which held him up because it also had too much salt. That's what his letter said. I have tasted my cuts and scratches, but my blood doesn't have any salt and tastes like metal.

This time we are all going together to Taxco—Primo, Amado, my parents and I. Mama always drives. My father tried to learn but he's too much of a dreamer to be a driver, always looking at what people are doing, seeing a story happening on the sidewalk. Besides he has a silver plate in his leg. It makes him cry out with pain when he uses the clutch. That's what Mama says. And it's true, Daddy never drives.

He is wearing a bright white shirt, open at the neck, and khaki pants with a brown belt. He looks so different from the man I see at home, who is in a long blue dressing gown, wearing flappy, leather slippers, or is in a dark suit, his balding head hidden under a brown felt hat, ready to go downtown for book business errands.

On this day, when we leave Coyoacán for Taxco, he is a different man. He looks free.

The blue Chevrolet rumbles and rattles over the cobbled hills of Taxco. At the top of a long narrow street Mama stops. From here we can see the trees in the plaza and the church of Santa Prisca rising like a pink sandcastle. Mama and Daddy are fighting. Most of the time I don't understand what they fight about. I am always surprised. They are just talking and talking and then like a firecracker there is an explosion.

Mama pulls the car over to the sidewalk and gets out. Daddy gets out too. They shout at each other over the roof of the car. Mama opens the back door for Primo and Amado. Absent-mindedly Daddy opens the back door for me to get out too. We all just sit there. We wait. I don't want to slide out onto their angry sidewalk. I look over the edge of the open door and down at the cobbles. They look like stone bubbles. I stare down so the voices over the roof of the car can get smaller. I look at the baby blue hinge of the open door. It is painted perfectly. Not a scratch. All around it dirt and grease are stuck together. The light catches the sheen of sky blue and for a moment I hear nothing. I want to hold on to the silence. I wrap my right hand around the hinge. It fits. The smoothness pushes cold and round into my palm. The seat squeaks as Primo gets out. It squeaks again as he pulls Amado out onto the street and slams his door shut. I don't move. The silence of the street and the sharpness of the arguments hold me in perfect balance.

"You are stingy," Mama says with her hands slapping the roof of the car.

I feel my socks rolled tight around my ankles. I hate them that way, but it is the way Mama likes them. My hair is too short, but Mama wanted to cut it because it is easier than making braids. My shoes are too tight but it is because she wanted to tie them and could not wait for me to do it because we were going to Taxco.

"I am not stingy. I'm thrifty," he says. "And you are extravagant."

"But the children must have riding lessons."

"We can't afford it. I know best. Please don't get the pony from the English girl."

"Primo needs something. Riding will be good for him, for both of them."

"Not now."

"And Soledad needs ballet. She's nearly seven. She must have it again."

"Eliana, she can dance next year when we have money."

"We have money now, Leo."

"You really must rely on me about this, Eliana. I understand about money and you don't."

"Oh, you. You, Leo, understand how to spend our money? On your students.... Our money as a hand up for those.... Oh, I don't know what to call them. I hate them."

"Eliana, wait."

"Leo, Leo. You can't save everyone."

I don't hear all the words because I am listening to the war.

It scares me, like Mama's needle when she sews, the thrust and plunge of it, too fast, finishing something beautiful, but in a rush, at the last minute, impatient. The shirring on my dress rubs my chest. She draws the needle through a thread or two and then up into the air, like a violinist with a bow. Her middle finger with the silver thimble draws back like a hammer, over and over, through the tightly gathered cloth, through the heart-shaped silver buttons, a hem, a lace. She does the details perfectly so she can keep her eye on ideas.

Glancing up, I see the look on Daddy's face. I am afraid she will plunge through with too many words, catch the skin, the flesh, make blood. It says Mama cheated in the argument, she went too far.

He starts to correct her as if she were a child. "Now you know I am doing much better.... That you're not thinking. We agreed to plan. To budget. You must listen to me."

He needs to be careful with money. He is afraid. His body says, Wait, Wait, Wait.

She's done listening. She wants what she wants.

The war scares me because they are both wrong.

I shift my weight onto the blue hinge and push on the seat. It is time for me to get out too. I see Daddy's hand. He is reaching down to the window of my open door. That's all I see, his hand flat on the glass, then he slams my door shut. A squawk comes out of my mouth. Then there is Daddy's face against mine, divided by the glass of the window. I have never seen that face. Our eyes wide. Our mouths hanging open. I can see a blur of Mama running around the front of the car and I hear screams like shots popping out of her mouth. Daddy is opening the door slowly, as if he thinks that if he's really careful everything will all go back to the way it was.

The door is open and all four of their hands are trying to reach for me but their words are firing into my body with pain, blame, pain, blame, so I don't get out and I bring my own hand up to my chest and hold it. It aches as if it had been ground up with chiles and glass.

I don't want them to touch it, but they both want to see it.

"I'll wrap it up. I'll disinfect it with mercurochrome. Gauze. Scissors." Mama is almost a nurse. She thinks one-two-three what to do in emergencies.

I don't know what I want, but it isn't one-two-three.

"I'll just do first aid, Leo," Mama says, "and then I'll go find a doctor. Oh, Lord, what if she gets tetanus." She goes to the trunk of the car for her first aid box.

Daddy is bent over my hand. "I'm so sorry. My brave Choli. But you shouldn't have...."

I want to hold him to fix his pain. He looks so helpless and sad for what he did. At the same time he is upset that I put my hand inside the door. When Mama comes back her eyes are spotlights of blame on his head. He gets out of her way so she can work.

"Hold your hand out over the street," she says gently. "I don't have mercurochrome. I have Merthiolate and iodine and alcohol. Those hurt too much. I have to use hydrogen peroxide."

She pours a bottle of peroxide over my hand. The bubbles burn and my eyes are flying from the red tile roofs to the doors where the silver men work on the jewelry, I close my eyes and think about the dark corridors of silver mines tunneling under the hills, maybe even under this street, under this car. The blood bubbles down onto the cobbles.

"That's enough. I'll just wrap it in gauze for the moment. Leo, put Amado in the car with Soledad and you take Primo for a walk. I'll get a doctor. Choli, put your button down. Don't open for anyone." Mama stops a little boy on the sidewalk. He says he'll take her up the alley to the house of the *doctorcito*.

I sit in the car with Amado. He leans against me and looks out with his beautiful blue-green eyes at the trees, the blue and white buildings, happy to listen to the birds and to say, *"Mira,"* as he looks around. I watch Daddy walk down the hill with Primo. Enormous round trees cover part of the apricot church and its double apricot spires with dabs of clay all over it as if it had been made with sand at the beach. They walk toward the cupola with blue windows like coins. Then the wide brown doors of Santa Prisca eat up my father and my brother. There is a round pond of sun in the plaza in front of the church. I watch it and wait for the white shirt and the khaki pants to come back.

Mama runs up with the doctor. He is dressed in a dark suit just like Daddy wears to go downtown. He is not in white so I'm not scared of him. And he is wearing a black hat like Daddy's, only smaller, and dark round glasses like Daddy's. His satchel is dark wrinkled leather. He sets it on the sidewalk next to him, unlatches it and opens its mouth wide. He takes out his own alcohol and rubs his hands. He looks at me as he puts one hand under mine, like a warm flat table. With his other hand, he opens up the leaves of white gauze my mother put on, then the leaves of pink gauze until he sees the red. I think of Pilar opening a special *tamal,* corn leaf by corn leaf. He holds my hand as if it were a small wounded animal. Then he starts pressing the knuckles, turning the bones, arranging each finger the way it used to be, the right shape under the cuts. It is not a doctor hurting me. His hands and mine work together. Each click and pain comes from a silent agreement, from his eyes looking into my eyes each time he puts something back in place. Tears come down my face but I am not crying. I ask him if he is a a *curandero.*

"My mother was a witch," he says with a frown and a smile. "She taught me in the old ways and then I went to university," he whispered. "Your hand is right for the old ways, and your mother was right to put disinfectant on you to keep away infection."

He takes a dark brown bottle out of his bag. With a glass wand he strokes the skin with something watery. "Arnica," he says as if I had asked. He takes an amber bottle out of his bag. It has a wand too. He paints my hand with something oily that stinks. "So the gauze won't stick," he says and covers my fingers with new layers of gauze and cotton. He puts five popsicle sticks, one against each finger, inside the next layer and adds turns and turns of gauze till it looks like a boxing glove, then he winds adhesive tape around my wrist. He snaps his satchel closed, straightens up, smiles at me, and taps his hat to Mama. She has not asked how much. There is a bill folded up under her thumb. She holds out her long white hand. I think he is going to kiss it, but he just bows over it and holds it lightly in his palm. The money disappears. He taps his hat again and goes back up the dark narrow alley.

When Daddy and Primo come back, it doesn't matter any more. Daddy's gone. Gone into the world he has with Primo. Cut off from the day, from Mama, from me, because he shouldn't have closed the door, and I shouldn't have put my hand on the hinge. Primo gets in and Amado leans on him not on me. Mama and Daddy lean against the blue bulge of the trunk of the car. I can't tell from their voices if they are cutting or mending. Their faces don't say anything when they get back in.

We bounce back over the cobblestone streets of Taxco and wind all the way home through the hours to Mexico City.

Pilar and my Mama are in the kitchen. They have set me up on the white tile counter to change the bandage.

"Pilar, do we still that that bottle of *bismuto?*"

"The one for diarrhea? Yes. It's always there on the shelf."

"My friend died last week, *la Sra. Estela.*"

"*Lo siento Señora.*

"*Gracias*, Pilar."

"Did she die from too much diarrhea?"

"No. She heard that good face powders are made with *bismuto*. She wanted her skin to be smoother, more white and more beautiful."

"Did she drink it in her water?"

"No. She made a paste of it and spread it on her face every night."

"*Dios de mi vida.*"

"I know. It's poisonous using that much. Let's throw it in the garbage."

"There are many other *remedios* for diarrhea, Señora."

They are done with the new bandage and they have left the popsicle sticks on my fingers.

Malintzin No. 19
Coyoacán
January 26

Dear Daddy,
    Tea was at Gillian's house. Remember for the war
we did parties and fashion shows to send money to the
soldiers? Mama made clothes and I had white gloves
and Gillian too.
    After tea she showed us her pony.
    The old man who takes care of him is like Rumpel-
stiltskin, He's all bent over with little eyes under
his huge hat.
    Gillian wants to give the pony to Primo and to me.
Mama says give. Not pay. We don't have to pay for him.
    But you said no horse so I don't know.
    Gillian's father is not the Ambassador in Mexico
any more so they have to leave.
    But not the horse.
    I am a little scared of him but the Rumpel-
stiltskin told Primo he would teach him everything
and Mama and me too. Bran, corn, clean his feet, hay,
alfalfa.
    Mama helped me to spell.

    Besos from your

                    Choli

12

A Heart from Tequisquiapan

God of two waters
rain and lake
mountain and flood
above and below.
Buried bells
fluted like flowers
keep silent.
Bells floating in towers
keep tolling
Tequesquitengo
but no one can go to church.

Soledad Paz

My father has brought me a straw sewing basket in the shape of a heart. It is a present for my birthday. He found it in Tequisquiapan near Mexico City. He went there on his way to villages where someone said he would find old books. At the same time he went to take the waters at Fortín de Las Flores. He told Mama that gardenias float on the waters to perfume you and to cover up the smell of rotten eggs from the mineral water that heals you. The water might come from a volcano. What if it changes its mind and sends up lava, like from Popocatépetl and Ixtaccíhuatl? He goes there to soak his bad leg. I imagine that, as he floats, the leg, weighed down by the silver plate along the calf bone, sinks into the hot, blue depths, drawing him to the bottom, while his hands make wide circles to keep him afloat among the flowers and the steam. I imagine that he lies there naked and alone, the way he does in his tub at home, though in the postcards Fortín looks like a spa filled with clumps of men and women standing waist deep in the pools and children in heavy diapers sitting on the steps of shallow pools. But I see him there naked, the black hair on his back washing up over his shoulders, his tobacco-stained fingers resting on the pool edge, the rest of his white body rising and sinking in the smelly water.

He never exactly told me about Fortín de Las Flores, or about the other place he loved, Ixtapan de la Sal. Maybe he never told me anything. I store what he tells others. I put it away here and there, in my ribs, inside the back of my head, rolled into the marbles of my spine. I fill spaces with pieces of stories, slivers of arguments, truth and lies, and spots here and there for his adventures.

He told us he took the bus to another village, in a yellow, dusty valley. There he floated in Lake Tequesquitengo that belongs to the god of its volcano. The waters are shallow and hot from rivers of lava that swallowed up the streets into the center of the new lake.

He took us there once. I swam in the water, staying close to the edge, and at the same time imagining that I could swim out, walk through the streets, and remember the town. You can see the cross on top of the spire. It's all that's left above water. Muffled by the lake, rocked by waves, the bell still calls, tolling to the dead in the world of the drowned, calling to everyone buried in the warm bath of their homes. It tolls and calls me as if a dry priest stood in the dry mud at the bottom of a dry town, his black cassock flying open and closed as he pulls at the long rope, folding and opening himself, up and down, to call us in from the edge of the waters, from the tops of the mountains, from the graves at the edge of town—to haul us in with each tone of the bell, which surely could really ring by itself, without him in the undertown, tolling and telling how the lava could not swallow its call, tolling how the volcano could not eat the cross, telling how the cross refused to sink below the waves.

By the lake I wait for Daddy. I feel submerged behind a window of the sunken town. I don't want to miss the moment he sees me, the moment he hears me. I don't want to miss it when he swims over to tell me the whole story of the flood, of the fire, and how he will walk almost without a limp after taking the waters.

The heart basket from the straw city of Tequisquiapan is almost the size of my chest. The bottom is hard wood but all around is fine woven straw. On the cover are pink satin roses with green buds on their stems. All around the sides, a pink ribbon weaves through the yellow straw. A straw ring at the bottom of the heart is the handle to open it. With my right hand still in bandages from the trip to Taxco, I hold the basket close to me.

"It's for your birthday that's coming," Daddy says.

I don't want to open it. As soon as I do he'll stop watching and the moment will be gone. Slowly I pull open the basket. The top and the insides are quilted with pink satin. Loops of pink ribbon hold a silver thimble, a spool of pink thread, a packet of needles and a tiny pair of silver scissors. On the pink tufted bed are two large spools of thick, soft thread, one black and one brown. They look out of place. Between them lies a large egg of honey-brown wood.

"Now you can darn all of my socks," Daddy says. "Such a big savings for us. Thrifty never to throw away a sock, don't you think?"

He didn't buy the heart basket for me. He bought it for him. The hurt is only because I forgot to be careful. I wasn't expecting a present. I forgot that I didn't want anything.

My thoughts make a large white sheet above me like the ceiling cloth hanging from the top four corners of my room. The large blank makes a good place to be.

After dinner Mama shows me how to darn socks when my hand gets well. How to turn the fat end of the egg into the heel of the sock and the small end into the toe. She shows me how to make the weaving, setting up a miniature warp of threads one way, up and down, then how to dip the needle and thread in and out across it. The black and brown threads match Papá's black and brown socks, rolls and rolls of them waiting to be mended.

The next morning my father plays baseball with my brother. Amado is sitting in a chair next to me. The sounds of the ball hitting the mitt please him. He seems to like Daddy and Primo saying, "Good throw," or "Well, you almost got it."

"I want to get the bat and we pitch, Daddy," Primo says.

"Not with Amado out here. He might get hurt."

I sit and watch from the steps to the kitchen. I ask if I can play three-man catch. They always say No, but today they say, "No, you'll hurt your hand."

I go into the kitchen where Pilar is experimenting with a faster way to light her charcoal fires. Instead of using her strips of resin wood, the *ocote* that smells of the pine forest behind the city, she makes tight twirls of newspaper and lights them. The paper rolls make black smoke and large, clumsy flames as she tries to get them into the square opening in the tiles of the charcoal stove. I hover close to her.

"*Azte, azte,*" she says, nudging me to move out of the way of her flames, out of the way of her efforts to get the coals started for lunch. She holds one rolled newspaper up high, ready to put it under the coals. She holds the other one out to one side, ready for the second fire. I am too close. The flame of the paper roll catches my bandage. The lightly wound gauze flares up, full of the ointments and arnica near the mending bones. The flames rise up and the heat burrows down into the skin. Pilar douses my hand in the cement reservoir of the kitchen sink. The steam drives the heat deeper into the flesh. I scream. Then the cold soaks in.

"*Ay, mijita, mijita de mi corazón.*" I am the little daughter of her heart. Then everyone else comes in and they are upset. Mama is mad because she's scared. Daddy comes in holding Amado, and maybe he's upset because we're interrupting one of the few times he gets out to the garden. My brother says he's mad because I'm so stupid. Pilar is sulking because it looks like her fault, but it wouldn't have happened if I hadn't gotten in her way. She gently cuts off the black and white chunks of gauze.

Mama always uses the same cure for burns, *Picrato de Butesín*, a bright yellow paste with oils and minerals. When Pilar is done cutting away the bandage down to the hand, Mama dabs the ointment onto the red skin. The daubs feel like new burns. To get it over with, Mama works with fast, hurting strokes. I hold my hand out for her to treat, but the hand, like my whole self, wants to lie curled against my ribs, the fingers turned up, wanting to be covered with the flat palm of my other hand, like two crabs protecting their undersides. I twist away as much as I can and push my foot against the sharp edge of the wooden chair to make a pain far away from my hand.

Pilar and Mama, are touching me but they feel far away. They stare at what they are fixing. When they are finished I sit in the yellow painted chair with the straw bottom. I feel the sharp edge of the wood against my arch, but I don't feel anything in my hand.

April 28
Malintzín No. 19
Coyoacán

Dear Daddy,

Now I can be in my room again. Mama fixed it after the
French people left. It's OK that you and Mama needed
the money and gave them my room. But now I don't have
to sleep with Primo and Amado. My room is like new.
My dolls have a place under the window. I can play
with them all I want.

I hope that every night you find a place to sleep on
your trip because you must not sleep without a bed.
One time you were sick. I don't like it when you are
sick because then I am sick too.

You said we cannot have a pony. But we have one. Can
you guess what color is the pony? You can guess all
the colors you want. But here is a secret. We call him
Caramelo.

But Daddy? Your writing room is gone. Mama made nails
in the wall for ropes and harness and bridle. Where
your desk was it is boxes with bran and alfalfa. Caramelo's brushes are also in hanging places. Caramelo
sleeps there and we clean every day. I'm sorry Daddy.

Love to Daddy from Soledad Paz.

                    Your
                        Choli

13

Doctor for Daddy

Lemniscus,
helpless in his nest,
twists zeros and eights,
on the wounds of fear.
The serpent, rises to strike,
freezes,
folds over soft undersides
and sleeps on its coils of rage.

Soledad Paz

So many names. First names. Last names. I store them like
books in my library head. Daddy and Mama invite people for
drinks. If they are hungry people, they invite them for dinner. If
they are from the British Embassy or the American Embassy, they
come for tea. If they are book people and might buy something,
they serve them coffee with buttered toast and crabapple jelly or
Pilar's bitter orange marmalade. These sweets are like the potions
and powders in the stories Mama reads to me. Maybe they make
the guests buy a book from Daddy.

Now that I am bigger, Mama lets me pass the silver sugar bowl
with silver pincers for the cubes. I pass the butter saucer with two
silver layers, one for ice and one for butter and a silver shovel to
serve the slices.

Mama knows how to do everything with nothing. She hardly has any money, but everyone thinks she's rich. She has Daddy's grandmother's silver tea and coffee set to help her, and the thick flatware with scrolls and flowers. Pilar polishes everything with special cream, and, if there is no money for real silver polish, then with Milk of Magnesia or toothpaste. When there is money, Mama calls the import store, La Ciudad de Londres, and orders silver polish, sardines, anchovies, tea cookies, sugar cubes and English tea. A shiny red truck delivers boxes to our gate and Mama feels like a queen. Primo and I learned the telephone number and ordered sugar and candy and chocolate just for fun but gave another address. When Mama found out, she took us to Ciudad de Londres and we had to tell the truth by ourselves. She didn't even say one word.

Enrique is their poet friend, the Catalán. Daddy says he escaped with his life from Spain and Franco, but I don't think he succeeded. Something in him is not alive. He is beautiful, not handsome. His nose is long and thin with a ridge in it, almost as big as the ridge on the nose of the matador Manolete. Enrique's hands, which had to kill to escape northern Spain, always lie quietly in his lap, one on top of the other. His suit is always the same one. The same tie too. He is a poet, but he had to leave other poets behind. He likes to say special things to Mama, like "*Helios*—Eliana O'Rohan de Paz—you are my sun." He says it as if he were tasting something delicious. When a new person comes to dinner, Enrique introduces Mama, and then Daddy, "Leo—Leo Paz, *bibliófilo*," as if the love of books were a passport to the world.

And everyone knows that Mama speaks Eyes.

Priests who have to hide from government attacks come to dinner. Mama says they are defrocked even though I have never seen them in or out of a dress. I save that word like a nut in the corner of my brain. Defrocked means they can't wear their black gowns on the street. One day a priest came in his dark sweater and gray trousers and put on his black gown inside our house after the door closed. Some can't go back to their churches. They live and hide where they can, with friends and with family. From the bits I hear, they run like human telegraphs, through villages in the mountains, across lakes, and through *barrios* in the city because they still want to bury people and baptize babies. Because they want to bless.

Once Mama invited a poor exiled count for tea. She also invited her Austrian friend the architect for tea. He's a count too. She found out that a count likes to be the only count in a room full of people who are not counts. It didn't matter. Mama and Daddy love them both. Now only one count comes at a time.

Dinners are the most special when the artists come. Enrique, the Catalán, reads from a little leather book of his poems, and then from loose sheets with new poems. As he finishes reading each one, he lets it slide down his legs onto his feet to the floor where it lies as if it were a pet or his child.

Fernando is a Mexican poet from New York who really only wants to live in Greenwich Village where he met Mama and Daddy. When Fernando wanted to leave Mexico and go back to New York, he asked Mama and Daddy to teach his children and to live in what was left of his hacienda after the revolution. They did that. Then Daddy found enough work in the city with an old book dealer. When the old man asked Daddy to buy the business, all the books, Daddy bought it. Eventually Daddy could buy our house in Coyoacán.

Juan O'Gorman comes, and his wife Helen. Juan is too tall and too handsome. It is hard to look at him, so perfect and sad. A hero in my house. In her own way, Helen dresses like Frida in clothes from Oaxaca, Veracruz, Tehuantepec. Her braids are different. She makes a kind of half crown, the braids like bricks woven back and forth above her forehead, the thick yarn of many colors coming in and out of her dark red hair. Frida's hair and her braids are more like a hat, a separate creation exploding in bows and flowers. Sometimes Diego Rivera and Frida Kahlo come to visit. Juan and

Diego both paint famous murals. They can't stop talking to each other maybe because they don't always agree. Juan built Frida and Diego their own studios in San Angel. Some people call the two equal towers "the twins." Siamese twins, maybe, because the towers are bound by a bridge at the second story so Diego and Frida can go from one studio to the other. Juan and Diego don't talk about the president of the republic because then glasses crash on the table and Juan or Diego pretend to walk out forever. When Helen and Juan are separated, only Juan comes, or Helen. When Diego and Frida are separated, only she comes or he, but not both. On those times they bring someone special instead of each other, and when they come through the door into Mama's living room all the air is sucked out. At the same time everyone goes on talking without air, pretending to eat and drink as if nothing had happened.

Mama talks to everyone. It's like watching ballet, or boxing, or even a bullfight. Men and women, but mostly men, speak to her as if she has studied with them, as if she knows what they do, even as if they could learn from her. I watch their dances. It's her eyes. If she talks to you, her eyes are yours. She is like a heroine in a story. No one knows the secret of her spell. Maybe it is because she stops watches. Her blood is magnetic, they say, or maybe she stops watches because her heart is electric. Maybe Daddy knows. Maybe that is why he and Mama fight.

I watch how Daddy greets Fernando. He just shakes his hand with a quick bow. He does not embrace him or pat him three times on the back the way Daddy does all the other men he knows, and he does not start a conversation. I watch Mama and I watch the poet. He has a delicate face with a long nose and a mouth that looks like pale charcoal as if an artist had rubbed it with his thumb. He wears his inside on the outside. If I could give him a name, his name would be pain. He is the picture of a man who might be ordinary, even nobody, but when he is near my mother, as anyone can see, he's suddenly extraordinary. He's a prince. He shines. He's a small peacock free to open his feathers and show off all of his colors. After a while he doesn't read his poems when he comes, and then he stops coming. He is not a guest for supper or for coffee, tea or drinks.

Here they are. Some of Mama's men—and I want them to be mine. Under my birth heart another secret heart of love is growing. I look down at the lacy silver dish. The miniature toasts with quince jam and *queso fresco* are disappearing. I look up and see Otto Butterlin. He says the same thing every time, "When you were a baby I held you like this in my arms," and he cradles his arms. "Now that you are growing up, shall I wait for you so I can marry you?" Some days he says, "I wish I were twenty years younger, Choli. I would wait for you." It's all right when he teases. With him it's all right.

Other people come. People who have left the United States or France to live in Mexico where they can write novels or study tribes and old art. They go on digs with Mama's friend Frans Blom and discover giant Olmec heads and small figures of men and women. Mama invites anthropologists who study with Frans Blom in Chiapas. He protects the stone-age Lacandons with their chopped black hair, their faces carved out of mahogany, and their man dresses of *manta* cloth.

"Nothing is more urgent than time," Blom told Mama. "The Lacandons are dying. Even though they have survived for hundreds, maybe thousands of years, now we are killing them." The Indians call Frans their protector Ba-lom. His name sounds like the call to a god.

Daddy doesn't have what Mama calls party talk. He finds a corner and smokes and watches. He doesn't like everyone talking at once. He's happy if one person sits down with him and discusses something important for a long time.

Salvador and his wife come to supper from across the street. Sometimes he brings his wife, sometimes he comes alone. She drapes herself in chairs like a model as if someone were going to paint her picture any minute. Her orange painted hair is too bright and she wears a magenta shawl. Mama says you never wear magenta with red hair, and, she says you don't wear a shawl that looks like a piano cover, but this woman does. I bring cream and sugar to her. Even though Primo and I play with her son Chava, she doesn't look at me. To her I am like a servant, so in my eyes her hands change into witch claws with long lion nails. When she drops sugar lumps into her coffee, I see dragon wings rise green into the air as if poison melted in her cup. Salvador shows his sketches and photographs of the new sculptures he is doing for the city. Some are still clay. Some white plaster. He is smoothing giant foreheads, breasts and soft bellies. He shows bronze pieces he is polishing for the sunlight that will fall on them when they are in their places around the huge fountains on the *avenidas*. In a corner of the drawings, hidden from the blaze of a nearly finished nude, is the newest figure in wet clay, the one he was shaping, pressing with his hands, washing, reforming, refining. From the pictures no one could tell, but I had been to his studio. I knew it was Mama.

The women who come to visit our house are the painters and writers from the club Mama goes to for shooting practice. Even though Mama shoots her gun into our eucalyptus every Sunday, we still have burglars who throw leather jackets over the wall poked with broken glass and climb over. Some of Mama's friends are the women who learn about how cars work. Mama found a mechanic to teach them how the main parts work, how to change a tire and check for oil. In the photos that Stevie took with his Kodak at these parties, Mama looks like the stars in the magazines, her red hair is a lion's mane, her face is like Hedy Lamarr or Deborah Kerr.

Stevie comes with his wife Annette and she brings a famous friend who says, "Annette, you are an artist, but your husband is an industrialist."

Annette defends Stevie the way she does when anyone criticizes him for being rich, "Stevie is a patron of the arts. He loves what we make. We all need each other. He's an exile too. Don't you know?

An immigrant, with no English; penniless. He is an artist—he created everything he dreamed of and now he shares it."

Mama says, "I love Stevie because he makes other people's dreams come true."

That is Stevie. All in one sentence that I can carry inside me with my love for him. Everyone knows that Stevie's heart is worth more than money, and that his goodness could pick them all up and save them if he had to. Annette is painting giant murals up on a scaffold with José Clemente Orozco with his big black glasses, and she has her own paintings too. Diego Rivera painted her with her hair on fire just like Mama's, and then he painted a portrait of Stevie, as he really is, a hero.

Anita Brenner knows everyone in Mexico City, even though she is from Aguascalientes where she grows avocados. She's also a half and half, *ni fu ni fa,* because her parents were from Europe. She was born in Mexico so she says she's a Mexican. She works as if a shaman had beaten her with wet leaves and told her to Write! Write! Write! Anita writes to help make *The Wind that Swept Mexico.* She takes photographs with Tina Modotti. She poses naked for Weston. She starts a magazine about Mexico, even though she is too busy writing *Idols Behind Altars.* I visit her house because her daughter is my friend. At night Anita brings us each a large hand-blown glass of *jamaica*—hibiscus blossoms boiled with sugar and turned maroon and sweet—even though Mama says no sugar before bed.

Helen O'Gorman goes to pistol class too. But she is busy traveling all over Mexico painting all of its flowering trees to make her giant book. She brings sketches and suddenly everyone wants a red firecracker flame tree, or a yellow *primavera* in their garden.

Mama wants only one of Helen's trees, a rare *clavellina,* with a bloom coming out of an acorn into the crown of a passion flower that blossoms pink like giant honeysuckles with butterfly antennas. Finally, she gets one.

Renate comes sometimes. Mama says she is also an exile because she was forced to leave Czechoslovakia. Renate doesn't bring her art to the house. She saves it for the giant puppet shows she makes for us in her garden. The puppets sound like trolls, with their words mixed up in Renate's language, and her funny Spanish.

Mama loves doctors. She invites psychologists, homeopaths, osteopaths, surgeons and psychiatrists. The doctors know what is killing the Lacandons. Tuberculosis, and diseases they whisper when I am near as if I can't hear them say syphilis. Mama says it. Daddy says it. I hear them talk about the stages and how someone had already died of last stages and paresis. Still, guests make it one of their whisper words.

Something about it in the family. The question Daddy and Mama ask in their fights is Was it madness? or Was it syphilis? So, Does it run in the family? or Did Grandfather catch it? And they go to specialists who tell them that madness does not run in the family. Their children are safe. It is a good answer and it is a bad answer because when I hear them talk about the specialist neither of them is happy. It means they know the truth about my famous, honorable, successful, fabulously rich Grandfather, who lost everything. Something about the women, and now the sanatorium, his memory gone, his eyes wild, the disease spread to his brain. A wealthy old family friend, who loves to own secrets, pays for the sanatorium so they won't put Grandfather back in the asylum. I can see my father shrink with disgust at how much they owe him and how much they have to pay in words and compliments and visits. He can come at any time to their door, for a meal, to tea, to talk. He likes to come for dinner, which at our house is always at two in the afternoon, because something in our family is southern, and Mama likes the southern way of saying that dinner is at midday and supper is in the evening. If he comes to dinner it means he does not have to stay very long because he likes to go home for his afternoon nap. After the visits Daddy washes his hands as if he and Mama had touched a thief. When they say that he is wealthy AND he is good, they say the wealthy word as it were sticky. Daddy's family was "wealthy." But the gold is gone, which is why this friend gets to pay for Grandfather and to visit my Aunt Soledad as if he were her *novio* and as if she would be his *novia* some day and then he could kiss her more than on her ear and she would marry him when Grandfather died.

Mama likes to talk to doctors about the latest cures and fakes. When she is talking to a doctor I can see how she looked at her father who adored her and who treated her as an equal, a chosen child, favored over her sister and her brother, even over her mother. She called him Father, but her sister called him Pop. I asked about Pop once. Mama said that was a silly name for "my-father-your-grandfather," and from her face I got the feeling that I could only borrow him for a second and then give him right back to her like a porcelain doll before I dropped and broke him, even though he was already dead.

One of the doctors is Dimitri. "I studied with Freud," he says, repeating always that he's a specialist in mental illness and art. He wrote a book about art and maybe also about the mind. He gave Daddy a copy of the book without a binding. Daddy said it was fine because he goes to the bookbinder all the time. He'll cover it in nice blue leather. But Daddy never takes the book to the binder. Mama thinks it would be perfect to get help from him because Daddy is a writer, which makes him an artist, and my father is depressed and unhappy and doing bad things, so he needs help. Dimitri, with his perfectly trimmed mustache just like Daddy's, and his black wavy hair, not at all like Daddy's, moves into our house with his wife. Into my room because my room is always the one. They are going to live with us. In exchange for room and three meals a day and coffee in the afternoon, Dimitri will be Daddy's doctor, his analyst. Mama thinks he can help. I move into the little extra room with my brothers. This time there are three beds. Primo and I each have our own and Amado too.

This doctor says he is Russian. They talk of White Russians and of Russians who aren't white. The conversations do not go well.

"For God's sake, Dimitri. Never mind. Let's talk tomorrow."

"You have secrets?"

"Yes. No. Not about Russians. I'm sorry. I am going to go back to work now."

"You go. We talk tomorrow for cure. Now coffee time."

Later Dimitri and his wife criticize my father because he has a business in his house and because his name is old and his roots reach into what they call society. They don't understand when my father says he ran away from all that and has to work hard for every cent.

He tells Mama, "Dimitri is the last man on earth to help me."

"We seem to have no one else. Can you try?"

"For you, yes, I'll try, but...."

"Wait and see."

The Russian and his wife eat alone. "We must eat in room," Dimitri said, "to preserve family. We are only two. But, so, we are family." Mama says Dimitri speaks Russian and French and Spanish. But his English is funny, as if he were walking down stairs and missing some steps.

Pilar takes their trays of food through to them. I thought he was angry and didn't want to be with Daddy or Mama. But after they eat they come out and have more tea and more dessert at our table. I didn't know you could be so hungry.

Mama says, "Maybe Dimitri doesn't really need more food. Maybe he wants to watch Daddy with us, with you children, with me."

Daddy wants help with his terrible nightmares. Dimitri has only one patient—my father. Dimitri says, "I must see you, hear you. No interruptions. I am yours alone." Dimitri waves his wife away to her room. We all have to go out, away, to the garden, or to someone else's house so the treatment can take place in the living room with its walls of books. One day, after Mama leaves, I come back and look through the crack of the long gold velvet curtains between the living room and the dining room.

The analyst sits behind my father in the brown velvet chair, which is really the story chair for Daddy to read aloud to me and to my brother Primo from *Kidnapped* and *Tom Sawyer*. Dimitri starts by talking and talking. He says Freud and Freud, and more Freud.

My father lies on the couch in his dark suit with his tied black shoes just off the edge of the velvet cushions. I close my eyes and tell my hands to move across the room to him. They slip thinner than a thought into his shoes. My hands give him a floor for the pain. His black eyes are open, staring at something beyond the ceiling. He holds his head as if to smooth his black hair over words, sounds, over scars from the fall that broke his skull open when he was six. I was six in Taxco, but my hand is nothing to Daddy breaking his leg, his arm and worst of all his head opening like a melon.

I hear Dimitri say, "Go on." Dimitri is treating my father for something in his mixed blood—passion from France, sorrow from Spain, and losses from Holland, England and New York all mixed up in his Mexico. I hear Dimitri say, "Your mind is stiff. You pretend to give up ancestral dreams and castles. You pretend not to care you are disowned by aunt, that you lose millions, but you give up nothing. Nothing. Maybe you are a fake—bad son and bad father."

I have never heard anyone say anything bad about my father. Dimitri says, "You are lost. I find you."

I know my father goes away all the time. I know I am afraid that one day he might not come back. But Mama always knows where he is. She doesn't think he's lost.

Dimitri talks about how he will treat him for a terror. He says, "We will go together to stones of your dungeons. We will ask Why, Why, Why?"

I forget about the curtain. I forget that Pilar might come and yank me back to her kitchen. I forget that Primo might tell on me. I forget that my father might see me. It doesn't matter. I have to hear. It's part of me.

"We must find why, when you hear No-This-is-Not-For-You, you want it. Why you want something bad and same time want family love. Why both?"

Daddy says, "But there is something else. I don't want to go mad like my father. I don't want my children visiting me and staring at my long hair and thick beard as if I were Robinson Crusoe. For God's sake, Dimitri."

"Well, maybe more you want be heroine like your mother."

"Don't be ridiculous. I am sick. I'm angry at my mother but I don't want to BE her. I want to be free of her. I want to stop disobeying her like a child. I want to obey, but obey the GOOD that I know. I teach my children to obey and then I DON'T do as I say! I live here in this house filled with light and sun. Then I run away to the secrets of the night. The night people are different. It's like a dream with no hours. Then I come home to sleep, and when I wake up it is day and another nightmare of regret begins. I don't know how to be a good... a good writer... a good man, a good father, a good husband. I never knew my father. No memories. No memories of my mother with her husband. What is a family? Help me! Can't you make me stop running? My son must not see what I've done. I must get well. I want to set a good example for my son."

He has forgotten. He's thinking Father and Son, like in his life. But we are three children. Why not Father and Daughter? Why not Father and Sons? Maybe he can only think of one at a time. Maybe his life stopped when he was just one son. Stopped when he could not see his father. In the story he wrote, he was little when they put his father in the "looney bin." Everything else he knew was what his mother said after she visited his father and her stories. Her stories scared him.

Dimitri growls at him, "Well, you are boy who love mystery and lies. Maybe no cure. YOU must work hard with me. Work— my single hope."

My father seems to sink deeper into the sofa. "You don't understand. I used to be like Don Quixote. I had dreams to do everything for my family. Hopes. Ideals. Now I am as sick as Dostoyevsky. "Can you hypnotize me and make it go away?"

"Very hard, hypnotism. Not hypnotism in my cure. We go together there. Follow sound of my voice. Close eyes. Never look at me. Speak. When you speak, say only truth. Tell me father story."

I lie down with the crown of my head against the velvet hem of the curtain. Half asleep, I follow Grandfather with my father to dark streets, to lies and danger and the passion to fix the lives of women who would be good if they could, if someone would just give them a hand, help them instead of use them, to save them, to save one. I hear Daddy tell how when he comes home he knows in his heart that those he loves most in the world, his wife and children, sleeping in his house, are unhappy in some way from what he does wrong and what his father did wrong before him and that's how his father got such a terrible sickness.

I thought Grandfather was a hero. They always told Primo and me that he had a nervous breakdown trying to repay the millions his partner stole. Embezzled, they said. And that Grandfather fell from his prize thoroughbred when he was racing through fields to clear his head. No. It was from something else, and then the madhouse.

"I can't sleep!"

Daddy says it so loud I shake on the floor. There is nothing but nightmares, his father behind asylum bars, eyes burning through long filthy hair—his beautiful mother dying of cancer—his own fall from the roof to the courtyard where the doctor crouched over him to take the brick dust off his brain with a chicken feather, and set his bones before he was carted off to hospital—the mockery and shame of having a limp, exiled from baseball and games of catch—and finally the addiction to his falls from grace.

Dimitri whispers, "So you are hero because you rescue female mice in filthy streets of night?"

I tried to rescue a mouse once. I knew if it went near the trap the metal bar would fall on his neck and he would be dead. At the last second I picked him up by the tail. He turned his whole body up in a loop and bit my finger to the bone.

"You think you are hero because you save woman cockroaches?"

"No!"

"Da! Hero pulls man his own size from ice. Hero pulls BIGGER man from fire. Pulls out giant! That is hero!"

"My father tried to help them too. To someone they were sisters or daughters. He tried to get them better jobs, learn to be someone, raise them up a little so they are not used up by...."

"DA!" Dimitri roared. "Is clear. Father and son. Same. Rat women give kisses. Men on knees to save RATS! You must rise. Stand up. Look UP! Save someone BIG. Save someone like you. Tonight dream HERO big like man."

Daddy's eyes are open and staring. Tears fall in a steady stream from the corners of his eyes onto the velvet pillow. He is shrinking, melting like butter into the couch, and my body is sinking into the smooth, polished floor.

It isn't enough that my parents feed Dimitri and his wife and hold them in the family and give them my room. It isn't enough that they have a home and that my father trusts Dimitri with his soul and with the hope of being cured.

After lunch one day Daddy goes to the bathroom to get ready to go to the post office. He leaves me by his typewriter with a short letter to copy for him. Dimitri walks by me into the room where Daddy sleeps, with the bookshelves in rows, made back to back by Daddy like the letter "A". I look up again. Suddenly Daddy is going into his bookroom just as Dimitri is coming out.

"That's my wallet, Dimitri."

"Your. Your. Your. For my work you pay me few pesos and coffee and this and that?" He takes bills out of the wallet and cuts the air with them. "Capitalist! Pig! Jew!" His face is ugly, all teeth and screwed-up eyes. "And my wife? Cook poisons her. When she comes in with a tray? She steals from us on way out."

He stares at my father and yells something like *ushnaya-gaDOST,* which sounds like a little dance, but he spits out, "Horrible garbage."

I watch my father Leo Paz being speared by Dimitri. Mama and Daddy aren't Jewish, but I think sometimes they want to be because they love their Jewish friends.

Daddy whispers, "Get out of my house."

Then Loud, like Hero, Daddy Shouts at Dimitri, "How Dare You Steal From Me after everything I've done for you? Get out of my house! Take your crazy wife and get OUT!"

Dimitri squeaks, "You are robber bandit capitalist. I will finish you." He sticks the money in his pocket, throws the wallet at Daddy's head and runs to his room, which is my room.

Mama gets phone calls and runs to find Daddy to tell him that Dimitri went to the police and told them stories about my father, that he committed crimes against Mexico. The next morning Daddy opens the newspaper he writes for and sees an ad full of accusations against him.

That night a friend of my father comes to tell Daddy he must run away immediately to another part of the city. Someone has been paid to kill him. I hear him tell Daddy, "Don't leave the city. In town they have to be more careful. We can watch out for you. We can find a place to hide you. Out in the country they'll shoot you for a few pesos and throw your body in a ditch."

Daddy is gone. In a few weeks somebody talks to the right person. I know it is someone who loves Mama. The dangerous ads say good things in the newspaper and my father is not put in prison as a traitor. They tell Mama no one is coming to kill him any more. It is over.

Dimitri and his wife disappear.

Daddy's nightmares continue. There is no one to help.

November 8

Dear Daddy,

Mama says after Honduras you are going to Texas
to the man who loves your books. Does he have more
books than we have?

The little spoon is in the salt pot on the table. But we are going to hide it when you come back
because we don't want you to die from too much salt.

I have no more letter today.
I am sick with sore throat.
I am going again to bed.
Are you in bed too?
Does your throat hurt too?
Sometimes I think when you are sick I am sick.

Mama helped me not to misspell.

Love from your Choli

14

Swimming under Salvador

You and I are one.
You shield me from the sun
and fish me from the sea.
You belong to me.

Soledad Paz

Mama plans the excursion. We're going to the hot springs of Cuautla, south of Cuernavaca. No. Daddy is not going. I don't hear all the reasons, but Mama is mad because she waited for him all night and he didn't come back, so Daddy is staying home. I saw the three suitcases that fit into each other and look like one until he separates them and keeps one for laundry and clothes and sends the others home filled with books. I don't want him to go away again.

"The children are going," my mother says to Daddy, "but not Amado. I don't want him near the hot springs. He'll stay home with you. Oh, don't worry. Pilar will take care of him."

So Primo is going with us and our playmate from across the street, Chava, which is the nickname for his whole name, Salvador, just like his father. I don't hear the reasons, but his mother is not going either. She is sharp and her hair is painted bright orange. Even though he is a famous sculptor, she screams at her husband—a high red scream with white fingernails in her mouth for teeth, and her green eyes too bright. She puts a bandana around her head and ties it like a gypsy when she cleans her house. She leaves rough, damp cloths spread out like rugs at every door in the house and tells us not to get her floors dirty. Across the street at Don Chucho's store, called "La Malinche," they say she's *zafada* to wash her marble floors on her knees when there are girls right around the corner who would do it because they really need the *centavos*. Mama says she does it because she is Polish and because of the war.

I think she's crazy. There is no heart in her long white body, except when she bathes her boy Chava. Right after the bath, she wraps him up in a big white towel and sits him down on a bench with cushions. She thinks I am nobody, so it's all right for me to watch. She doesn't know who sees out of me. She dries her boy with the white towel, then she takes out a round box of talcum powder with a white velvet puff. She smoothes powder on him, moving the puff around on his body, on the back and the front. With two long white fingers she picks up his *pajarilla*, his little caterpillar—that's what Pilar calls it when my brothers are in the bath and their two pink caterpillars are bobbing in the water— and Chava's mother powders under it and pats his little lavender sack. It is wrinkled like a walnut with a raised seam between the halves. She dusts it and puts his worm back down on it. She powders his thighs and lifts his arms, ragdoll limp, to spin the powder puff in his armpits. Then his neck, his toes. I learned to powder the newborn baby next door. I didn't know you would powder a large boy with no diapers. Something in her is calm. Her eyes ride all over his skin.

Little Salvador sits still as a doll on the white towel. He looks like the naked chickens Pilar props on the tile sink, washing them inside and out, rubbing lemon on them and wiping them dry. He is not fun and mischievous like he is with my brother. There is nothing in his eyes. He's like a puppy waiting for his bath to be over. The large white towel covers the bench and falls across the floor like spilled milk. At last his mother pulls up the corners of it and wraps him. I think she wants to pick him up and carry him to his room, but she lets him walk by himself. I can go too and wait while she dresses him. She points him to a long bench of dark green leather under the window covered in green vines. She pulls one thin white sock over one foot and then the other, smoothing the sock like a skin, her hand passing under his arch, over the instep and up his ankle, stopping as if she does not want to stop. She puts his undershirt over his head, pulling his arms through like the arms of a baby. Then his sweater and his pants. He doesn't even have to tie his shoes himself. The thin leather is caked with white polish. Afterwards, he and I walk down the long black corridor toward the garden where the sun leaks through tall vines onto ferns and over the green moss on the bricks of the walk. We walk like soldiers to the gate and out onto the damp yellow earth of the street.

After the gate closes, we run to where my brother Primo is waiting on his bicycle, and we dash screaming to the corner store "La Malinche." We jump when the side door of the store opens. I think it is La Malinche herself, mummified, electrified, her black hair turned grey from too many years with Cortés, and come to live at Her Name house. But it is Chucho's mother who isn't even supposed to be let out. She is scared of us and jumps back behind the door. We buy *paletas Mimí,* our favorite suckers of burnt sugar. We rough up Chava's perfectly combed hair, kick dirt on his heels and step all over his white polished shoes. Chava grabs my brother's bicycle and jumps on it backwards. Making clown faces, he rides wobbling down the street to the wrought iron gates of our house.

Mama asked Chava's mother to paint Primo's portrait. Then Mama asked her to make my portrait. Her paintings are famous. Not as famous as her husband's sculptures, but big cars with chauffeurs bring people to her house to be painted.

The day of the portrait Mama walked with me across the street to leave me with Chava's mother.

"*Dios de mi vida*," she said, staring at my face near Mama's waist. "Look at her eyes. What color are they? Well, don't worry. Maybe she'll be beautiful like you someday."

I followed her to the dark studio at the back of the house and sat down on the straight wooden chair with painted flowers. I looked out at the garden through the small panes of glass set from floor to ceiling. The trees had wet, twisted black trunks. But their blood came out in new green leaves. The red bricks under the trees grew moss. Primo and Chava and I knew how to skate on the moss when no one was home. I wanted to look far away through the branches to where shadows moved.

"Over here!" she said, moving her thumb in the air to make me turn my head. I looked at her without blinking. She sat in a leather chair with green cushions, and her long gown of green silk spread out over her feet. A small canvas was already on the easel. She stuck her thumb through the hole in a round sheet of wood. It was covered with coils of paint as if birds had flown in and squirted colors on it. She took two brushes from one bottle and stuck them in her fingers under the board of paint. She took more brushes from another bottle, held them, looked at them, and then looked at me. She stared. I stared, trying to see her as a mother, an eye, a person. But she was made of thick glass and there was no way in. I waited. Suddenly she screamed, "I cannot paint those eyes! I cannot paint those yellow eyes! Get out!" She threw a handful of brushes at me and I ran home.

Later she asked Mama for a photo and she painted me from that. She didn't want to lose the *centavos* she would get paid. When Mama brought it home she looked at it and said, "This isn't a real portrait. It's not a likeness if you don't sit for it," and she gave it to my nurse Pilar, and Primo's portrait too. We both hang in Ixtapalapa in the large room where Pilar's sisters sleep. The little girl in the painting has two long, dark brown braids over her ears, the way Mama braided them. I like them behind my ears the way Pilar does it. Crooked bangs come down to her gold eyes. Her face is there, but there is no one inside her. She looks out into Pilar's room in the village where Pilar takes us sometimes. Pilar does not really live there. She lives at our house, in a small room off the kitchen.

Big Salvador is going to the springs with us at Cuautla. Mama says he studied in Paris with Maillol, and now his women lie in large bronzes at the edges of gigantic fountains. His women, smoothed and polished by his hands, rinsed and gleaming under sprays of water, are goddesses of the wide *avenidas* of Mexico City. They sit at the top of tall marble steps, their gold breasts pressed between long, round arms. The city is like his own sculpture garden. I saw one of them in his studio. The enormous room was full of clay figures, wax miniatures and bronzes ready to polish. I saw the beautiful white woman he was carving in marble. She was alive. The stone glowed. The breasts were like skin filled with water pulling toward the ground. One thigh lying heavy on the other looked soft. Even though the face was different, I knew that inside her, in the neck, in the shiny bones of the knee, was my Mama.

Salvador is special. I don't remember his voice but I remember his body. He let me lean against his firm belly, his soft gray sweater against my face when Primo and Chava were mean to me in his car. When they pulled my neck hairs, I didn't tattle because then his red-hair wife would turn around with her eyes of green ice. If I said anything, the white nails of her teeth would slice out of her beautiful face and bite me. But when the car stopped, the boys ran off, and she got out and went through her gate, then he opened my door and I fell against him. He didn't ask what the boys had done. He let me cry for a moment and I hugged him. Then I reached back into the car for my school bag and went home where Pilar waited holding open the gate.

My mother has packed a picnic. There is something distant and excited in her. In the car she and Big Salvador sit in front and I have to sit in back with Primo and Chava, but I get a window and don't have to sit between them. Today the boys are laughing and punching each other and they leave me alone.

The spa is covered with trees. The hot volcanic waters come out of a white grotto and spill over gray-white rocks into pools strung on steaming rivers winding down the hill. The eucalyptus and pepper trees trail their long leafy arms in the blue pools.

Water rushes in the river, speeding faster and faster as it goes downhill. A leaf drops. We run along on the mossy edges following it. We can see it caught up by the water, spun, swallowed, thrown against a blue-white rock and stuck, then washed back into the deep and out of sight, gone, faster than we can run.

Mama has picked a middle pool. Next to it a wide grassy lap spreads out under the pepper trees. She lets the wind loft a teal green cloth and then she lowers it to the ground. She takes two whole roasted chickens out of the basket. The aroma of fried onions comes out of a tall paper bag still steaming from the rotisserie on Avenida Insurgentes. There is bread from "La Malinche"—*bolillos,* the sour two-pointed loaves like feet in ballet shoes. Pilar has stuffed them with sweet butter. They are crisp outside, and white as cotton inside. Mama is serving Big Salvador. She pulls off a slab of breast the same size as the roll and slips it onto the butter. She adds a handful of shredded, deep-fried onions. Before she passes it to him, she wipes her hands clean on a big white napkin. I don't think they see us. Primo and Chava and I grab drumsticks and some *bolillos* and run through the trees to the river. The water is clear. We can see rocks below the blue stream. Above us we hear the yelps of the people trying the hottest water straight out of the grotto. Below we hear the cooing of those resting in the cooler pools.

The boys play games in the trees. They don't want to play with a girl. Under the trees the shade is cold. I go where I want to be, by the edge of the warm water, to feel the river that rises up the side of the grainy white rock, lifting lips of waves at my legs. It runs its hands over my feet and over my ankles. It spins hot and firm around my calf, pushing and turning, rising to the knee, pulling

me, wanting to bathe me and hold me. It comes higher on my thigh.
It is so clear on the bottom that I can see each grain of sand around
the gray round rocks. I want to reach down and bring up one small
rock just for me. I bend forward and reach in as far as I can.

It's too deep. I can't touch the stones and I can't hold onto the
edge. The water tips me, turns me, swallows me.

I cry out, but I am pulled and swept away. I'm upside down. I
come up just before the river pours itself over and begins its fall on
its way to the next pool. I cry out again but I choke, and now I'm
in the long, straight part of the river. I don't close my eyes. I think
of Pilar praying about death to Our Lady—*ahora y en la hora de
nuestra muerte, amen.* I watch with my eyes open. All the froth
and bubbles like the flowered skeleton of La Calaca, La Muerte,
with her wide-brimmed hat flapping around her hollow skull. And
Pilar in my head saying, "See? *¿Ves? ¿Quién te lo manda?* What
were you thinking?" The warm blue water twists me and throws
me. I am face up then I am face down in the water. My arms and
hands flail. I hit rocks and swirls and turns and deeps. When my
head comes up through the water, I yell.

Suddenly I see Salvador running on the bank beside me. The
river turns and plays. He runs straight along the edge but he can't
keep up. He calls to me and I turn my eyes against the rolling of
my neck to see him, to keep him with me. Please don't stop. Please
don't stop running. He sees me. He's coming. But the river teases
me to the other side. I turn again into a swirling eddy. Now he's
running ahead. He's over the flat of the river. I see his legs strad-
dling the water. I try to keep my eyes on his gray head shining in
the sun. His arms are open. He is motionless like one of his statues.
The river is suddenly shallow and it shoots me forward, stretched
out, my hands and hair flying out behind me, my feet pointing
toward the bridge of Salvador.

He lunges forward from the waist. I fly up into his arms. Stum-
bling and toppling, he carries me to the grass and sets me down.
I don't know if I cry. My mind is full of him waiting to fish me. I

only see his large sure head, his gray hair with pieces of sun on it, his wide brown face solemn. Panting, he bends over me on the grass.

I am safe, lying on my back on the grass. When my mother comes running up, he has to comfort her. The words they have are for each other. They take me back up the hill to the cloth of the picnic. They wrap me and sit me. Maybe they feed me or scold. They comfort each other. They don't look at me. What he did, he did it for her. What she feels for me, that I did not drown on the day of the picnic, she feels for him who saved me.

Even if they don't see me, the blue above me is mine, below me is a hot white river, which is mine. The race when he carried me in his arms is mine, and the moment he leaned over me, on all fours, panting, is mine.

Primo didn't see me. Chava didn't see me. When we come home Mama doesn't say anything. Pilar sits next to the tub with me and keeps an eye on the new water heater that is using petroleum instead of wood. She doesn't trust it and is waiting for it to explode over our heads. I whisper to her that I fell in the river.

"Dios de mi vida," she says. *"¿Quién te lo manda?"*

I hug myself on the way to my bed and I think about being saved, rescued. Like in a story.

Daddy tells us at the breakfast table that he is going to New York. It's true. Another one of those men wants him to tell him how many dollars his library is worth. Daddy says he will see my aunt, and he mutters something about going to see a doctor, but it's a good thing. He's not dying. It is about that old time when he was little when he broke his head. In my bowl of oatmeal and milk are slicks of places that must be New York and the bus on the roads and my father alone. I move my spoon to make turns and rivers. I don't look at Daddy because he'll see I don't want him to go, and anyway, when it comes to telling him to stay, I don't have a mouth, or arms to hold him, or legs to run to the other side of the table to lean on him.

When Mama goes into the hospital, I go with Pilar. We have to take her fast in a taxi. We wait for the doctors and Pilar sits with me on the hall bench. Her rosary beads climb up and over her fingers keeping up with her prayers. When the doctor takes us in to see Mama, she is crying. Pilar cries too and pats Mama's foot. I hold Mama's fingers limp as baby fingers and I think about the white bowl I saw under her bed filled with pieces of blood. They won't let us take her home so Pilar goes next door to the old doctor. He makes the telegram to Daddy. We come every day on the streetcar because we don't have enough *centavos* to take a taxi all the time. Daddy is rushing back from New York. When he arrives, he takes Primo and me to bring Mama home, away from her high white bed and the nurses. He holds her hand high against his chest, balancing her on the way to the taxi. She lies in back with her head in his lap. In the front seat, Primo and I have to sit next to each other, which we hate.

Mama whispers, "Choli, you were almost born in a taxi."

"This one?"

"No, silly. Your father kept saying 'Faster! Faster! The baby's coming!' And the driver kept yelling, "Not in my taxi! Not in my taxi!'"

At home, Mama lies all day on the sofa. Daddy sits near her and holds her hand. Mama sobs sometimes, and they talk softly to each other.

The baby, Leo, the baby.

Oh, my darling, don't cry. Too little. Couldn't.... Poor little halfling. I'm so sorry I was gone. You could have died. It was so hard with Amado, remember?

Oh. Oh, I remember, and I also forgot.

The doctor told us, "Never again."

I know, Leo. I'm sorry, I was lonely. I needed you. I needed... everything. But you were rescuing some dreadful woman.

She wasn't dreadful. She was a librarian.

I gave up, Leo. It's my fault.

No, darling, mine.
I shouldn't have. So foolish.
I was gone too long.
I thought you were never coming home.
I didn't know if you would take me back. Did you love the man?
Oh, yes. I loved him.
Can we fix our lives?
I don't know. I'm so tired.
Can we try?
Yes. We can try.
Please, let's try.
Leo, I got so confused doing everything. It was too much and I made mistakes with the books.
Don't think about it, Ellie. Not right now. I would have raised the baby as my own, you know.
I know.

Big Salvador packs the car and goes away with little Chava and the portrait woman—the house emptied in one night. No one knows where they went. I want him to come back.

Mama has a key to Salvador's studio. After Salvador and Chava and his mother have driven away forever from their house across the street, Mama takes me to his workroom a few blocks away on Higuera Street. We pass the red house of Malinche. The house of treaties, dialects, agreements and women. As we pass the open door, I stumble as my body almost falls into the cool patio, pulled in as if that was where I belonged, where I spoke all of Her languages, where I was needed and not needed, seen and not seen, where they used the name Malinche for me, and for Cortés also, just like they used it for Her.

Mama and I enter the studio. Her jade robe is on a hook near the door. A white curtain is pulled open between the clay women he is forming and the plaster statue ready to be cast. I look around for the marble where I have seen him with his hand on Mama's translucent hip—Mama inside a larger woman, with round eyes, larger breasts and giant hands. His enormous wooden work stand is on its side.

Her marble self is all in pieces on the floor.

In my mind, I see him, alone, waiting for word from the hospital. Was his baby killing her, or would it, half-made, tear itself away and spare her? I see him, her Maillol, bellowing, crying over the white skin he had carved from the sight of her thighs. I see the mallet coming down, taking toes, elbows, flattening her stomach, smashing ribs. With his feet set firm to break, undo, reduce, the hammer slashes at the swoop of her spine. His gray hair is filled with white dust. Dust powders the sweater that comforted me. My eyes stare at the marble pieces and I hear him groan, then roar, knowing the exact moment his baby went to God. My own chest hurts as if it remembers how a piece of his heart tore out in a clot, how a slice of his chest broke and rose like a cradle to lift the small wild ribs of his unborn lamb to heaven.

I see him falling over what is left of her, cuts on his arms, blood on his face, kneeling to kiss her white Carrara palm.

Mama is sobbing. She sees the blood on the marble fingers. She sees in her mind what I see in mine. She pulls giant drawings off the table and rolls them up with rubber bands and we go to the car. There are certain things she burns in our fireplace at home. I know she will feed these papers to the fire.

15

Waiting for Daddy

Giver of Life, I look for you.
Should you
not look for me?
Giver of Life, I wait for you, afraid,
as you should wait for me.

Soledad Paz

The iron gates to the street clang in the dark. I get out of bed and watch Daddy put the chain around their iron necks. The padlock clicks, then I hear the soft padding of his limp as he starts down the street, walking on the stitches I darned into his socks, away from Malinche 19, toward the corner, to wait for the bus, to go to his post office, his binder, his printer, his night. My spirit arms reach out and call to him, "Daddy!" They want him to come back, but tonight I can't remember how to float and follow him. The night swallows him up. A thought, wide and black, lies in my brain—a night wish to keep him close. I am the only one who will keep watch through the night till he comes back. Pilar sleeps on the other side of the house. Mama sleeps on the other side of the wall of my room. My brothers sleep in their own rooms now. Mama and Daddy made a brick room for Primo with a round ceiling like in a chapel. The house and I keep vigil. We both stare unblinking into the dark. We listen through our pupils and keep track in our hearts. I never wonder where he goes. I know. I have been there. The night is full of harms. They move large and dark past the plane trees, above the storied houses across the street, along the wet sidewalks and up against the wrought iron gates. Harms rise flat and black against the house. I press my ear to the wall. I hear a whisper and a step—bats and owls and the night birds that say "Psst" like people and then pretend to sleep after scaring me.

Night after night he goes. I imagine that I never sleep, but near dawn I sit up wakened by the pling and squeak of his key in the gate. He clicks the padlock shut and limps up the walk beside the garden of roses, under my window and up the stairs. Sweat cools on my face. My long shadow arms that waited for him now return to their regular length. My head shrinks and my hair falls into my eyes. I am little and cold, standing by the window in a huge, shadowy cube of a room. Now that he has closed the front door, I run across the room and jump into bed before anything under it can catch my feet. I hear his footsteps limp and fade on the waxed floors. He goes to the bookroom because these days Mama won't let him sleep in her bed.

He never tells me he's home. He never checks my bed. He never opens my door. Does he remember I am here? Does he know my watching brings him back? My Daddy, with the sad fold at the outside corner of his eyes, is home. I curl up under the covers. Leo Paz is back, with his mouth that turns down when he smiles so that I can see white teeth and gold and silver. When he laughs, his mouth opens as if he were screaming, and he says, "Don't you think that's funny? Aren't you going to laugh too?"

In the morning I wake up and go to the bookroom where he sleeps. Mama is mad at him. He is asleep, deep and distant, outside of our life, riding his terrible nightmares. I watch, startled by a yowl, a moan, and his tortured turning in bed. What does he see?

Is it his mother, his old rich aunt, the other women called Soledad? I want to help him. I feel very old. There is a doctor inside my body, trapped by the witches in the masks of devils from Michoacán,

by my storybooks, by the *nahuales* that haunt the valleys past Ixtapalapa, Pachuca and Toluca. If I watch and wait, a special, kind
wizard will pull the doctor out of me and fix my father. I take the
socks he dropped on the floor and check them as if they were gypsy
cards revealing where he has been, good places and bad. I look inside
his shoes and turn them over for a sign. I put them back near the
bed with the toes pointed toward the door. Sometimes Mama finds
me standing by his bed. She sends me back to eat my oatmeal and
brush my teeth. She doesn't see that I have to be there, but I obey her.

In the sunny alcove of the dining room where the light falls
like water down the three long windows, my mother is still painting the copy of the Sahagún. It is that printed copy of an ancient
Codex made in Tenochtitlán hundreds of years ago. It is pages
and pages of drawings, lined in black. Every scene explains a war,
taking a prisoner, making a house. It shows priests giving advice
with *tlatolli,* with long liquid commas which are the signs for words
coming out of their mouths. Words cross to the other person like
pieces of a spiral, of breath, of air, of meaning. The pages show
midwives, seers, blood from cuttings they do on themselves, from
cuttings done on them, cuts for punishment, for bravery. Mama
and Daddy had a real Codex on fig bark once, but they sold it. It
was eleven meters long.

The one she is working on was copied onto pages one hundred
years ago and opens and closes like a regular book. The printer
forgot to print the colors on dozens of pages. Mama has been
painting for years making each page the same as the original on
fig bark with thousands of painted miniatures.

Under her brush, the white clouds become lavender. The *pet-
ate* mats made of woven straw turn gold. She dips her brush into
the oval eyes of her palette, turns the bristles in circles inside the
red. She deposits the color on a sheet of glass next to her, wipes her
brush on a towel in her lap, and then dips into the brown porcelain
eye to add it to the glass spotted with red. Now she has the color

of the mask of Death covering the black face of the figure and she has the clay color of the strap of his sandal. She has the red of the silly hat Life wears on his headdress. Her brush paints the red tongue sticking out, the tassel under his skirt and the tiny red crowns at the base of his long gray nails. She moves from place to place, checking an old copy that is complete and copying where red has to be. Red is in the fish that drinks blood from the body piercings in sacrifices. Red is the one long tongue shared by two children. Mama washes her brushes in shallow, porcelain cups of water around her palette. As she works, the water gets redder or blacker. She uses the blackened water to paint the gray in the river, gray tiles and mosaics making a pool where a man dives onto the sticks that will pierce him.

Three people sit on the ground together, wrapped tight in white cloth. They look like *tamales* with human heads. Two face each other. The third figure speaks out in the word signs, the black curls of words that float above their heads. The priest speaks on one page. A medicine man on another. The messenger speaks and dies under the small black scrolls of his last words. Mama points at the word curls in the air. "Volutes," she says. "That's what they're called. Remember? Volutes. This is a mother talking to her child to teach her. This man is telling a history, maybe a report about a war. I have to finish this book for your father. I think someone wants to buy it, but right now it feels like mine."

"Can Daddy work on it also?"

"No."

"He knows other things."

"Yes."

Mama tells me as she goes. "Xochipilli here is a deer even though he is the prince of flowers, and of musicians and he's a poet too." She paints the red corners of his eyes. She adds deep black onto a tiny brush and paints a dancer splitting open the head of a clown. She says the dancer is a god, but he is wearing a comical suit of red and white stripes and the feet of a jaguar. He is juggling headless yellow bodies. On his elbows and knees are more heads that eat the feet of red and white messengers, and of gray and yellow messengers, caught before they can say a word. Mama takes a new brush and paints white feathers on an eagle, white paint on a man swinging two monkey heads.

"It's restful to do white," Mama says.

She turns the book around and around. Figures point every which way, hundreds of white teeth, dozens of white bones falling out of the chopped necks of the captured. Mama rests, painting the white belts, the white stripes on the face of the sun, the white loincloths of little men falling into heaven or out of it, depending on how she turns the book. I watch her work around and around. She is a magician, knowing where the cactus flower is blood red, where the marrowbones are gray and where to make emerald in the feathers of a peacock. On a loose page there is a drawing of Malinche.

"This one is after the *conquistadores*. Someone wants it added, but we have to leave it loose because it was done long after the ones I'm working on.

La Malinche is standing next to Cortés. She's doing her work, re-saying his words, forming and re-forming the languages of the runners and ambassadors and sending their messages out of her mouth in Spanish. The volutes in the air say she's finding words for everything.

Mama says, "This one is a scribe, a *tlacuilo*. Remember? You can tell. He's wearing a mantle, the *tilma* tied on his shoulder." Mama is a scribe too because she colors him in his right colors, and paints him in the right temple. Her brushes make blood and the cream of eggshell. My favorites are the tiny black footprints going somewhere, maybe saying goodbye or marking a road. Mama's favorites are the words like commas coming out of special mouths. They are the story of a true sound in a tadpole shape, like scrolls of black smoke, like signs for music. It is better to see all this talk after seeing so many spears into eyes, a child eaten by a priest, a baby born backwards out of the mouth of a god.

After a time Mama no longer speaks. I don't think she hears either. The figures are small and powerful, and the acts are horrible and mysterious. She is very accurate. What she makes is just like the Codex she is copying. Soon she seems to be the one who made the original Codex hundreds of years ago. She is wearing an invisible *tilma* tied at the neck. She is far away, doing the work of the one who told the life of the gods, who told the work of every soul on earth.

Daddy and Primo are carpenters on the sawhorses in the backyard. They have a project. I sit on the steps where I can see and hear them, but they don't talk. The planes and saws are talking. Screws squeak. Hammers on thumbs make yells. Nails bend and make loud words. The wood plane is the best. Daddy's whole body slides along the board, pulled by both hands. When he backs up, he leaves behind long gold curls of wood just like the speech marks Mama is drawing into the Codex. I run down to gather their silent messages. I collect the waves that crest with each drive of the plane, that fall out onto the grass on the return.

Broken words still speak. I listen to them. The thin, tawny wood is the same color as the stain Mama is making from her watercolors for skin. But these pieces of tree meat are scrolls. These have grain. I lay them on the steps, curl after curl, waiting for the sentence to form itself, for the tree to make a last sound, for the secrecy of the speech curls in the Codex to explain themselves. Just like in the book, every volute for speech is slightly different. A language lies on the cement steps. It becomes music in my head. The figures in the book are singing too. A priest is droning, filling the man in front of him with his law. I hear moaning. My chest trembles like the deerskin of a drum. I gather up all the golden sayings and take them to my room. I lay them carefully in a shoe-box, in rows like lines in a book. I hide the shoebox in the bottom drawer of my blue armoire. The sound of words from long ago makes me tired. I fall asleep.

16

The Head in the Gate

No lloro, pero me acuerdo.
I'm not weeping about it, but I remember.

—Mexican proverb

Daddy is going south to Yucatán, Guatemala, El Salvador, the place names he teaches me as he packs, as he checks maps to choose which villages he'll visit to ask about books. Pilar reads to me from her comic books, from her romances on rough tan paper. She taps her tongue for spit to pinch and turn the pages. When I get restless she grabs my arm. Then she starts sawing on it with the edge of her hand. She chants and saws: *los maderos de San Juan.* I know what is coming but I can't get away. *Piden pan, no les dan.* She stares up at the ceiling sadly. *Piden queso, les dan un hueso que se les atora en el pescuezo. The carpenters of San Juan, beg for bread but they get none—beg for cheese and get a bone—it sticks in their throats and then they're gone.* I try to duck but her hand is at my throat before I can lower my chin, and I "choke." She laughs. It is the end of reading.

She checks on Araceli sleeping on the bed in their tiny room. I peek at the altar to Our Lady of Guadalupe on her dressing table. A silver chain hangs over a corner of the picture. It holds a sealed token, a prayer stitched in. On the other corner is Pilar's rosary. Seven wrinkled bitter oranges are all pushed together on a piece of turquoise oilcloth printed with peaches and red hibiscus. Next to the oranges is the blue and white lady on the can of Crema Teatrical. In the bottom corners of the picture of Our Lady are two wallet photos, with stains of white light eating away at the heads and shoulders. One is me. One is another baby that I don't know. I don't ask. We go back to the kitchen to wait for our soap opera and to sing ads as they come on the radio, *Palmolívese, embellézquece, Palmolive le da suavidad, con aceite de olivo y palma....*

Pilar has a secret knowledge known to her bones, in her deep flesh, that round brown pillar from which she accepts me and teaches me things apart, nothing to do with school. She teaches me about fear. She makes mysterious comments to tell me things men do. What happens to women and why children cry. She teaches me from the *noticiero policíaco*, the gazette of police stories at the back of the newspaper and in her magazines with black and white covers showing bodies, the sheets pulled back from the face by a policeman. The pictures are in black and white but in her words the blood is red. From how she reads and adds her details, the eyes are purple smashes all the way down the cheeks, and pink marrow shows at the broken bones just like the scabby chicken feet she roasts for soup with their red tendons torn at the knees, like the pigs' ears we buy from the market to make thick broth, like the tattered red and white hip joints we boil for the dog.

She teaches me about life in the *barrio*, which begins, at least on one side, just outside our walls, on the dusty street south of the villa, where the real adobes begin. We can hear screaming. Brooms bang. The mother yells. Children and chickens and pigs run because they went where it is No. She hits, children cry, pans bang, pigs squeal. The bad words we hear make Pilar's mouth go down at the corners and her tongue makes sucking sounds on the roof of her mouth, sounds I hate if they are for me.

I hunch up my shoulders and listen to the accusations and the thudding of sticks on little bones. When the father comes home the children are silent. He yells. He shouts at the mother and says things. He beats her and makes her cry loud and high. Somewhere the children are hiding. Through the yellow wall of crumbling *tepetate* crowned with shards of colored broken glass I see their eyes, lidless and blank looking at her screams.

In the police *noticiero* they show pictures of a woman found with her lover. One of her eyes is swollen shut, the other is just one of the holes her husband shot into her. A white rag has been pulled away from her feet for the camera. Near her ankle a tiny hand comes up from under the bed, a hand alive, reaching out of its hiding place to touch the mother.

Pilar reads me the stories. A little boy has been missing for days. They are looking for him in the scary lava flow, in the *pedregal*. Every day they mention him. His family is wealthy. They live in the fancy Lomas. Every day we read their cries for their child to be returned.

The *pedregal* is red and black lava, yellow and orange and purple rock. Nothing smooth. Every surface is marked with miniature craters. It goes for miles, a hardened river, here and there piling on itself, making caves and hills. In the crevices small cacti grow. On the crooked faces of the tumbled rocks, lichen paints its flat flowers, yellow, green, and gray. There are deep *barrancas* and hidden places for outlaws, and caves for coyotes but no sand to see their footprints. It is a place where no one can follow and there are no directions. Pilar says the killers and kidnappers go there, the bandits and robbers. They are not afraid. They can run over the volcanic cracks and boulders like lizards in the desert. No one can see them but they can look out. She says no one can find them, but in the night they come into the town to kill and steal and take children from their homes. *Robachicos.* The stealers of children. They are everywhere. Pilar sees them when she tells us to wait on the corner. She sees them coming when she tells us not to go out of the gate without her. She knows they will get us when we want to run to the corner for candy. In the market I keep a handful of her apron locked in my fingers.

Pilar has a new *noticiero policíaco*. While my mother takes her afternoon nap, while my brother carves on his miniature ship from the Spanish Armada, while my baby brother Amado sleeps in his playpen, and Araceli has had her milk from her mother's breasts, Pilar reads to me in the kitchen. It is our time. The dishes are washed and put away. A large clay beanpot boils on the back burner of the charcoal stove. Now and then Pilar tells me to fan the draft hole in the tiles. Sparks and long blue flames flash up around the pot as I flap and flap, my whole body swiveling to move the straw fan, though when Pilar does it she stands like a quiet prayer, only her wrist furiously fanning. We are in our afternoon silence. The program we like on the radio is about to begin. Somewhere the new gardener is quiet, not pushing the lawn mower, not clacking his shears to trim the honeysuckle and bougainvillea, maybe sleeping in the big dark hole next to the water heater where no one can see him.

"They have found the little boy," Pilar says.

"How?"

"With a dog."

"From the police?"

"No. The boy's dog. A German shepherd. *Un pastor alemán.*"

"Not a coyote?"

"They say a dog."

"Was he in the *pedregal*?"

"Yes."

"In the barranca?"

"Yes."

"How did they find him?"

"They sent the dog of the little boy out in the morning."

"Do they say about the coyote?"

"No, of course not. I'll read you what it says. "They released him at the edge of the rocks and he ran away out of sight with his nose to the ground."

Slowly Pilar picked her way, syllable by syllable. "The German shepherd wove through the lava as if he knew where he was going.

He was lost from view at the edge of a deep canyon. He was heard whining and barking. He crawled up to the edge where the family and the police were waiting."

"What about the little arm?"

"Wait! Wait! It doesn't say about an arm." Pilar frowns at me for interrupting.

She continues reading so quietly I can barely hear her. "The dog came back. In his mouth he carried the arm of the little boy."

She's silent. I'm silent. In my mind the shepherd no longer moves. He turns a deep yellow and freezes at the edge of the red and purple lava, obedient, his head pointed at the sky, like in my dream, as if to howl, but he can't because he is holding something of his little one. In my mind the arm of the boy stands out, stiff and white, a broken piece of a doll. Nothing moves. I can't get the coyote to go to the police, or turn back into a police dog, or lower his head for the leash. I can't get him to come close to the father who is waiting, seeing, recognizing. Pilar does not read any more for a moment.

Then she reads quietly again, as if I were forcing her to, because she sees me staring at her without moving. She thinks I am waiting. I am not waiting. I am seeing my dream and it doesn't let me breathe.

"Because they didn't get their money in time, the kidnappers threw him into the *barranca*. Following the dog through the rocks, the police gathered what had not been eaten by animals and turned it over to the family for burial."

Pilar crosses herself and prays. Absent-mindedly she kisses her thumbnail where her forefinger folds under it in the sign of the cross, and then she crosses me too and kisses her thumb again.

Padre Nuestro. . . Our Father. . . questasenloscielos. . .

Bendito Sea. . . como en la tierra. . . líbrenos Señor. . .

Dios Santo. . . Amen.

While Pilar waters the pink roses rising up around the double staircase to the house, she stands motionless, one arm across her breasts, the other holding the hose. A car goes by with four men in it.

"Are those the *robachicos*?" I ask her.

She looks surprised. I wonder if now I am the only one watching for kidnappers.

"Yes, yes," she says impatiently, turning her head towards the car going by. One of the men inside wears a white hat and he turns to look into our garden through the tall wrought iron gate. Pilar opens the gate and goes out on the street to water the dirt in front of our house, the house at Malintzin, Nº 19. She waters under the plane trees that are cut into large balls above the trunks painted with lime to keep away the ants, painted white to keep away the burn of the sun. She stands outside the gates, in the evening, peaceful, watering down the dirt street. I sit close to the gate, or play hopscotch near the house, ready to run if she should signal that they're coming. Sometimes I don't believe her. I am curious how she knows. And why sometimes like today, she doesn't seem to be worried at all. I want to see them and know for myself.

One day, when Pilar has watered the street, put away the hose and locked the iron gates with the fat chain and the brass padlock, I stay in the rose garden alone. I climb up on one of the rungs of the gate and hold on to the iron rosettes on the bars. Little by little, working this way and that, up and down, I slide my head between the bars and look out up the street along the line of plane trees toward one corner, and down the street toward the barrio. Now and then a fat old car slides past on the side streets. Then one turns the corner. As it approaches our house slowly, I try to pull my head through the bars, but my head is stuck. My ears will not come back through. I try to reach the doorbell, but it is too far away on the brick pillar.

The car is backing out of the street and turning around. They have seen me. They can tell I am helpless. They will come and steal me right here from my house and I will disappear with the *robachicos*. Now I know what a kidnapper looks like. I have seen for myself how slowly they move looking for children and I imagine how fast they will speed away through the dust into the *pedregal* after they have captured me.

The sun is going down. The light is getting gray. In a few moments they will be making another sweep through the city and I will be gone forever.

Pilar comes to look for me. She laughs at me for whining.

"I saw them. They were going to steal me."

"And how were they going to steal you with your head stuck like that? Or were they just going to cut off your head and take you screaming away? Were they just going to leave us the parts that get in my way in my kitchen?" Her jokes make me feel small enough to pop out of the iron hold of the gate, but I can't.

My mother comes and the new gardener and my brother Primo. Primo sits near the rose bushes, laughing and laughing, and doesn't come to help. Mama struggles to free me with face cream, turning and tugging with Why did you? and Why didn't you? and Why? Pilar smiles, waiting for my mother to give up, just like she did when my mother had the tapeworm inside her.

Mama turns exasperated to Pilar, "Can you get her out?"

Pilar pours warm olive oil all over my ears, then puts one hand through the bars over my forehead and another hand under my chin and she jerks me back through the bars. I think she has torn off both my ears, but she hasn't. They are *her* ears anyway. When I was a baby she taped them back against my head all those months so they would not stick out like my father's. After my bath, she makes fingers out of a towel, rubs off all the olive oil and dries my ears to a pink, hot, painful shine. "*Quién te lo manda,*" she spits out over and over. Who told you to do something so silly?

And this night, the night of the head in the gate, after she groans herself down onto her knees to get ready to pray by my bed, she takes soft flannel packs soaked in a tea of arnica, holds them gently to soothe the sore head bones and my red ears. She knows I was scared, but she laughs because she knows I am stubborn to

learn, to see for myself, and she says "God help you" every time. She
knows that out of curiosity my body forgot to think. She knows
how mulish I am, just like her, and maybe just like Mama. But
even when Pilar is angry with me for being pig-headed, she says
it will save me from madness, from destruction, from the edges
of the cliff. There she is on her knees, and on this night when the
eyes of knowledge don't sleep, her teachings speak. She prays in her
sweet soft voice, and all of her ancestors hear her say *Santa Maria,
Madre de Dios. . . entre mujeres. . . bendito sea. . . blessed be . . .
el fruto de tu vientre, Jesús. . . .*
      "Did you pray for Amado?"
      "I blessed him," she says.
      'Did you pray for Primo?"
      "Yes."
      "Why?"
      "Because everyone needs blessing."
      Three or four more times, for whatever she has hidden in the
day, for her sins and mine, over and over, the sounds of her prayer
come like a remembrance into the corners of my sleep. Her voice
loves and trusts the Blessed Mary close in her heart. Sleepily I see
the gleam of nightlight on her glossy brown hands praying together
on her chest. On the backs of her hands are four dimples of fat.
Her eyes are closed as she whispers to Her, to Him, for them, for
us, lost in a rosary of repetition.

17

A Gold Watch and Women in Hats

Even when they have parents,
children know they are orphans.

Soledad Paz

I am in the kitchen with Pilar. She's teaching me to make *chiles rellenos* to celebrate because Daddy is back from Guatemala or maybe Bolivia, and because I am old enough to help cook for him. Daddy came home with more rare books for their book business. Later, Primo and I will get our jobs to roll up and save all the string that Daddy says is twine. We'll smooth and fold brown wrapping paper and stack newspapers. Daddy uses everything again when he sends books to his customers. He calls them collectors. When Mama and Daddy lived in the United States, he loved old books, all books, all words, paper, ink, paste to mend books, and gold leaf to mend titles. Now that they live in Mexico they say his dream has come true. Our whole house is books. He finds, collects and sells them. There is a lot to do to make new packages, invoices and inventories. Someone has to hunt for books for the people who asked for something very special. Mama and Daddy have been working in the dining room for hours. I hear their scrambled voices in the dining room.

Pilar bumps my arm. "Soledad, take the beaten eggs and make beds for the *chiles*." She wraps my arm around the bowl mounded with beaten whites, yolks and flour.

I spread a large foamy spoonful in the iron pan. Pilar comes behind me and lays in a dark green chile, roasted, peeled and stuffed with walnuts and goat cheese. I look up to listen. Something is wrong.

"*Ándale*, Soledad!" Pilar laughs. "Put a nice blanket."

I cover the chile with yellow froth. The edges snap and hiss. I give Pilar the bowl and run to look through the crack in the kitchen door.

Mama says, "Where's your watch?"

Daddy's answer is lost in a sizzle of oil.

"What do you mean you lost it?" Mama says.

"I lost it. I just lost it."

Mama smells a story. For a moment her eyes are bright, as if it might be interesting. Then suddenly she looks disgusted, as if she knows he's lying and getting ready to "spin a yarn."

He says, "I left it under my pillow in the hotel, and when I got to the bus station, I realized it was gone, but when I ran back to the room the bed had been made. The manager called the maid and she said she'd found nothing. What could I do?"

Mama says things about women in his room stealing from him right by his head. And I can see the white bed, with white puffed pillows. Under it lies my father's beautiful gold pocket watch with a door that flies open to show a white porcelain face and black Roman numbers. It gleams with rays of light like in treasure dragon stories. I see some sort of ghost of my father in the edge of my sight. He's lying up to his neck in hot water, in a large tub, with the door open and steam floating out. On the other side of my sight I see a woman, maybe the one who makes my mother cry. She's gold-skinned and black-haired and she's crawling slowly out of his bed. She's wearing a man's hat and carries a baby on her back held up in a dark blue rebozo. I know she'll reach under the pillow and take his watch, then tip-toe out of the room while my father still talks to her through a damp and steamy door.

Daddy always has trip stories. He likes funny stories and he likes to tell when things go wrong. But this one is different and I know to listen for what he leaves out—things that burn in my mother's eyes, and that later I hear in their shouts and see in her tears, especially when he is late returning from a trip. There are stories in the arguments over what he received in payments for his rare books, how much he paid for purchases, how little he brought back, and why he got home late. There are loud "theys" and "shes," and always something about "last time" and "never again."

My skin is covered with eyes that listen to what they say. The words are like shapes. I know some of them. Other words are like strangers in dreams. They are real but I don't know what they mean. That's when Daddy's loneliness, sadness and apologies move into me. After the arguments, the shape of pain is so black and mysterious that it could devour him or fill me. The feelings slip in through my eyes, enter my bones, mix with my blood, till I can do my part, take care of him, and bind my mother and father together—till I am old enough to find the words to make them happy. There isn't an inch of my body that doesn't hear and see. Every inch, like feathers in a peacock's tail, has an eye. A million irises soak up looks, words, movements, hurts. I flinch from their anger and blame, relax in their silences, warm up in moments of forgiveness, stiffen with accusations and explanations. Even if they can't see me— even if he doesn't see me—I watch. I don't want to miss the split second when something fractures in his face and he needs me.

Another day, in the bedroom next to my bedroom, the argument is even louder than the fight about the watch. I think it can't get worse, but it does. It's like when a long storm ends, and suddenly there are new, louder claps of thunder.

"I can't protect myself if you keep lying. Why did you come home?" My mother's voice is high and tired but filled with anger.

"I came home because I love you. You are worried about nothing."

"It's NOT nothing. You give... people money that we need desperately. First it was your students but then you stopped. Finally. Then it was your assistant, after he had been drunk over and over for days. And you probably still give him more than his salary. And now. How can you spend our money on those.... Oh, I don't even *want* a name for them!"

"It's only when I think I can help."

"Help? Help them?"

"They are people too."

"We are people. We need your help. We are your family. We have needs. We have AGREEMENTS. You don't even drink. What are you doing in those places? Don't answer that."

"I know. I'll stop going to those places.

"You want to be to be just like your father."

"No! I never even knew him."

"Well, it's what they say about him. For God's sake, can't you remember it's why he died in the sanatorium?"

"Yes."

"I know why you called the doctor. I know about the creams in your pockets."

"I promise to stop. I spent weeks in New York with the analyst. He's helping. I want to be with you. Just with you. I will keep my promises and be a good father to our children."

I lie on the wooden floor of my room to read the sounds. Mistakes, sorry, won't, and answers against anger. I am lying on forbidden ground. I hear things I am not supposed to hear. I can feel my father's lies and wishes and maybe my mother's too. I don't know. My mother requests, begs, demands. I lie paralyzed by the sense of need, hers as passionate as his. Loud mysteries. Their intensity scares me. Their voices are like knives, then soft as kisses, warm as embraces. But I can tell that they are not one. Now they are two. I don't know why they are so strong and loud and why they are also soft and filled with memories. I am afraid. I don't even want to stand up to get into bed. I crawl under my bed, even though usually that is the scariest place in my room.

"What kind of father can you be if you can't control this obsession? It's so far *beneath* you, so far beneath the man I married."

"I want more than anything to be a good husband and a good father. I am not the only one. You and I are both trying."

"You're not trying hard enough."

After the fight my mother closes her door. My father walks around to the back of the house, and up the rusty fire escape to his other room, where there is another bed, a bathroom, another hot water boiler, and hundreds of books stacked from the Persian carpets up to the ceiling. Later he comes downstairs. From the kitchen where I have been drinking a hot milk with Pilar I hear him on the phone. "Harrington, my friend. I've been banished," he says.

I have seen the word in books. King Arthur says, "Banished."

18

Women in Hats and the End of the World

Huir y correr no son la misma cosa.
To flee and to run are not the same thing.

—*Mexican proverb*

On the days when my mother and father don't speak, women in black bowler hats fill my dreams. When my father doesn't spend the night in my mother's bed, I dream of ghost women who reach into his jacket for his wallet. One slips silver pesos from the pile on his dresser. One takes his passport from his briefcase and searches under his pillow for a gold watch. Sometimes the women are wrapped in rebozos of navy and black. Sometimes they wear tall glass heels with gold ankle straps and their breasts bulge out like on the women in comic books. All of them wear hats and carry babies on their backs, faceless babies tied on like dead bundles. White arms, brown arms and black arms come out from under his pillows with coins and precious papers. Their silence fills the hills of Bolivia, the shores of Veracruz, the ruins of the Yucatán, the towers in Salt Lake City, the snows of St. Louis and Denver.

One day at noon we do the usual things we do before each meal: we clear the table of fresh piles of books and the typewriter so we can all sit together to eat.

To help Pilar I come in from the kitchen with tortillas. The winter sun from the bay window shines on my father's shoulders at the head of the table, and its light makes the silhouette of my mother sitting at the foot. She is always elegant, vital, beautiful.

She would never wear curlers to the table, but this day her rich crown of red hair is wrapped in pink rubber curlers. She seems distant, as if she is visiting.

I miss the first part of their conversation because all of my eyes are too busy. They are watching a fire. The fire is going to roll up in two balls and split apart. The eyes know it. I sit motionless inside the division of their words. I hear her say, "I'm leaving. I am going to take the children and go."

For the first time, the pain I have watched for years in my father stands up and moves. For the first time, it is real and awake, not in the howl of his nightmares. For the first time, I hear him sob. He gets up from the table. Covering the sounds in the hunch of his shoulders, he goes through my mother's room to my room. I get up and follow him. I have to comfort him. I sit down next to him on my bed and cry.

"Daddy, please stop crying."

"I'll stop if you stop," he says.

But I can't stop. I sob and he sobs. Something is broken. Something has changed forever. Beside him on my bed, I sit holding my head and he sits holding his head.

"I'll stop if you stop," he whispers again.

We both wipe our faces. We stand up. I look up at him next to me. He is a little stooped. I am a little stooped. We start walking slowly along the wood floor of my room, over the floor of my mother's room and across the Persian rugs of the living room. I walk close to him and my body rocks slightly with his limp. Then, we face the open double door of the dining room. My mother has her back to us. Amado is in his high chair. The light from the window makes him a cherub. Primo stares up at us, but none of my eyes are reading him or my mother. I am only reading my father.

I slide into my chair. Daddy sits down and puts his napkin back on his lap. The rest of lunch is like the room where the mummies are stacked against the wall in Guanajuato. Maybe we raise food to our mouths. Maybe we reach for a tortilla. Maybe we chew or sink down deeper into our chairs. Like the mummies, with their mouths open, their nails seeming to scratch at a box closed by mistake, we are all caught in the light falling like dust on something that no longer breathes.

We eat what Pilar cooked. It is a meal to finish. The last family meal.

19

Wrong Side of the Gate

Amor con amor se paga.
You repay love with love.

—Mexican love song

Mama launches herself like a bright comet through the house. Her red hair leads a filament of clothing that flows over her white skin. It's what she does before a car trip as if she doesn't really want to leave Mexico City, or she doesn't want to get where we are going and this time it is because she's not coming back. She flies out the wrought iron gate to the car, checks the tires, opens the hood, puts water in the battery, comes back up the white steps to unpack, re-pack, give orders. She runs out to do errands, is suddenly home again, sits in the bookroom to write reminders for my father, and lists for Pilar. She picks through her purse, and leans into the hall mirror as if it had said something.

Now the wrought iron gates to our house are closed and we are on the street. The round blue Chevrolet is loaded. Mama parks it right in front of the gates decorated with sleeping S's on top. I don't like the car out on the street. The pink rose bushes climb up the twin staircases to the white columns at the edge of the porch. We should be back in the garden, on the safe side of the brick wall, on the side of the father, on the side of the kitchen, near the rooms filled with circular stacks of books, under the cool shadows of the pine tree, on the side of Amado's cradle and the playpen Mama filled with toys and blankets trimmed in pink satin for Araceli, Pilar's baby. On that side of the gate is the path where I learned to ride a tricycle. There is the cropped lawn where Amado took his first steps, the stone bench where the puppies lost their tails, the garden where the broccoli grew snails and the snails grew fire, and where on ivory plates the green flowerets lay in a pool of butter till I hid them in my mouth. I want to be inside the gate, where mornings come through the bay window, where we work with Daddy. We untie knots in twine and knot the string together to use again, listening to how we mustn't waste. On the outside of the gate is the street where I feared the kidnappers, where a funnel of dust rises when cars pass, and where the road begins which my mother wants to take one way north to Jalisco.

Mama is going to make me do what I don't want. I try to make them all stop. Or wake up to see it's only a dream that Mama is a tornado getting ready to leave Daddy. My brain sees how to fix everything, but I can't make her stop. She is like the monkeys that wind up and play a whole song, with drums and triangles and cymbals and there is no switch to click them off. Her movements are jerky, in and out of the house, quick and mechanical. A thermos jug goes into the front seat. She is flapping blankets and poking pillows in the back seat, banging them into place with unnecessary pats. Her gestures are jagged. She is going to take us away.

We are on the wrong side of the gate.

Near me, my nurse Pilar holds up a corner of her apron. She keeps pressing and drying her eyes, but tears pour out anyway. Amado is against her knees and her smooth, shiny brown hand, dimpled and fat, rests on his head. He leans on her like a carved cherub at the foot of the Madonna. He might feel her pain, but he knows there is something special in the need of her hand to rest on his head.

I fall into her wide waist.

"*No llores, mijita,*" she says. Neither one of us stops crying.

My mother puts her purse on the front seat of the car and goes back into the house for something she's forgotten. Daddy and my brother Primo are standing in the sun in front of the car. I look over my shoulder to see what they're doing. Daddy is saying things to Primo. Daddy things, like "Brush your teeth," "Don't use too much shoe polish," "Take care of your mother," "Be good," and maybe even "Be a man," though Primo is only ten.

I let go of Pilar.

Daddy is looking at me. The sun shines on his black hair slicked back. The sun is on Primo's shiny light hair. Daddy's bent forefinger gestures to me. For a moment I think he's really calling me to him. I run the few steps to him. But his eyes are on his hand. I am too close. I step back to look at his fingers. He is holding a large silver peso, a blinding silver coin with a sunburst on one side. He says it is pure silver. The wings of my arms fold to my sides. The petals of my heart fall. I can't hear what he's saying. Anyway, Primo is listening so I don't have to. I am back inside my other body, the one who waited for Daddy in the night, slept when he got home, learned to darn his socks, bleached the fox stain in his copy of *Travels in the Yucatán,* patched a worm hole in *Huckleberry Finn*, waxed the leather back of *Don Quixote,* mended the broken corners of Cook's *Voyages,* choked on the smell of book paste for *Chesterfield's Letters,* stood next to him in his chair, breathing in the smell of tobacco and staring at the black hairs in his ears. I think of the red leather book by Peñafiel where I traced the ancient drawings that gave each city and town a sign, a symbol—before Columbus. For us, for our house, in these streets of Coyoacán, it was the sign of the skinny coyote, a full moon in his stomach, his jaws hungry for food.

I can't leave Daddy. There is still so much to learn. I want to ask him again, "Well, am I a Mexican?"

And he'll say, "You were born here, and you have a Mexican passport, but you can be an American some day if you want to because I was born in the United States."

And I will ask him again, "Well, am I an American?"

And he will say his same puzzle, "Soledad, you are imported wine, bottled in Mexico."

The edge of the silver coin shines. It's not mine. I don't want it. I want him.

Primo has taken his. "A whole peso? Wow!"

I look down at Daddy's brown shoes between us. He's wearing the white shirt and the khaki pants he wore to Taxco the day he closed the door on my hand.

He and Mama have an agreement. I don't like it. I want to stay. I don't want to leave Pilar, or my shaggy Tigre, wagging his tail and waiting inside the gate for all of us to come back to his house. Tigre, the son of Liffey-The-Cat-Killer and a striped mastiff that jumped over the wall. The mastiff and Liffey got stuck together. I pulled at them trying to get them apart and yelled for Daddy. I remember his white shirt and his hands on my hands as Liffey and her stuck-on dog trembled. I was crying. He took my hands in his and said, "It's all right. I know it doesn't look all right, but it is. Let's leave them alone and go back to the house."

I looked back. Both dogs looked so stupid, their tails stuck to each other, shaking all over, their long pink tongues dripping with saliva.

Now here's his hand with a coin in it, and here's the white shirt again. I put my head on Daddy's chest and smell the yellow soap, even the heat of the iron and the smoke of charcoal fires. He won't let me leave my head on him. He reaches for one of my hands and gently pushes us apart.

"Choli, take it. Here. Take it." He uses my nickname. He never uses it. He always wants people to call me by the whole name, Soledad, because I am a namesake, for his sister, his mother, his grandmother—all of them Soledad.

He presses the coin into my hand. His voice speaking English to me is the softest ever, with his Spanish mixed with a Southern drawl even though he never lived very long in the South. "Choli, go to Pilar. I need to talk to Primo." Primo is not crying. He knows he is going to come back to Mexico City sometimes, by himself, to help Daddy.

I go back to Pilar and hug her. The coin hurts the tight throat of my fist. I push my closed hand into Pilar's waist where her large back sits on the square stone of her hips. My hand with the coin squeezes as hard as it can. I want it to cut the skin, slip the coin into my blood and do magic so that suddenly we will all be back inside the house, in the living room where Daddy reads to us in the velvet chair. I will pull the silver coin out from behind Daddy's ear and compare it to Primo's coin and laugh when his vanishes. But my hand only sinks into the space between the two shapes of Pilar where the apron string disappears. My other hand presses on the familiar long, black trunk of her single braid, a million living threads that run through her to the ground. My throat like a snake chokes on coins. Payment and silence strangle each other inside it. I make fists of my eyes to shut out the pain. Pilar and I rock together and Amado rocks against her knee. She hides her face in her apron.

Mama comes around the car and picks up Amado and puts him in the back seat with a soft cloth story book. Mama is arranging him in the seat as if we were going on a picnic instead of on a long trip to another life.

Memory lifts me back into the house, waking me in time for crabapple jelly like liquid carnelian on hot fresh sourdough rolls and Pilar's coffee in my milk. I can tell Pilar my dream about The Wrong Side of The Gate and she will listen to everything about the tears and Daddy's coin burning in my hand, and how I took it out of obedience, because he said to. Then she will tell me her dream about her *bracero* singing to their baby then asking, What's her

name? I don't want my Pilar to feel alone so I whisper, "Araceli."
And now, with our dreams out of the way, we can go to the kitchen.

There we'll have *nopales*, and eggs and hot tortillas patted
between Pilar's damp hands, the *masa* circling, falling, and growing large enough to slide in a soft caress right onto the heat of
the griddle. Pilar will send me to get Tigre so he'll stop barking
through the iron gate at the children who tease him.

The egg basket will be in its place on the counter, and in it,
under the brown and white *blanquillos,* lie the pesos she has saved,
for when she forgets something at the market, for when I run to
her because Primo has kicked me—coins for when she hears the
whistle of the popsicle man and she buys us tamarind ice, or hibiscus blossom ice when we don't even ask—coins for when Daddy
does not take me and goes into the night with Primo with packages
of books to mail, at the post office that is open all night, and the
movie page from the newspaper.

Something has to wind things back. I will be good. I promise.
I know how to walk quietly past my sleeping mother, who looks
weak, white, nearly dead, as if she had fainted in her bed, her arm
flung up over her head, her elbow bone drained of the blue veins
from her long white arm. I know to pick up Amado—who is my
baby anyway—and slide out the back door to sneak up the stairs
into the kitchen. We both fall into Pilar and laugh at her mean-
ingless scold. We soak up her overjoyed disapproval that we are
up early and in her kitchen that smells of *cilantro* and oatmeal, of
coffee and scalded milk, of tortillas toasting, of black beans and
epazote sputtering in the *olla* at the back of the charcoal stove.

What will happen to the times we spend in the afternoon
when I lean with Pilar into the black radio on the counter, watching its black holes tell the news, give out the lottery numbers that
won, play *Pálmolivese, embellésquese,* Palmolive jingles over and
over, how soap will make you soft, beautiful with the oils of olive
and palm, then a report that a woman's head was found outside
her lover's house. The kitchen is the place where I sit in the straw-

bottom chair and hold up my legs so Pilar can sweep under me. I cuddle Amado and spoon-scrape bananas for him and let him taste my bread dipped in coffee with milk and sugar, giggling because everything we like is in this room.

Other afternoons I listen to passionate soap operas with Pilar. Some days I visit friends from school. I never want to miss ballet. It is a real place, where I sit reverent near the sullen arrogance of the older girls while they cup their toes in rabbit fur, bandage sore joints, slump toeless socks around their ankles, slip on toe shoes, and cross the satin laces around their wide solid calves. I want to stretch and bend. I would even break my back, lying on my stomach on the floor when Madame pulls my feet up to the back of my head. I don't mind the cane that zings against my thighs, burning me with Madame's insistence on perfection, because I want to learn, and my legs ache for repetition until I am like the other girls, old enough to go on toe.

It was supposed to be that I would sleep the whole night and wake up to find the piano in the dining room. The piano did come. Mama heard me. I begged and begged. Quietly. Carefully. Truly. And it finally worked. Mama found the German woman, Frau Blauheim, sad, maybe one of Mama's exiles, a concert pianist, poor, lonely, with her hair in a gray knot like a bullfighter's at the back of her head. She looked at the piano and started to play. Her fingers were a whole world, filled with scenes, words, songs, and memories. They were small sacred flowers, a flesh fan of kelp swaying in water, a gathering of fishes that would dart from her wrist up and down and everywhere in the black and white pool. I saw her eyes on the keys, on her fingers that were laid gently as if on a wound waiting to be healed. She looked at her hands the way we watch the hands of a magician. She surprised the mahogany piano where there was no music laid out. She played Mozart and Beethoven and Schubert. Mother recognized the melody. Said it was about a trout. Frau Blauheim smiled and her hands swam. Her smile was so small it must have been hiding a long time with no hope for this joy. Next week was to be my first lesson. Next week I was going to sit next to her on the bench in a speechless promise to learn, to listen, to repeat and to watch her fingers run over the keys to say themselves. Instead, the men who brought the piano are coming back to take it away, and I will never see Frau Blauheim again.

I want to wake up and run to the back, to Daddy's writing room that Mama made into a stable for Caramelo. The pony will let me rest my face against him breathing in his sweet and sour smell, chew his bran with him, lift up his hooves and clean out the frogs with my special stick. It's my job to rake away the wet straw, protect his feet with new hay, give him fresh water and slip the leather thong of the brush over my hand to curry him over and over, one hand brushing, the other sleeking. I imagine that I am not afraid to gallop, not afraid to jump, not afraid he will run away with me again. I will pull on the reins and imagine I CAN make him stop whenever I want.

Mama bumps the horn. We all jump. She hates horns. She did it on purpose. She wants things to fall into place. She wants Daddy to stop talking to Primo and she wants me to stop hanging on Pilar. She wants Daddy back in the house with his rare books. She wants to get behind the wheel and take us where she is going, whether we want to or not. Daddy can't hold on. Pilar can't hold on. No one can stop her.

I see something in Pilar that is not anger, nor the pretend disapproval when we squeeze her. She is hidden in her apron, large and round but small and helpless. One arm is folded across her waist to hold up the hand that wipes her tears. At the same time I see her kneeling in the dark church of San Cayetano in Coyoacán, bickering into the beads of her rosary, her eyes whispering to Jesus' feet spattered with blood, to his knees with sharp red cuts and blood dripping down his shins. She's talking to the red slit in his ribs, thick with blood that does not fall. She is whispering to his fallen head, to the spots leaking from his forehead under the wreath of thorns, the *Corona de Cristo*. Pilar on her knees, her prayers softly spitting and hissing. Her eyes, half open are on His eyes half open. She silently begs. She looks into His eyes as if they were ears to hear her *ruego,* to hear her plea.

Her prayers won't save me. Pilar—my large other mother, my scolder, holder and withholder, my serene punisher and giver, my nurse and comforter, my healer and teacher. I see her, bargaining with and shaming the market women who are trying to charge her too much—then at our gate wrapping the soft sour roll of bread filled with beans for the beggar who sometimes rings the bell for the breakfast she brings in her apron. In the late afternoon she holds the hose like a gun against kidnappers she taught me to fear from the newspapers. I see her in her house on those Sundays in Ixtapalapa, laughing, her long hair wet and falling around her face, letting me try to braid it, shiny, blue-black, smelling of soap. I see her standing solemn, applauding tortillas one after the other, her head tilted to one side as if there were no hope.

Mama is going to take away all of my Pilars. These are the moments of goodbye because of her agreement with Daddy. Now goodbye is over.

There is nothing to do. Nothing to say. Mama wins.

I can't move the house. I can't push the car back into the garage. I can't put Mama back to bed, deep on the wide white mattress where Daddy no longer sleeps. I can't take Pilar and run with Amado in my arms to the back of the house. I can't push Primo away from Daddy and send him back to his carving of the Spanish galleon I am not allowed to touch.

Pilar holds my face in one of her soft brown hands. She says the special words, *"preciosa... consentida."* With one hand she smoothes my tears over my cheeks, down one side and down the other, anointing me, the way she smoothes *Crema Teatrical* over her face at night. She smoothes the tears as she soothes my skin, thinning the pain, holding all of me in the cup of her hand, healing the separation, salving it with my own salt, feeling the loss and sharing it, handskin on faceskin, over my eyes, my mouth, just as she did when I was a baby to rinse the soap from my face, not with a cloth, but with her hand, sliding the soap from my eyes so it wouldn't sting, sliding over my mouth with fresh, clear water. My tears slow down. My cheeks begin to dry as she comforts me in her wordless way for the last time.

Daddy gives each of us a hug. I don't want to let go. But he lets go. I turn to the gate and hold silly shaggy Tigre's head and let him lick my nose. Then I hug Pilar again, so warm and fat my hands can't meet behind her, then I slide into my place next to Amado in the back seat. Half of everything I love will be on the other side of the gate, in the large white house, with all of Daddy's books standing in rows, their gold letters like map-words to the countries inside them, the books he loves more than anything, books we dusted and cleaned and bleached and mended, and which I think are mine, like my dolls, like my babies, but which are truly his, his real and precious children.

Before the car starts away from the gate, Daddy quickly leans in Mama's window. I want him to kiss her so she'll turn off the engine and we can unpack and go back into the house. He says, "Ellie?"

"Don't call me that."

"Eliana, please don't drive after dark. It's not safe. Stay on your schedule." Then he stands up and away from the car and we start to move down the street. I look back. A white triangle of apron falls from Pilar's face. Daddy stands as if ready to walk through the gate, but his head is turned toward us. He is holding one hand to his face. I try to wave through the little back window. Then I roll down my window and reach out to wave hard, but it's too late. Mama has turned the corner. The car rumbles over the dirt road, the cobbles, over the trolley tracks of Coyoacán, taking me to a village I barely know, to a life that is not going to be a vacation after all, but permanent, where Daddy will not live, where Pilar will not even visit, where Mama will love someone else, and where Tigre can't come because he has to stay home to protect Daddy.

Once we are in the car Mama is more compact. She doesn't want to miss anything. It takes two days to drive four hundred miles from Mexico City to Mama's new life without my father. We will go west to Morelia, then to Lake Chapala and on to the village of Ajijic. She promised Daddy we would be in Morelia before dark, but before we reach Mil Cumbres—the Thousand Peaks—I think we'll stop in the mushroom hills she loves. She's going to make the same stops, maybe even new ones, just like she did when we drove up to the lake for vacations, when we borrowed a house from our best friend Stevie who knew Mama needed something.

In the back of the car I coil on myself. Mexico City flicks past, pole after pole, with long stripes of yellow street-cars, green blurs of fir-trees, and then the long gray-green climb through the Desierto de los Leones, through the forests, onto the soft round hills. I look up at the creamy velvet roof of the car. I watch the ivory tapered handle of the gearshift that my mother moves up and down as she takes the turns. I hold the silver handle on my door as if there is still time to open the door, roll out and run back home. My mother says "Buttons down," and Primo and I push down the buttons that lock the doors. I close my eyes. The coin in my hand is hot. I can't squeeze hard enough to melt it, and I can't squeeze it hard enough to cut me. My mind takes my body where it knows. It goes to sky.

I jump when Mama says, "Soledad, do you remember there are four dots in Ajijic?"

"Mississippi has four dots," says Primo. He gets to sit in the front seat. He's ten and the eldest.

"But not in a row," Mama says. "Our village has four in a row."

So it's already ours. Theirs, maybe. Not mine. My place is in Mexico City, in the barrio of Coyoacán, inside the thick walls of Malintzin No. 19. I look back. My city is being buried by bridges and turns and hills. I have to carry it in my heart. I'm eight. In the backseat Amado leans against me.

Mama slows down. I think she's going to turn around and go back. I open my eyes. She is not going back. She has come to one of her most special stops. The green hills are blinding. It scares me to look at them covered with the criss-cross of grazing paths with no animals anywhere. Part of me sees things growing, sees light leaping from the earth. It is like the long green folded sides of the volcano they used to call Matlacuéyetl, the wife of the rain god Tlaloc. In stone carvings and in the records of ancient time, his words are commas curling out of his mouth. Godwords of storm and rain. On top of the volcano there is always snow. Below the snow, Matlacuéyetl has forests and endless folds of green. Springs run down her skirts. Thermal waters bubble up hot from her fire heart. Other pools are as cold as ice and pure enough to drink. But the volcano has a new name now. She is called Malintzin, like my Malintzin, the woman given to Cortés.

La Malinche. The woman of many voices, of so many lives that they had to give her different names. Maybe she was like that volcano—hot, treacherous, powerful. La Marina, Malinalli, Doña María. Maybe she was as cold as the constant springs. My heart says No because inside me I feel her as warm—La Llorona crying out in the night for the children Cortés took from her because they were half Spanish.

Mama pulls off onto the side of the road, gets out and opens the trunk to take out two pillowcases. We walk the hills with her. She knows how to pick wild mushrooms that sprout out of the cowpats in the grass. We drag the pillowcases behind us. She fills them with her little one-legged men. She feeds her children mushrooms from endless strange hills and never makes a mistake. She doesn't poison us because her father showed her how to choose. She tells us the secrets and shows us her choices. Near the shade of a tree, Mama makes a campfire, and over the flames she sets up her wire frame for the cast-iron pan. We go back to the trunk of the car for a mayonnaise jar full of rough, gray salt, a giant square of raw butter wrapped in brown paper and a bag full of two-pointed *bolillo* rolls. She melts the butter till it's frothy, then fries the mushrooms. We pour them onto our sour *bolillos* from Don Chucho's store "La Malinche," on the corner near our house. Malinche. That's what Cortés called her, his woman, his interpreter, his helper, until she was baptized, then he called her Marina. People say she took the wrong side. Some say her womb was the mother of the new Mexico. She and Cortés called their son Martín for a saint. Pilar said it was for San Martín Caballero. But she also showed me San Martín de Porres who was a *mestizo*—almost black. Pilar said Martín was a good name for a *mestizo,* but that Cortés wanted it to be San Martin Caballero who was named for a Roman soldier. Before I could read or write the words, I liked the story about San Martín Caballero who slit his Roman cape in half to cover a beggar, because in the morning Jesus told him, Thank you for covering me from the cold. Malinche should have given her children royal names from Coatzacoalcos where she was born. Still, to Cortés everything was his, all he had gained from her gifts and from the fruits of her womb. Or maybe they only say those words for the Virgin Mary.

We eat the mushrooms like piles of tiny steaks, salty and chewy. Mama talks and talks about her father, the farm with his enormous beds of flowers, the books, and their own green hills in some faraway world where he taught her about mushrooms and wild edible weeds. I don't want to learn my grandfather's secrets. I keep forgetting whether the mushroom with the ring on its stem is the good one or the bad one. I know that if I get it wrong someone will die.

Anyway, that's her father.

I want to talk about my father, but I don't.

The hills and turns of Mil Cumbres are coming, a thousand curves around a thousand peaks. The endless passes make me sick, winding back and forth, up and down through the highlands. I don't want my button down. I want it up so my door can open on

a steep curve. Primo and Amado will be asleep and I'll roll down
the green mountainside hidden by pines for miles and miles.

When we get to Morelia we are halfway there and halfway gone
from home. Even though she promised Daddy no night driving,
it is after dark when we arrive at the Hotel Virrey de Mendoza
where Mama always stays. I walk Amado up the marble stairs
over and over again and hold him on the wide bannister so he
can pretend to slide all the way down by himself. Primo explores.
Primo always explores.

20

After a Thousand Peaks

> Years and minutes
> tick together
> in the heart.
> Memory clocks
> and filigree dreams
> take time apart.
>
> *Soledad Paz*

When I wake up in Morelia, nothing has changed. We are still halfway from home and halfway to the new life.

We sit down to breakfast, which is why Mama loves this hotel even though we can't afford it. Daddy says she spends money twice and he doesn't understand how she manages. Either she gives up something or she owes someone. She wants to make dreams come true, the way Stevie does. Money seems to come from somewhere. It's probably better if I don't spend my allowance, because sometimes when she needs money I give her the coins I have.

The table is covered with a thick white cloth. Napkins stand like pyramids in the middle of our plates. The waiter has a white towel on the black arm of his suit. He bends over to place a silver tray in front of Mama. She pours her coffee from a silvery pot, hot milk from another and hot water from a third. She can make her coffee just the way she likes it. He brings us a basket filled with *pan dulce,* sugar-coated sweet bread, crescents, and angel ears of thin caramelized pastry. He asks if there is anything else. There is. Mama wants jam and butter, and we all get orange juice just like at home, squeezed fresh and full of pulp. Eggs and beans and bacon. Going north or going south, Mama's stop is the Virrey de Mendoza. It's different this time. It's not a round trip. Mama will drive the last lap north to the lake and I don't know when we'll ever go south again.

Later in the morning we stop at Mama's special tree. It's hidden. You have to know where it is. High up in the mountains she pulls the car partly onto the feet of the hillside. We climb with her up the wet slope, over roots and through vines. She is not worried that we will slip or fall. She knows we can get there. We hold Amado and the four of us climb as one. We're quiet. We push through veils of Spanish moss as if we were entering the ruins of an old church. Then we are in front of the tree. It is covered with cloth bags that look like heads of garlic, each tied onto a twig or branch. Some are gray and sagging. Some are so old there is only a thread left to hold them. Once, Mama found one on the ground. She knew it was wrong, but she put it in her pocket. Later, in the car, we opened it. Then Mama started the engine and she drove too fast around the curves as if the parents of the packet were behind us and could catch her. It was true what someone had told her: inside we saw a piece of birth cord, green mold of torn tortilla and the old rust of soaked blood. Each bag was for a baby. Some of them lived and some of them died. In the villages high in these mountains the family sends an offering to the tree for each child born. Sometimes the mother comes, if she's alive. Many times it's a grandmother. Sometimes the father brings the birth bag to the tree, hangs it on the arms of God, and leaves his prayer.

Mama is always sad at her ghost tree. Somewhere in the hundred hands of its branches is something of hers. I can feel it in the air that rises out of her to the babies, the mothers. It is like a dream that she too had come, in her way, with her fingers, to put birth cords fed with tortilla into muslin pouches for the souls of her own little ones that had not lived. At this tree-cross I always see three children, their backs to me, playing in a bluish garden like Mama's thoughts above my head.

On the second evening we come over the hill and get the first sight of Lake Chapala. It's so big there is a horizon. I think it's really a sea because Mama showed us a map drawn by the Spaniards and they called it *Mar Chapalac.*

"Look," Mama says. "You can see the curve of the earth. And the Rio Lerma we passed? That is the river that feeds the lake at the other end. Remember someone said there were hot springs in the lake?"

"Volcanic," says Primo. "Last time we were here a guy told me I could cook an egg at San Juan Cosalá 'cause the water boils right there at the edge of the lake."

"Let's go there," says Mama.

"Let's go everywhere," says Primo. "I want to see the waterfalls again too. The one called El Tepalo falls right into Ajijic."

Mama says, "Ajijic. It's a Tarascan word meaning...."

"...village of the running waters. Yup, I know."

"Don't say 'Yup'."

They are happy sitting there in the front seat with their plans. I am tired. Amado is flopped over on me sleeping. I pat him gently over and over as if he were a baby though he is almost three. My hand is like the hand of my nurse Pilar, patting to comfort me, patting to comfort him.

When we get to Ajijic, someone shows us the house with one room. We'll stay there until Mama can fix an old, big house she found down the street with a long room full of corn stored like a pyramid up to the ceiling. In a few months Mama says the granary will be our living room.

I can't see, not even in my dreams, how life will be when we live here forever. The only thing I want to do is write to Daddy at *Calle Malintzin Nº 19, Coyoacán, México D.F., México.*

PART TWO ~ LAKE CHAPALA

21

Losing Amado

> Behind us is the land of bricks,
> walls with crests of broken glass,
> iron gates and iron locks.
>
> This is now our house with cane roofs,
> scorpions in the adobe and
> doors wide open to the lake.
>
> *Soledad Paz*

We are unpacking everything we brought to our temporary house in Ajijic. Behind us are the mountains. In front of us is the biggest lake in Mexico, and on the other side, above the checkerboard farms at the feet of the hills, is Mount García, its round head like the dome of an old elephant. If I have to live here, then that hairless mound will be the place for my heart. My soul can travel from it to our side, to the sister mountain behind us, the steep, pointed Chupinaya. I don't really have to be in this house. I can live in other thoughts.

Mama has hung a cloth over the front of a closet to make me a room. My bed is an army cot we used to sleep on when we drove to the United States. I sit on it to listen to Mama who calls Primo and Amado into my "room." I pull Amado up to sit next to me.

"We're not going back," Mama says. "We've been here several times on vacation. But this is not vacation. We are not borrowing a house from Stevie. This time we're staying. We're going to live here. Make a life here. That's why I'm going to fix up that old adobe house down the street. I just want to be sure you understand that."

She must have known that until that moment I didn't really believe we were going to be in this village forever. My heart breaks again. I didn't know it could do that. It's knowing I have to sleep in that cramped room, with boxes at the back and clothes hanging from nails in front of me, and the long rod of the army cot digging into the backs of my thighs. It's knowing that everything we did to unpack was more than we ever did on the vacations when we came here before, when Mama used the lake house for those separations that she called vacations. Mama brought us into "my" room for the finality of the change. She should have told us in one of her places, not in mine.

"Will Daddy come here? I ask.

"Of course your father will come here, once in a while."

"I'm going to be nine here. Will he come for my birthday?"

"I don't know, but if he comes he can't stay with us."

"Why not?"

"He'll have to be in a hotel."

"Why?"

Mama is looking impatient, as if she thought we were just going to listen and then she could leave. "Because that is what people do when they are separated."

"Is separated before a divorce?" asks Primo.

"Sometimes."

"But I'm not separated," says Primo. "I'm going to visit Daddy and help him in Mexico City," Primo said. "Daddy and I planned it."

Daddy and I. Daddy didn't make plans with me. Maybe that's what they were doing the day we left Coyoacán. Today is like the day we left when I wanted to push the car back into the garage and stop my mother from leaving home. Primo and Daddy were already fixing things between them. I feel the same now. The water is too deep. The stones are too big. I can't fix the break in the dam. I'm like a bag of rocks myself. No way to make the arms swim. No way to go back to the shallows. I have no more questions.

Primo is glad to be done with the conversation about separation. Anyway, he's two years older and he has his plan to go to work for Daddy in a few weeks, so he runs out onto the street. "I'm going to explore," he yells.

Mama is done. She goes back to putting things away in the kitchen, to trying to figure out how she is going to cook over these charcoal burners, who's going to help her, who's going to go to the plaza for drinking water where there is one tap with spring water from the mountain. Who's going to carry the egg-shaped *cántaro* on her shoulder to bring water that Mama will put water-purifying pills into and then boil anyway. Who's going to watch Amado while Mama goes down the street to oversee the work at the "real" house Mama rented from Don Jerónimo, our new landlord.

I sit by myself in the sag of the canvas cot. I only want to do one thing—write to Pilar. Maybe she doesn't know we're never coming back. I have to tell her the way I'm telling myself. In the other room are three other cots. Mama says I'm the only one with my own room.

In this village we can walk anywhere. Because we come from a city of gates and walls and kidnappers, I hardly know how to step out of the door alone to go to the store. I hardly know how to go with no Pilar, but I do.

Suddenly Mama runs in. "Where's Amado?"

"I don't know. I thought he went to you."

"Soledad! You're supposed to watch him!"

We race under the grape arbor of our temporary house and through the mango trees to the old well. It's closed. Mama opens it anyway and I think we'll see him at the bottom even though he couldn't have lifted the cover. We run down to the gate that lets out to the lake, but it's locked and the fence is high. We look in the outhouse. Mama opens the door into the black, smelly little room to see if Amado is in the corner. I don't want to look down into the dark hole we sit on. I don't want to look into the big pit filled with the piles we made, sprinkled with the white lye Mama puts on it to keep off the worms. Mama looks in.

When we get to the front door Mama is calling out to others to help. I go away on my own. I want to be the one who finds him. At the corner is the Camino Real. It's the road the missionaries took after Columbus, and after Hernán Cortés. The fathers traveled the north side of Lake Chapala, west to the ocean and up the coast. The buses go on it. A few cars. Amado might have liked that because it's the street to the stores with lollipops and cheese, the barrel of gravelly sea salt, and bins bigger than he is, full of raw peanuts in their shells just dug up from the next town of San Antonio Tlayacapán. He likes those soft peanuts.

He also loves the middle of the plaza under the purple jacaranda tree and the yellow *primavera* tree. There is a round cement bench around the water tap where he can get a drink out of his hands, or wade in the drippings inside the fountain basin that has no fountain.

Next to the tap is the little chapel they still call the *hospitalito*. They say the Franciscan monks built it, well, told the Indians to build it, to have a place for sick people, and the monks cared for them on benches under the tiny altar of the chapel. Amado likes it there because he and I went into it alone and got scared. That day we opened a little door cut into the giant front door and saw the man in the coffin. The coffin was all of glass even on top so we could look in and see him, half naked, just with a cloth of plain *manta* covering where you are not supposed to see. There were scratches and blood all over him, even under his nails. His mouth was open and we could see his perfect white teeth. There was blood all over his chest where there was a deep hole from a knife, and blood was in his beard too. We stared and stared. Amado wanted to open the top.

I wanted to open it too because I thought he was not really dead. I needed to touch him. And if he was alive, I needed to lie on top of him to warm him and cover him. We couldn't open it. It was glued shut. In a few minutes we were not scared any more. I looked at the holes in his hands and the pieces of thorns still stuck in his hair, so I made Amado kneel. I knelt too and I moved Amado's little hand over his face to make a cross the way Pilar showed me, and I held his thumb for him to kiss it and say Jesu Cristo, and put it on the glass, then we ran out.

I didn't think he would go in there without me.

To the north are the hills, just three blocks away, and at their feet the giant pools in the mango grove where women wash their clothes and where the pipe to the plaza begins at the springs. He likes the pools and the women loving him with their eyes. But behind me is the big water, the lake.

It's easier to walk downhill to the lake. He would have gone down the hill, past the store with candy and ham and gum. I walk slowly down the street looking into each door in case he stopped for a *taquito* with someone. There are dogs on the street. Funny little dogs, on their own, walking their strange village walk, crooked. They walk up and down the streets, and even along the Camino Real, at an angle. Someone said it was from walking up and down hill, that it was easier if they walked sideways. The people also have a walk I've never seen. They don't walk like people in Mexico City, who bend forward to get someplace fast. Here everyone seems to rest on the spot where each foot lands for a split second. Then too, almost no one wears shoes. Everyone wears *huaraches,* just like the ones in Daddy's Codex, which Mama colors—sandals with intricate weavings. In this village. people know the exact person who made their *huaraches.* They say, "Oh, these are from the workshop of Don León."

Amado already has his first pair of *huaraches* we bought from a bunch strung up like fish at the store on the corner. Mama is going to have some made to order for him from one of the special leather weavers because the store sandals bunch up his three-year-old toes into a pyramid. We'll each get our own. We can pick who will make them and with what weave. The soles are made out of old tires. Maybe that's what makes people walk in the special solid way of the village.

I don't see Amado anywhere. I have to think he's been stolen. That's how we thought in Mexico City. I don't know where Mama is.

Wherever she is, she's scared. She'll get help, this beautiful new woman, back in the town with her three children, her brilliant head of red hair half contained in a pile of curls on top of her head, and half falling around her neck and face, her eyes flashing and talking faster than any words can come out.

I get down to the long stone pier. On either side are clumps of willows, and around them tall, rough-hewn poles holding up the giant fishnets to dry. At the edge of the lake are the long-nosed fishing boats with the oarlocks made of the elbow of a branch. There are notches along the pier with steps down. The water has been higher. When the water rises again, launches will deliver passengers to the steps. But the lake is low. Set after set of steps lead down to the mossy grass of the beach. I weave back and forth looking down the steps on each side, and looking far away down the beach, down to the sand where the small waves lap. There is no Amado.

Near the bottom of the last set of steps a blue eye looks up at me through a kind of gelatin. The whole head is jelly. Even the body seems soft and transparent. It is a complete baby burro, born too soon, dropped and left, like a large-eyed, four-legged jelly fish that dreamt of being a kind of horse. His mouth is slightly open and the light moves on his ribs as if he breathed. His eye is pointed right at mine and it seems to see me, so I can't move. I can't stop listening to that eye, feeling the shine of his see-through body, held by his almost-born and almost living self. Something in him has hold of me and is pulling me down the steps to him, into him. I have to fall backwards against the stairs and stumble back up to the pier to get loose, but he doesn't really let go. I just have to forget him and go find Amado.

There are fishermen working around an upside-down boat. I see smoke from their fire and I smell the tar they use to caulk the boats. The willows break up and move the smoke and the men, laughing, talking, and hammering at the cotton wadding soaked in the hot black liquid. I run along the soft moss on the beach to the willows. People. Laughter. Fire. Water.

Around the boat are large rocks white from the hair of dead moss, white like the stones the women use at the edge of the lake to do laundry. There is a petroleum can full of boiling tar on the small circle of rocks with the fire. With their backs to me, two fishermen sit on white rocks. They wear huge hats, the hats worn only by men on this side of the lake, wide brims and small pointed crowns. Each man tilts his hat in his own way to suit his walk or his weight or to say who he is. Opposite them, on the other side of the fire, sitting on his own little stone, with his hands on his knees just like them, is Amado, talking, as if he's spent his whole life on the shore with them. I am still scared when I run up. For a moment I think I have to snatch him up and rescue him and run all the way home and lock the door behind us.

The tallest fisherman of all turns from the boat he's mending and says, "*Hola. ¿Cómo te llamas?*"

"Soledad." I tell him I can't stay because my mother thinks my brother is lost.

They tell Amado to come back tomorrow. He takes my fingers. We're saying goodbye when Mama runs up. She talks with them. They say, "*Tranquila, Señora. María también buscó a su niño, cuando andaba con los sabios.*"

Even with tears on her face, Mama laughs and tells them she's glad they're fishermen and wise men, so they know she understands that Amado has been as safe as little Jesus was when he wandered off.

We walk up the hill, Mama walking free, Amado holding my hand. In his baby talk Amado tells us he was not lost. He was with his friends.

That night there is a fight under our only window. This is not Mexico City where at least rose bushes and a high wall divide you from these terrible sounds.

"They're drunk," Mama says. "Go back to bed."

But we're all standing against the closed dark wood of the window listening to the blows and the grunts just inches away from our faces. Fear keeps us paralyzed on our feet. We hear the *chinga* word that we can never say, with *madre* and the *puta* word and the *pendejo* word. If they are boxing, then their fists are going right through their ribs and almost through the adobe into our room. The last sound is not a word, just a thud like a horse falling against the wall, and then the sound of feet running up the cobbled street.

In the morning Primo shows me the blood under our window. It's not red. It's wine-black, thick and shiny in the grooves of the bricks where someone tried to sweep. The people across the street know the murderer. They know the dead man too. They say his sister came in the night and kneeled on the bricks by her brother waiting for someone to help.

At least we know where we're going to live later on. I'll have my own room. Primo and Amado will share. Mama has a room next to what will be the living room. The well is already dug. To get water you loosen a giant rock tied to one end of a thick bamboo pole and let the pole lower a square petroleum can into the well. You have to stand on the wet edge and catch the can and pull it over to empty it into buckets. Mama says we can't live there until she has built an edge of bricks around the well, and even covered the inside of the well with bricks, leaving steps along the inside of the wall so it could be dug deeper later, or to retrieve buckets. She wants two brick posts holding a thick beam for a rope and pulley, and the carpenter has to put on a wood cover that's too heavy for Amado to open. There is an open kitchen, no electricity, and a tiny bathroom. We'll use a bucket to flush. A bucket to heat water for a bath. With the clay from the well she has adobe bricks made right on the flat space that will be a driveway. She has enough to make one more little room for an office for when she figures out what her work will be. To make the adobe bricks they stirred the mud with cow manure and straw and some powders the man wouldn't let her see.

"Is that salt peter?" she asked him. "Ashes?"

"Something like ashes," he said. "This is the *chicle* of the adobe. In this village, this is how we make adobes. Others don't have our secret."

"What is it?"

"It's a secret. The *adoberos* of Ajijic, they know it. Your house will be strong. The old adobes in the old rooms you are plastering, they were made more than a hundred years ago with our same good adobe. Don Jerónimo built it with time in mind. He's like a priest, but he knows walls. He knows his fields and the harvest. You will be sleeping on solid ground."

Mama likes our landlord. He's handsome, with a thick black moustache and a hat that covers most of his face. When he raises his face to look at Mama, his eyes are beetle black and seem on fire with intelligence. He uses so few words that she says he must have taken part of a vow of silence. He is of the old way. His word is law and his honor is his life. There is no need to sign papers. Mama knows it. "Such men," she says, "are noble." She repeats it in Spanish, "*Noble*," respecting a rarity.

She needs new cane for the ceilings, but the moon is not right, so for the moment the roof is not on and the old mission tiles are stacked in what will be a garden. If you cut the cane in the wrong moon then the bugs get born and eat it, dropping dust month after month till your roof falls in. If you cut it in the right light of the night, then the cane can last you your whole life and hold the weight of a thousand tiles.

Mama needs a long beam for the living room. No one has one to sell her. She went to Guadalajara, but even the lumber places did not have one, not one that would span that long roof of the room that had been a granary. Her ally is Don Marciano the stone mason, who is now a builder and brings his workers to the house, and who looks at the picture books Mama has for her ideas. Just from memory, with a measuring tape and a string, he can make anything she wants, so she says he is a great artist, and *curioso,* which she only calls people who are gifted and can do things others can't.

"Don't worry about the beam, Señora. I have it arranged," he says.

In a week some men across the street in the hotel garden are holding up one end of a huge beam. They had to go across the street and into the hotel to try to fit it through the hole near the ceiling of our house. The beam is tapered, thick and fat at one end, but still solid and strong at the other. A giant, straight and perfect pine. But it is not a plain pine. It is covered with black creosote.

Mama doesn't want anyone to hear. She tells Don Marciano to walk up to our little temporary house to talk to him. She is almost running up the street. Don Marciano never runs. He gets to our house when he gets there.

"You stole it," she said.

"No. I told you I would arrange it."

"But it's illegal."

"Señora, por favor. How do you know?"

"Because I can see them on any street and along any highway. It's a...."

"Señora!"

"Take it back."

"Señora, I am barely not in jail for bringing it to you. There are no other beams for your house. We went in the night."

"To the depot of the electric company?"

"I cannot make my men go again. They have children. Families. They did it for you. I said No, but they said, *No hay otra.* There is no other solution. Or, I can make your granary into two rooms and put little beams and short pieces and cross-pieces and lower the ceiling and...."

"No. No, thank you. All right. But you should have told me."

"Told you what, *Señora?*"

Don Marciano was the only one who knew how to talk to Mama. Mama learned how to listen to him, the way she learned to give bribes. Never to the man she was bribing. Always for his children or his grandchildren. Real truth was never spoken.

```
April 23          Ajijic, via Chapala
                  Jalisco
                  Domicilio Conocido
                  Mama says the boy
                  Vicente will give us
                  our letters at the
                  post office inside his house.
```

Dear Daddy,
   How are you?
   Primo is getting worse and worse in Huck Finn
language and contradicts me. For instance I say some-
thing he does and he says harshly   Didn't   Don't
or   shaddup.
   Mama found a house but it is not ready. It has a
dog in it. Her name is Mariposa and she had puppies.
Mama says we can only keep one puppy.
   How is Pilar?

   Amado is ok. He did not really get lost. The fishermen took care of him. They told Mama it was like
when the virgin Mary found the little boy Jesús in
the temple.
   Mama is worried because of the man they killed under our window last night that maybe he was alive and
she should have gone out and saved him but the neighbor says no They would have killed her too.
   Here they call the little church the HOSPITALITO
and the big church they call it the TEMPLO. But in
Coyoacán when I went with Pilar to see the Virgen of
Guadalaupe we went to La Villa, and if we went to the
church at the plaza it was the IGLESIA. I don't know.
Then there was the Catedral you showed me downtown in
Mexico City, and somewhere else there is the capilla
near the piramids and they are talking about a Basí-
lica. Will you tell me about that? You or Pilar?
   I don't know what to say but, that, do you know
when you are going to visit?
               love and this many kisses to you
                   XXXXXX   XXXXXXX
                       Choli (Soledad) Paz

                   Choli

22

Standing in the Coffin to Call

In the beginning was the word,
and the word was No.

Soledad Paz

The telephone in the village is a few blocks from the house. When a child comes to Mama with a scrap of paper with the words *ocurra teléfono* scrawled on it, telling her to go to the phone because there is a call for her, Mama usually sends Primo or me to take the calls. She sends one of us to stand in the brown wooden box waiting for the operator to connect the call.

The box is like an extra big coffin standing on end. There is a door in it, and in the door is a glass window the size of a face. That's how we watch the operator in the next room as she turns the handle and grinds at the phone waiting for our call to come through. The phone rings with each turn of the handle until finally, someone answers, sometimes the one she was grinding for. She nods and points and we pick up the black tulip-shaped ear piece on the wall of the coffin and yell up into the black cup of the receiver, trying to hear the message for Mama, trying to answer the person calling her. It is almost Christmas, and the only thing I want to know is if Daddy is coming. Sometimes we have to go two or three times till the operator finally makes the connection for us, till we can hear

him on the phone and he says Yes, he's coming for my birthday, or
before school starts again, or after Easter. Or, No, he's not coming
after all. He's going to miss Christmas. He's going to miss Primo's
birthday. He has too much work and he has to make money. Someone has to earn a living. But he's coming soon. Tell your mother.
Tell your brother. Be a big help to your mother—words, words,
entering my ear but landing hard on the bones of my heart. I nod
and nod. It doesn't matter if I say anything in the brown wooden
box with a window that looks out at the woman with the grinder
phone. Long after he's stopped talking, I nod so she'll think I'm
still on the phone,.

I look up at the mouthpiece. It is full of small black holes. It
smells of spit and cigarettes. He has said Goodbye, and I already
said Yes, Goodbye, I know, Daddy, yes, and he's gone, but I keep
speaking. You're not coming. You're working hard for us, you're all
alone, coming soon. You have to wait till after New Year's. You're
sending money for Mami, for Christmas.

But I don't want to be here. It's Christmas and I want to be
in Coyoacán with our own evergreen tree in the living room, and
under it the small package with the green ceramic Esterbrook
fountain pen with a gold nib because I can spell and Primo can't,
or because you gave Primo a blue one so I got one too.

You gave me a pen to suck up blue-black ink because you knew
about the letters. You knew before I did that we would be gone
forever, gone to where we have to write to Daddy.

I put the ear piece back on the silver hook. I stand there looking
at my feet. The box is warm. Daddy's voice is still turning inside
me, humming in my head, in my chest and in the golden walls of
the box. I stay as long as I can because when I come out someone
else will talk to me and they'll erase the sounds of the drum.

I leave the telephone house and walk past our door without
stopping. I go down to the shore. The sun is about four hours away
from dusk when I am supposed to be home. The lake is calm,

lapping at the sand and the scattering of rocks. At sundown the waves will rise and froth like an ocean. I teeter on round white rocks covered with dead moss. Maroon crabs crawl from under them. I like them. They are mine. Pilar said that because my birthday is in June it means I am a Crab. Primo remembered and one day he caught one near the beach and tied its legs on a string and threw it into my hair. I like their blood-red shells, but they are also horrible.

Tiny moss roses face up with five lavender petals. The whole flower is smaller than a fingernail. Today I step on them. I listen for the crunch of their crisp stems. When I walk in the sand I twist my foot at each step. That way there will be no print. More like a smudge, more like a hoof print. This is the damp sand that is perfect for horses to run on. If I were on a horse now I would let go of the reins, hug his neck, and kick for the gallop. He could jump the low stone walkways, avoid the deep sand and leap the poles piled up after the drying of the nets. I would let him stop when he wanted to. This time I would not be scared.

At the long sandy point in the beach is the *chayotera*. The green roof of the vines is letting smoke through. I walk under it. The vines grow up from the ground and then across the reeds and sticks woven for them. The large green globes of *chayotes* hang down easy to pick. Empty boxes lie in rows ready to fill and load on the bus to send to market in Guadalajara. Some *chayotes* have long thorns on them, some have soft beards all over, and some are the new breed, smooth and shiny. I love this vineyard ceiling with the broken sky coming through the leaves onto the sand.

I head for the smoke. I hope I know who is there. If not, I have to pretend I was looking for someone and go home fast. A big fire is in a clearing near the *chayotera*. I can smell the catfish. It is Sunday and a whole family I know and the fishermen who work this part of the beach have come down to cook fish soup and laugh and talk.

They are sitting around the fire, each one slowly doing something that will go into the giant black pot. *Chayotes* cut in quarters

are thrown in, then *jalapeños* from the bushes near the vines. On
an old slab of boat wood, the catfish are strung like a necklace on
a long stem with green leaves. They are taking gulps of air and trying to swim on the dry board. The fishermen know how to pick
them up without getting stabbed by the catfish spikes. Heads and
tails go into the boiling water first with onions and whole heads
of garlic and a handful of rough gray salt. Then the cleaned fish
bodies go in. One of the women throws torn leaves of *cilantro* into
each enameled bowl ready for the broth. The oily scent of coriander
means we are ready to eat. Someone hands me limes and I cut them
and squeeze juice into each bowl. One of the children scrubs the
spoons in dry sand and I run to the lake to rinse them. The *caldo
michi* is done. The soft white meat with fine gray veins is in my
mouth and in their mouths. The hot chile is in my mouth and in
their mouths. We are all sucking in our breath to cool the burn of
the hot soup, and blowing out to cool it. Someone sprinkles salt
on his tongue to stop the burn of the chile. I suck a slice of lime.
And we start all over with a fresh spoonful with a chunk of boiling
chayote. The smoke from the mesquite branches under the pot and
the steam from the broth lick at the circle we make. No one speaks.

I forget about the telephone. That night I dream about the
real things that happen. The things I don't like. The things I don't
understand. I hate the dream but it feels things for me.

In my dream we are children. There are three of us just like
Primo, Amado and me, and there are two big people who are
supposed to drive. Someone is going to hurt the children. The big
people make me drive. There is a pig in the back seat and the big
person is supposed to keep the pig from eating the children. I need
someone in the driver's seat. I try to get someone to help.

I dream it because of the real, black sow at Doña Tere's house,
up in the high streets of the village, that ate a real baby. It was
not a dream. It was from the girlfriend of the horseman, the man
in white they call Tacho. But she was only twelve. Lara. She was

not really his girlfriend, he just made her have a baby. She didn't want her mother to know. They say she took a *remedio*. She even screamed when she took the medicine it was so bad, and the *doña* who cooked it took her to the back corral, behind all the corrals of the chickens and the goats, all the way to the one near the pig corral. That's where we saw her when we were hiding behind the outhouse because somebody knew what was going to happen. We watched Lara throw up and throw up, and then, when she was standing in the mud crying, with blood on her legs, the baby fell out. I saw her pick it up. It was tiny and made the smallest baby noises I had ever heard. The *doña* ran out of a shed and cut the purple rope that hung from the baby. Everyone knew the girl had to do something, but these things are secret. We watched the old woman slide the baby through the mesquite beams of the fence in front of the large black sow so no one would know, so no one would find out or tell Lara's mother. But we saw, and we could not close our eyes. The sow snouted at it till it was gone. Crooked and bleeding, Lara ran back to the house, holding her stomach with one hand and her mouth with the other. And it's true—they say Lara's mother never knew about the day of the baby.

The black pig sits inside me and can rise up in a dream any time, with her red angry eyes, and she can eat me or any small thing I love.

Ajijic   Lago de Chapala.   Calle Colón.   14 May

Dear Daddy,
    14 de mayo --- Happy Birthday and I never forget
you!
    Mama says if you can send money because we are
only eating oatmeal in the night and sometimes we
can't buy eggs. Mama says if you can send it in a
telegram.
    We are not in our new house. That one will be on
Calle Morelos.
    We are still in the mango house and in the back
is a whole little roof of leaves hanging with grapes.
Primo and I went in the nights and ate and ate
grapes. Mama says our landladies the Pérez sisters
counted all the bunches we ate.
    The Perez sisters came to see Mama even with the
priest in his long black dress and he told mama how
much she owes because we stole. She owes a lot. Sorry.
Now there is not enough money.
    It is different here and we all have to help. Well,
not Amado, maybe. So Primo and I help Mama. Someone
called Chona comes to clean but she spanks. Tell Pilar that Chona is not not not my Pilar.
    When we move to the really house Mama will start
our lessons.
                  Love to you and Pilar and Tigre.
                  But, Daddy,

In a few days is my birthday.

                  Choli
                  Junio. Sign of the Crab
                  El Cangrejo

23

Blood in the Brain

Memory sits at the table. It fills
a hundred eyes, stores
a thousand bites, waits
to taste life again.

Soledad Paz

Daddy is in Mexico City. We are still in the temporary house with one room and my little closet. It's all right. It's like camping. Even though Daddy used to go away a lot, this is different. He and Mama plan if he is going to visit or not. His absence lives in my ribs like the ache after eating a China plum that is too green or tortillas that are too raw. He lives in my other stomach. No matter how many sweet *tunas* I eat, how many meatballs in *albóndiga* soup, how many angel hair *fideos* in a sauce with cream and butter, how much hot bread with goat cheese, how much perfectly fried *bistec* from the cow they just killed, or chile sauce from green tomatoes I roasted and ground, this other stomach, which is for him, cannot get full.

Now that he stays in Mexico City he signs his letters "Father." Maybe it is just for him to understand that his house is empty, that he can pile as many books as he wants on my bed, that we don't have to clear his papers off the table so we can all eat together.

I don't die from the green truth that I can't see him when I want to, or because he is planning when Primo will go to visit him. I don't die because of everything I didn't say, or from everything I didn't ask. I don't die waiting for the dust of his smell to reach me, for the tobacco to come up from his clothes, for his fox-stained book to send the scent of paper mold and shaving soap into my face. I don't even die from knowing he is still bleeding from amoebic dysentery and could die far from us, far from me who doesn't know how to help, but who used to know how to watch over him.

He still has Amoeba histolytica. My mother says the name of his sickness and says they are still looking for a cure. In Mexico City the doctors have nothing for him. Amoeba histolytica. Like a short drumbeat the word prints itself on me and I see the red and brown spots in his underwear, the blood clots in the toilet. I step on the pedal of the sani-can and see the toilet paper soaked with red. The amoebas are eating him alive and then they spit out his blood. My father's blood.

Mama says he's in the hospital again in the United States. I read the letter he sent to Mama over and over. He lost 28 pounds. The blood is still coming out. Even the sores in his mouth are bleeding. I think I will see him again because they have found the medicine. It is a miracle drug. Mama calls it Tetracycline. That's the cure. The amoebas can't stand it. They are going to die. Maybe there will not be any more blood in his clothes. But the letter says he will be thin. I have to remember. there will be less of him

When he goes home, how will Pilar take care of him? She has her rules of "hot food" and "cold food." Will this go with the medicine? It is not the temperature of food. "It is its nature," she says. Even a boiled, hot cucumber, is "cold" food, and should never be eaten after noon. "Each food has a personality, *su carácter.*" Rice is warm and generous, adaptable, *no insiste,* adjusting to the body it enters. Broth is a second blood, gentle, reassuring and comforting. Peppers are hot, warlike *guerreros,* like medicine, good for you even if they hurt, like tequila which is really for healing not for getting drunk. She says peppers and lime juice enter you to make the agreements, and to cure colds, sweat out a *gripe*, even fix a hangover, *la cruda,* to balance and seal you. But the important thing about hot and cold foods is that cold is for before noon and hot is for after noon. She says every food has its time of day, though chocolate seems to go well any time. Foods are like people. Like the butcher—you don't speak to him except in the morning. Like the postmaster who is "raw" from his night of beer and pool—you don't speak to him until late afternoon. Then there is the bus driver we don't speak to at all, though he grunts and spits and looks as if he talks to himself under the large black mustache. Morning foods come to release the night and prepare for the day with a soft roll with beans, and coffee with milk and sugar. No fruit until the sun is well up in the sky or you will have arguments in your stomach. No meat or eggs until you are ready for long, solid work and have plenty to drink. After sunset, no salads to chill your *tripas,* stiffening your innards with their firm, grainy coolness. At noon everything is welcome. Pilar said that in the middle of the day we can eat a "cold" and a "hot" and even food that doesn't seem to have a name or style at all, neutral food like cream sauce and flour tortillas that come without personality from Sonora in the north. You can have "cold" eggplant, tomatoes, "cold" cactus, "warm" rice to pad the stomach and tortillas as receivers of the aggressive "hot" foods, meats with sizzling sauces full of *picante.* At night it's time for the neutral, to lay the body down in a bed of bread, a thick corn drink of *atole,* even a hot chocolate, because it is sweet like a kiss even though chocolate itself can be acid and "hot" if it has too much cinnamon.

She doesn't want us to be sick like Daddy.

I forgot to ask her if it is true that watermelon is "cold," and papaya.

We have to go eat with Mama's friend. He invites Mama, and she invites us. We go to where he lives near the lake shore. It is a small hotel. Very cheap. He says he is a starving artist, but the way

he says it, it might not be true. The way he says it, starving artist
is something good. He wants a prize for it. He has a mustache,
and even though he does not have a beard, people say he looks
like Hemingway. He thinks that's good too, as if that makes him
halfway a writer whether he's made a book yet or not. Anyway,
he has a belly, and he eats a lot at our house, and supper is also
always waiting at his *pensión*. The hotel where he lives is owned by
a German and his sister. We watch them on the beach. Everyday
just before sunset they walk on the sand in front of their *cabañas*
with their hands behind their backs. He is thin as a stick, wears
a striped bathrobe and walks in tie-up shoes without socks. She
wears shorts and a tight white shirt over her big stomach and over
her breasts that show through, and she walks in tie-up shoes with
socks. They don't speak. They just walk. When the sun sets he takes
off his robe, puts on a shirt and they go to the kitchen to bring
up dinner, dish after dish, from the little kitchen in the basement
where they taught someone how to cook their German way.

I can't write Pilar to tell her how delicious their soups are. It's
all right, because they make them out of potatoes and caraway and
dill. She never uses those things. In the dark dining room, painted
shiny black, the only light is from petroleum lamps hung on the
pillars. We sit at long brown tables with all the guests. Sometimes
we do not have to sit with Mama. After dinner the German
brother brings out his guitar. He plays beautiful music for half an
hour, then he goes to his own little house on the mountain side
of their land. Mama says he plays like Segovia. The sister goes to
her miniature house near the lake side. Primo and I always go to
the outhouse because this one has two holes. We drop matches in
and we use their light as they flicker down to the bottom to see
how the worms move in the mud. They don't put a lot of lye in the
outhouse like Mama does, so there are more worms.

We go home and have to go into the one room where we live
and close the door because Mama uses the patio outside the kitchen
for a living room. She found two narrow beds with ropes to hold

the mattresses. These are her couches. She found small round leather tables, and two leather *equipal* chairs they made right on the street outside our house. They stink of pig hide and chemicals so they have to stay outside.

She and her friend light petroleum lamps in the kitchen. Mama brings one in to us and she leaves one on the wall near the entrance. We can hear them talking. Late in the night he knocks his pipe against the ashtray and leaves. Mama comes to the room smelling of tobacco. Now that he's gone I should be able to sleep, but her dreams keep me awake, and also the way he puffs on his pipe by snarling at one corner of his mouth, and also because he raises his eyebrows and narrows his eyes when he looks at us and pretends that he's getting smoke in his eyes.

                                        Domicilio Conocido
                                        Ajijic, via Chapala
                                        June 5 and June 6
Dear Daddy,

Mama's friend is here all the time. And they hold
hands.

He doesn't live here, but he comes for lunch and then
at night we go to where he lives for dinner. He gets
soup in his mustache and doesn't wipe it.

He thinks he is very funny. And teases. He calls
Primo a wiseacre and Amado a weisenheimer. But if you
tease him? He hates it and his eyebrows go up and he's
mad like when Primo told him he had fleas in his moustache.

Where he lives every guest pays for his own little
tiny house. Mama's friend says he likes it because he
can type and write his book even all night.

He says his bed is so uncomfortable it might be filled
with baseballs. So he stays a long time at our house
at night and then goes home in the dark.

Daddy, I know he teaches us a lot of things like Plaster of Paris and how to do ping pong and badminton
and tennis and chess. I know and I like all of it. It
is a lot of fun.

But do I have to like him? Because I think I hate
him.

I don't think he does things because he likes us. He
does them because he likes Mama.

                         Your
                            Choli

24

Las Mañanitas

El día en que tu naciste
nacieron todas las flores.
En la pila del bautismo
cantaron los ruiseñores.

The day you were born
every flower was born with you.
Around the baptismal font
nightingales sang for you.

Las Mañanitas (Early morning birthday song)

We were going to have my ninth birthday at the new house, but it's not ready. Mama wants a septic tank and my uncle hasn't come yet to help her make it the way they do in the army. So we are still here where there is an outhouse.

There are paper streamers strung along the roof ends of bamboo and over the edges of the roof tiles of the open kitchen. On the counter is a huge glass pickle jar with lemonade and a white enamel ladle hanging over the side. A bottle of white tequila is there for those who like something extra in their lemonade. Mama's clay dishes from Tzintzuntzán with fish painted on them are filled with crackers. Mama went to that village with her friend. He bought her a necklace with the same long white fish carved in silver. He didn't see that she never wears jewelry. A board of many colors from the high forests of Michoacán is covered with chunks of salty cow cheese, and triangles of goat cheese. A whole circle of gold quince jam from Ixtlahuacán de los Membrillos is on the cobalt

blue plate we found at the glassblower's in Tlaquepaque, and in a
cup are the glass flowers of pale blue he made for me when Mama
told him it was going to be my birthday. The musicians lean their
dark bottles of beer against the wall near their feet.

I stand in the doorway to our room and look at everyone.
Mama is near the kitchen watching the tin box on top of the
stove. The box is our oven. Mama's waiting to see if a cake will
come out. On a plate are nine pink candles in little sugar flowers
to stick into the cake. It will not be Pilar's cake with thin layers,
each spread with apricot jam and then covered with pale, shiny
frosting of butter, sugar, lemon juice and one drop of color. Today
Chona is supposed to watch Amado but she wants to talk about
the cake so she pretends to talk about me.

"Don't worry about Choli. She has skin like a baby, and has
a little red in her hair. She gets that from you." She doesn't really
want to work for Mama. She wants to be her friend, but this is the
Chona who smacks our behinds and laughs.

Mama smiles. She probably hopes Chona is right, but I think
she worries like I do that my eyebrows meet in the middle, and
my teeth stick out so I am worried they'll call me The Tooth when
they come to giving me a name in the village. Primo has braces,
and there's only money for one person with braces.

Primo is picking up the guitars against the wall and trying to
play. Each of the musicians has brought two or three instruments.
Vicente can play guitar, but right now he is against the adobe wall
of the little patio with a big bass fiddle. He has long dimples going
down his cheeks. He never looks at his fingers as he plays. I want
to stare at his face because he is something like beautiful. I want
to be close to him because he might be as good as his face, but
he might not. So in a way he scares me and I don't talk to him.
I only look at his brown, smooth cheeks when he is not looking.
He keeps up with Domingo on the trumpet and with Juanjo on
the guitar. Domingo is teaching all of his sons to play instruments
even though he is really a carpenter and is making doors for our

other house when it is ready. Mama is waiting for the owners to take a mountain of corn out of the living room, then she can put in a floor of blood-red tiles and maybe even a smooth brick fireplace in the corner like the one she saw in her Italian magazine *Domus*. When she has money she is going to put one of those fireplaces in my room and also in the studio for her friend so he can paint in her house and then he'll be there almost all the time. There is no mantel on the fireplace she wants. It is a smooth, plain pyramid of brick from the floor to the cane roof, just with a square mouth for the fire.

Domingo is the head of the musicians. He is tall and thin. He is handsome but his face is also mean. People who love him say he has to look like that because he wants things that are better for his family. His boys are not going to be fishermen and they are not even going to be carpenters. After they finish elementary school he is going to save to send them to school in Guadalajara. They don't play on the beach after school. They go right back home and take turns on different instruments. Friends of Mama's who play jazz in the restaurant gave him a clarinet and someone else gave him a violin. Instruments come to him because he is special in what he fights for. Just in case, his boys know how to plane wood, and saw it too, and they know how to glue and nail and measure. Also, they don't dress like other children even though they are poor. Amado and Primo look poorer than they do because the boys of Domingo always wear white shirts and black pants. It is part of his dream. I don't know how it works, but it is true that you can always recognize them and they always look nice. We have clothes that Mama makes or that people give us because right now there is no money since we live here and Daddy lives there and Daddy says it is expensive to have a family in two places and Mama doesn't have a job yet. Still, she got me a new embroidered shirt for my birthday with little people cross-stitched on it. I went to the woman who makes them and picked it out alone. Books in English come in the mail from a man who does good for people, and Mama is going to teach us. In a second-hand store Mama bought a lilac linen dress so I can look nice when we go to Mexico City to visit Daddy and to see Stevie and his family. She is saving the lavender sweater she found for when we go, but today I get to wear the lavender dress for a little while. I have to be careful. It is very old and I already stuck my hand through a hole in the pocket, but on the inside. It doesn't show.

I watch Domingo play his trumpet. He has hips that come to the front more than his shoulders. He wears a big silver buckle. I watch it go up and down as he plays the trumpet. The harder he blows the higher the buckle goes up and his hips come to the front even more so his trousers come up and his cuffs go up and down on his *huaraches*. The easy notes he plays with the trumpet close to his chest. When they are high and sad the trumpet goes up into the air and I watch his pants moving with the notes.

Mama says, "Don't stare."

"I'm not."

"Yes. You are."

"I'm not."

"Well, what are you doing then?

"I'm looking at him on his inside."

Juanjo has a belly so big it looks as if someone blew him up. His shirt fits tight all over it but the buttons don't pull apart. His wife must have made him his shirt just right to fit his balloon. On top of it he rests his guitar, and sometimes the *guitarrón* which is leaning against the adobe. The *guitarrón* has just as big a belly on the back, so when he plays it his arms are all the way out reaching for the strings. It looks as if he is playing on a table balanced on his chest. His hat is too big for him and makes a big shadow over his eyes. It is his style. Even from behind, if you see him on the street, you know before you see his belly that it is Juanjo because of his hat.

Chona, who comes to work for Mama a few hours a day, is in the open kitchen leaning on the counter waiting for glasses or dishes to wash. I stay away from her because she hits my bottom for no reason any time I come close, and then she laughs hard. She is not like my Pilar. Chona has chairs in front of the bedroom door so that no one can go in where Mama shares with Primo and Amado and where my closet is. Right in the middle of the patio is a square of smooth red tiles, and Mama says it is big enough for dancing. If someone has to go to the bathroom they have to go through a narrow door, and back under the grape vine to the out-house. One thing Mama always has is toilet paper, not like some people who use comic books and newspapers. Mama says there are some things you can't do without. Right now the roll is on a coat hanger, but when we have our house it might be on a real holder like in Mexico City.

It's like what they say about Mama, that she looks as if she has a lot of money. No matter what, everyone always thinks she's rich, and it is not just because she is beautiful. Now that we are not in the city and Mama does not wear suits any more, she is wearing peasant blouses with meters and meters of lace. She makes belts out of leftovers of satin from a second-hand store. Today she is wearing a white lace blouse, a green satin belt and a skirt of three tiers of gold plaid that she made from some old gauze curtains our neighbor Lorena was throwing away. Because Mama makes her own clothes she doesn't look like anyone else. She is always the only one. Her hair is up in red curls on top of her head. She doesn't need ear-rings or necklaces. Her eyes are her jewelry.

Suddenly the music is really loud and they are singing the *Mañanitas* to me—the early morning birthday song that I like best, about the day you were born when all the flowers came to life and nightingales sang. I know it isn't really about me. I like it because we sing it for lots of birthdays, especially Mama's.

I don't see him come in.

But there he is. Daddy—walking up the last few cobbled steps of the steep entrance, and then I have my first real hug as if he had been waiting until today when I am nine years old to give it to me.

He is wearing khaki pants and a bright white shirt, just like when we went to Taxco. Pilar and the Tetracycline have fixed him. He is not thin like a skeleton the way he was. He looks almost like before he got the amoebas. Now I don't feel worried.

The *músicos* start a waltz. Daddy says, "Would you like to dance?"

I don't know who else is there or if anyone else is dancing. I am only seeing him. I am worried that I have to move a certain way to help because of his limp. But it's not like that. He doesn't sweep over the floor. He doesn't do fancy steps. He moves to the music and he makes his limp fit in so I hardly notice it at all. I look down mostly at my feet, and at his feet in the brown shoes I polished so many times. Maybe inside them are the socks I darned with my wooden egg in the heart basket. We dance all the way through to the end of the song, his white shirt cool under my hand, and the tan pants bending with his knees. If he says things, I don't know because I am too happy to listen or to speak.

                              Dom. Con.
                              Ajijic via Chapala
                              Jalisco
                              June 29

Dear Daddy,

Thank you. It was the best birthday because you were
a surprise. I want to write you in spanish because
that is how I hear it. Pero, pero, pero, but
you said to practice our English. I am reading English
every day.

It was the best birthday!

Daddy, Did you know Mama was going to marry That Man?
He lives at our house now. No one even asked. Just
like that. Now he is very bossy. Mama said you said
it was OK with you. Maybe you knew already. Next time
maybe someone should tell Primo and me before they
get married.

If Primo thought I was bossy, this man is REALLY
bossy. The man has a cat called Jerky. Jerk is a big
word these days. Also he uses g+d++m+it for everything. Mama does not even say GOSH. You don't either.

Her husband says Primo is a jerk. But you can't say
jerk to him. He does not call me a jerk. Maybe only
boys are jerks.

                    Love,
                    Soledad   your Choli

25

Piñatas

Blindfolded.
His stick hits a rope.
Voices spin him the wrong way,
tell him to strike hard.
A boy's head cracks.
No candy.

Soledad Paz

This is Christmas in our real house. Mama fills clay bowls with candy and coins. As children pass by the door she hands them out. More and more come. The word spreads and in minutes children are packed from our huge front door all the way to the other side of the street, screaming and flinging their arms out so Mama can choose them. She starts to throw handfuls of candy, then some coins, and more candy. The children become wilder and wilder, screaming for more, stealing from each other, pushing against her, grabbing at the edges of her bowls. I watch from the top of the entrance. Suddenly I see she is afraid. She throws what is left in the bowl as far away from her as she can, closes the door, turns the giant key and leans against the wood.

"I had no idea," she says. "I thought they would like it—there was enough for everyone."

Her husband says, "You did it for your ego. Acting like some rich outsider. You are so thoughtless. Sometimes I wonder if you are actually human. Did you think they would just obediently catch what you were throwing at them? You were THROWING things at them, for Chrissake!"

I hear her crying in her room, then quiet, maybe napping the rest of the afternoon. He sucks on his pipe in the living room with a look that says That'll teach you. Maybe he's right, but that's when he is the meanest of all, when he's right. I can't go hug my Mama, because her room is their room. There's no place to go and still be close to Mama, so I go to my room and bathe with the pitcher and ewer. In the wardrobe I keep an amber glass filled with milk separating into whey and making a kind of cottage cheese. When I am hungry I can spoon it out, sprinkle it with salt from the corner store and eat. I am always hungry. There are new rules since Mr. Mustache came to live with us. One, I am not allowed in the kitchen between meals, but only to cook for the five of us at night or to bake pies and make fudge to sell. Two, he's going to rip out the purple ivy if we don't stop calling it Wandering Jew.

"It has a botanical name, you know. Call it Zebrina, for Chrisssake!" he growls.

Mama says he's Jewish but not to mention it because he's funny about it. I want to say that he's the one who is wandering, and that's why he doesn't like the ivy name. I don't have the right botanical name for him either. Mr. No Name is good enough. Anyway, I don't want to say anything because I love Stevie like a father and he's Jewish, and he doesn't talk about it either as if he belongs to another group now. My tutor—Creighton, a Welshman—explains a little about Jewish people. It sounds as if God blew on a dandelion bloom and their seeds flew circling the world. I didn't know we all have to move from tribe to tribe.

I don't belong to Daddy the way I did before. I feel like Malinche. First she's in one family with her father and mother, and she is called Mallinali. Maybe like Grass Flower, the goddess Malinalxóchitl. Then when Malinche's father dies, her mother gets married and has a little boy. Her husband doesn't want an *hijastra,* so her mother gives her away, or sells her, or lets her be taken to another group. Miss Galindo said the new husband wanted his own child, not a stepdaughter. Her new name is Malli because she is a captive in this new tribe. Miss Galindo said Malintzin was born in a bad luck year. Mama showed me the years in the codices. One Reed year was not good.

After Mama's bad day with the candy, the priest does not embarrass her by coming to the house to talk. Everyone would see him and gossip. He finds a way to help even though she isn't a Catholic, and she doesn't go to church. There is a funeral procession leaving the church. We stop. Mama even turns off the motor and we listen to the muffled banging of the death bell. The priest leans in her window and asks her for help during the upcoming Christmas. During the *posadas,* when they enact how Mary and Jesus are turned away every evening from an inn, the priest sets up his events of piñatas for all of the children in the barrios. He picks Mama to be in charge of everything he needs for the piñatas for that night in our barrio, on the corner of our house. There is a real inn across the street, where Mary and Joseph will bang on the enormous wooden door and no one will give them shelter.

Starting in the afternoon of the day the priest picked for Mama to be in charge, the priest and his helpers string ropes from house to house and older boys set up each piñata and get them ready to swing up, down to the ground, and up again out of reach. Older girls fasten bandanas around the children's eyes, and give them a stick to break the clay *cántaro* full of fruit and peanuts. These girls get to spin each child around till he's dizzy and waddling like a drunk in the direction of the piñata. Boys yell that it's to the left, and others that it's to the right. When the child finally breaks the piñata, he's the last to get a good haul because of the bandana. Some learn to dive blindfolded right after the sound of the breaking pot. I hate piñatas. At first, at birthday parties where there was always a piñata, I stood at the edge when the piñata broke so a piece of the clay *cántaro* wouldn't fall on my head. So I got nothing, no tangerines, no candy, no coins, no miniatures, no wrapped surprises. Then I watched Primo, and even if I broke the piñata, I dove into the center scooping everything I could into my arms. I got stepped on, scratched, bruised. Hands reached in and grabbed candy and presents right out from under my throat. I got tired of Primo's way too. Someone always shares and I don't have to have my face on the cobblestones. Also, I hate the bandana over my eyes.

A few days before our Posada, we go to Guadalajara to the wholesale open market. We buy small paper bags in bunches of 500. We bring home candy in bags of five and ten kilos. In the fruit section we pick up huge string sacks full of tangerines already weighed and counted. We bring shopping baskets from home and shovel them full of kilos and kilos of roasted peanuts in the shell. In Tlaquepaque we fill the car with cracked or chipped *cántaros* that are no good for carrying water. Friends and neighbors come to our house and cut kilometers of tissue. We make glue out of boiled flour and water and paste streamers and colors all over the jugs. Some people know how to make heads and ears out of newspaper. We cover those with tissue too. The beams of the verandah are filled with hanging donkeys, clowns, strawberries, and pigs.

Mama's table seats fourteen or more on our porch. People from the houses around us help fill hundreds of little bags with some of everything, even now and then a coin, or a chocolate coin or a cheap miniature toy we bought by the dozens. My favorite candy is a sugar-coated sliver of orange rind. As I fill bags I pluck those out and pop them into my mouth. They last the longest and at the end there is the tough bittersweet skin to chew. Then we fill piñatas. In the evening the piñatas are strung up on the street and children sit on all the sidewalks. Hundreds of children from this *barrio* and from nearby. The priest in his black cassock marches up and down the street keeping order. He has some kind of magic, a word here, a warning there. They obey even when they can't see him. Like God. Piñata after piñata is broken. The first is for the toddlers, then come the ones for the youngest ones, and so on up to the oldest who are ten or eleven. Each age group has its own piñatas. After the piñatas, it's time for the "Navidad," the extra little Christmas, the paper bag filled with fruit and nuts and surprises. There is a bag for every single child so that even if they have been too scared to dive for things under the piñata, or if they have been trampled and had all their loot taken from them, each one gets something.

When the priest gives the signal, we come out of the house with *chiquihuite* baskets filled with bags. The ritual is so known and the priest so clear in what he expects that no child jumps or grabs or takes the "gift" of another. In the shape of a cross, the north, south, east and west sidewalks are filled with children waiting for their "Christmas," laughing, joking and talking. The priest like a giant black bird flies up and down and across. When it is over, as if flocks had landed in a field and found all the seeds, with a high and low chirping and chattering the children fade along the streets away from our corner. We bring in the empty baskets and put them back in their places, in laundry corners, by the fireplace for wood, in the kitchen, in the garden for picking fruit.

This is Mama's village now.

The priest helped her find her place.

13 de julio
Sorry. I forgot to mail it at once.
The letter stayed in my room.

Casa Siranda Blanca
Calle Morelos

Dear Daddy,

First I wrote the house name for our new house. It
is only my name for it. Do you like it? It's because
we have a real siranda blanca tree. It comes from far
away at the sea. No one else has one except the people who live on the Pacific.

Now I can have a cat. Mariposa and Azúcar don't
bother cats.

Ernesto, a friend who is a painter, said to come
because he has kittens from his girl cat. Her name is
Oedipus. Ernesto gave me 2 kittens not one.

Cenizas is the name of one kitten because she is
grey like ashes of the carbón.

Agüilote is her sister's name because she is black
and because also we actually have an Agüilote fruit
tree in the garden. It gives fruit black like olives
but very bitter. Do you like agüilotes? I don't like
them, but our agüilote tree is especial and everyone wants the fruit even though it makes your teeth
black. We give all the fruit away.

But Daddy. When I left Ernesto's house with my kittens I said thank you. Then he said don't mention it.
So I cried all the way home. Did he not want to give
them to me? Was he mad?

Mama says it's ok because that's how he talks. She
says it is like when we say your welcome.

I want you to see my kittens because I take good
care of them and I love them.

Choli

26

Keeping Angels

New eyes are mine.
Soledad Paz

Mama doesn't use her gun in the village. We have a eucalyptus tree, but she doesn't shoot into it every Sunday the way she did into the tree at our house in Mexico City. Here what she needs is her Kodak. No one has a camera, so when a baby dies they come looking for her. They call the lost babies *angelitos,* because they are still pure. They died before being baptized and there are no pictures of them. For baptisms and special days the photographer comes from the next town on the bus, bringing his tripod and his black hood and rude directions that poke like fingers into parents, godparents, or a wedding party. He gets off near the church, shoots a wedding, a funeral or a baptism and then leaves. But for the *angelitos* there seems to be no money. Instead, there is fear. Fear of no memory, nothing to hold on to, nothing to cry over or point at to remember a son or daughter, a brother or sister. The infant will fade, just like the baby biers in the cemetery that melt slowly with each rainstorm till no colored streamers fly in the wind and no little thrones of cane honor the mound.

"*Señora, si nos hace el favor,*" someone says at the door. Sometimes it's the mother herself, asking Mama to do her the favor of taking a picture of her baby that God has taken.

I go with her. We walk a few blocks, following the mother or child or relative. We always ask the same questions. When did he die? What did she die of? Did the doctor come? What did the priest say?

Once we are with the baby we have no more questions and we don't want to talk. One baby boy has a soldier suit on. He looks at me through slits in his eyes, but when I come close I see that it is only the whites that are showing. They have woven for him the usual bed of split cane. On one end, where his head is, the bier is tipped up so you can see him better. A canopy made of cane strips arches over him, making a cross in the middle and curving down to the knots at the corners. Tissue and crepe paper are cut into thin streamers decorating his bed and the canopy. Around him are carnations and roses and petals of daisies. Vigil lights flicker everywhere, as if death and life can gutter or gleam, turn on or off, as souls ride whispers of air.

At a little table next to him, Mama takes out her camera and opens the front of it like a door. She stretches out the black accordion with its large bulbous eye surrounded by silver rings etched with numbers. There are levers she pushes up and down and a wire that has a tiny plunger like a syringe on the end. She walks around to see how to take the best picture. She stands looking at the baby. He is a miniature carved out of yellow beeswax. There we are, trying not to stare at his little fingers turned up, wanting to swat at the flies on his slightly open mouth. I watch one fly walk right in. I don't see it come out. Everyone is watching us because what we are doing is magic. They know that in a few weeks Mama will come back with a black and white picture of this baby. The red stars on his uniform will be black, his yellow hands and face will be gray, but what is black today, like his hair and his tiny plastic boots, will still be black. They will have something, and when they hold the only picture in the world of their baby, the tears will come again.

We are there to take pictures, but around us there are so many bent heads, sombreros held in hands, shawls pulled to hide what you can't hide, tears through fingers, noses wiped on sleeves, the father, already slightly drunk, the mother falling to one side and held. I looked at the baby's dimples made of wax and the tan cap a little crooked on his forehead. I want to touch him. I want to put the light back in his skin. I want to pick him up and wake him, but I am scared, too scared even to wave flies away.

A baby girl we photograph on another day is in the dress they bought for her baptism. It flows over the edge of the cane bier and touches the ground. I can see how she would have looked in her godmother's arms at the font, the dress trailing lace to the floor, the holy water falling from heaven, her name spoken over her head and into the hearts of her parents.

Another baby is so tiny I could have cupped her in my hands. She wears a party dress of taffeta with pink bows embroidered under a layer of organza. Her hair has been combed with fresh tomato juice into one curl on top of her head and is fastened with a miniature pink bow. Inside the curl is a tomato seed, but I can't figure out how to take it out without upsetting someone. Pilar always told me to be sure the juice was strained before I used it to keep my hair in place. No seeds.

This is the baby girl's last party. No first communion. No *quinceañera* when she turns fifteen. No one will ever dance with her. The drink today is the drink of wakes, hot cinnamon tea with grain alcohol from the vat at the grocery store. The food is this and that, plates the neighbors bring, sweet bread, hot coffee, tortillas to warm up. Something happens to Mama on the day of that baby. I can see her camera shaking. She's trying not to cry. She's trembling so much the picture will be blurry and the family will be scared when she brings them a photograph of a gray ghost of their child. Carefully, I get the camera out of her hands and take the pictures. Mama has seen something else. Her own secrets are shaking her. Her own deaths are draining her. Mama never again goes to photograph an *angelito*.

Now when they come to the door, Mama sends me, and after a

while they knock and just ask for Choli. Mama gives me her Kodak and then my own Brownie that takes beautiful, clear, square pictures. I go alone to make the memories. Later, when I visit houses where I have been before, I see photographs tucked into a frame of El Santo Niño de Atocha, into a painting of San Cristóbal or of Nuestra Señora de San Juan de los Lagos, my favorite, with her halo of flying baby angels. The photographs are faded. What was black and white is brown and gray, lacquered with fingerprints, etched with kisses. I finally know this is my village because now they ask for me, and I have my own camera.

Mama tells her husband I will be taking the photographs because she's getting too busy. It's true. She's learning to weave, to design from cones of thread, to the shuttle, to the weft. She hires more people to fill the spindles and to learn to weave, to turn the design into cloth. Now there are more seamstresses to learn how to drape and fit her unusual patterns. Our ping-pong table becomes a cutting table. Each time she invents a new outfit, long hooks hold the patterns in thick layers of shaped brown paper tied with scraps of cloth. She creates fabulous clothes. Even the wife of the governor of Jalisco came to our house and Mama made her a whole suitcase full of carefully lined handwoven cloaks, capes and evening dresses for a state trip to Paris.

It all started when Mama and her husband saw four handmade treadle looms thrown away in the garage of the hotel across the street. When the hotel was built, eight stalls were set up for cars and trucks. Two of the stalls are for the hotel horses I take care of. In two other stalls were the looms, covered with dust and spider webs. They still had bolts of warp on them. Melquiades, who made them, had moved to Guadalajara when no one showed interest in his placemats and napkins. After Mama and her husband bought the looms, Mama went to look for Melquiades. He came back and taught her everything about weaving. He was a master weaver and loom builder. He stayed with her for years, building eight more looms, wide and narrow. She and her husband learned to make everything from belts to cashmere for men's jackets. I wove on all the looms, even the ones so wide that half of me was stretched over the warp trying to sling the flying shuttle back and forth to make the woof.

Mama makes beautiful subtle designs, blending the rarest hues for women, for men, for children. She teaches me that no stripe should ever be the same width as any other. Her husband, on the other hand, orders the weaver to make even, boring stripes and squares of black and white and brown—no drift of shades. They do look like the lanes at the bottom of a pool. Someone compliments him on his awnings.

Even though she's busy, something in Mama needs to go back to rescuing. One day a woman called Victoria comes to her. "*¡Señora!*" she says, "*Favor que le pido.* Please heal my baby. Your children get sick and you make them well. They are dying and you save them. You know what to do. You get the nurse. You get the injections. This is my last baby, my thirteenth child. I give him to you. He's yours. Just save him. Please!"

"But, Victoria, what's wrong with him?" Mama asks.

"He is only sleeping and sleeping. And I am so tired I forget if he has eaten or if there is milk in my breast."

Mama opens the rebozo. She picks up the little boy's arm. It is limp. "I don't think he's asleep," she says. "He's unconscious."

"Doña, he's dying. Please take him. Save him."

Mama lifted him out of the rebozo and held him close.

"I don't know. I will try. But what if it's too late?"

"Doña. I know you can do it. I give him to you. It is the only way." Victoria turns to the godmother of her other children, her *comadre* who is with her. "*Comadre,* you are my witness. I give my son to the Señora. Now he is her son. You have heard me." The *comadre* nods, crying hard. Victoria sobs, kisses the baby's forehead and his limp fingers, makes a sign of the cross over his face, then covers her mouth with her rebozo.

Victoria has green eyes and grey wavy hair. She is already in middle age. It's true. She will never have another baby. Mama takes him. Not to keep. Just to try to help him.

"What's his name," Mama says.

"Victor."

Both women pat Mama's arms as if to reassure the powers they know are there. Then they bless her and walk away up the hill.

First Mama takes Victor to my room and puts him on the bed and undoes his wrappings. She tries to get him to open his eyes as she speaks to him in the soft purring voice that is only for puppies and kittens and babies. She looks at his mouth. She moves his legs and arms and presses on his skin. "Look, Choli, his skin doesn't come back when I push on it. Look at his mouth. It's sucking in. He's starving to death. Victoria let him sleep too much. No one woke him up to feed him. He has to eat. Quick."

In the kitchen Mama boils water and invents something like a formula with powdered milk, oil and egg. She feeds him the warm milk from an eye dropper. "Choli, run up to the plaza for Blanca the nurse and buy a baby bottle. Go!"

When I come back, Mama has made diapers from her old flannel nightgown and wrapped him in clean pieces of a torn sheet and more flannel. His arms are still floppy but his eyes are beginning to move in his head. Blanca and Mama look him over and agree he's not sick. There's no fever. No marks. It's true—he started to die of hunger. Mama and I, and anyone else who wants to help, feed him and hold him day and night. My room is his nursery. I can hold him for hours, watching the veins in his pale eyelids as if his beating heart were there. Then one day I see his life when he opens his eyes and looks at me. In the night I listen for his little sighs and his sudden intakes of air which make me jump out of bed and hold up a candle to see if he's still alive.

Someone makes a bath out of oilcloth sewn onto sticks. Someone else brings an oval Moses basket of pale *tule* reeds from the marshes of Sayula. Mama lines it with flannel for his bed. My bed is his changing table. He lives with us for many months. We feed and bathe him. Then, when he is six months old and healthy we go to Victoria's house and return her son to her. We give her tins of powdered milk. Mama shows her how to boil the water and mix his formula. She tells Victoria a million things. For months after that, Mama takes sterilized pots of applesauce she makes herself, more cans of milk and boxes of Pablum and little jars of food even we can't afford. She makes Victoria swear to give them to the baby. Victoria always promises.

"I will borrow him from you," Victoria said, "because he is blood of my blood. But his soul is yours. You saved him. You didn't have to come take a photo of my dead baby. I didn't have to visit his grave in the *camposanto*. You are giving him back to me alive."

She borrows him from Mama, with his beautiful green eyes and the beginnings of wavy hair. Then one day she brings him back. Whatever she feeds him comes out in green and yellow juice. Whatever he drinks comes out in spurts of dark water. Mama gets the doctor. She makes Victoria take the baby home, but Mama goes every day taking everything the doctor said. She crushes charcoal tablets between two spoons. She mixes bismuth powder with rice milk that we boil and grind ourselves. Mama tries to give him boiled banana water with cod-liver oil. The nurse comes and hangs a translucent bag of *suero* from a floor lamp, and tapes the needle to his tiny arm. It doesn't matter. Cloth after cloth fills with the colors of his stomach. His green eyes turn to gold. Then to coal. Then he's gone.

Mama and Victoria fall together at the shoulders, making a tent. Each one takes half the weight of the pain. They stand that way until Victoria steps back, wraps her black rebozo over her mouth, pats Mama on the shoulder and walks us to the door. Mama will not come back. But I have to. When they have bathed him and dressed him and put him on his bed of cane strips with a crown of paper streamers, I'll come back with my camera.

                    Casa Siranda Blanca
                    Calle Morelos
                    Ajijic

                    10 de mayo (It's Mother's Day so
                    with my friends we brought mariachis
                    to our mothers in the dark dawn.)

Dear Daddy,
    Mama saved Baby Victor but he died.
    I have to go to his house now and take his picture
for Victoria his mother because even that he got well
she didn't get the money to baptize him. Daddy, I will
take the pictures. Mama can't do it so I have to.
    You said that Bernal del Castillo wrote about ev-
erything he saw in Mexico. Can you read it and see
that Malinalli had a stepfather?
    They say that when her mother had a baby boy with
the stepfather they didn't want Malinalli any more so
they gave her away. Then she was Malintzin. But can
you read and see about that?
    She was only six, Daddy. She wasn't even Malinche
yet. And it is still lots of years till she helped
Cortés.
    I like my lessons. I wish they were all day but
they are only in the morning.
    Then Primo and I go up the hill to the caves. Mama
doesn't know.
    We take candles. Primo says when the candles go
out there is no air for us. We take food. I am always
hungry. I like to sit by the Tepalo waterfall and eat
bread and cheese.
    At the bakery they let me help make birote bread
in the evening. My pay is bread for my family, but
I keep some for me because Mr. I Need A New Pair of
Shoes To Match My New Suit keeps the lock on the
kitchen.
    You didn't keep a lock on the kitchen. Pilar
didn't. Mama didn't. This is the new way. So between
meals when we get hungry I buy ham or goat cheese
with the money I get for taking care of the horses.
And also I share with anyone else that is hungry.
    I am sad about the baby. Your

                    Choli

27

Stop!

Cada quien es dueño de su miedo.
Everyone is master of his own fear.

—Mexican saying

Mama's husband is beating at the inside of the chimney with his pipe, knocking out the tobacco. He is angry or he would be using the palm of his hand to tamp out the cinders. Through the adobe walls I hear it. Again. Louder. The pipe on the bricks on the inside of the fireplace. I sit up in the dark, light a candle, check for scorpions in my shoes and slip them on. Tap. Tap. Tap. Faster. Harder. Louder. But it is not the tapping that has wakened me. It is the voices. I can hear that they have risen, hers higher and higher, his louder and louder. They have risen up against each other so that both voices clash in the middle, spilling up loud above the buzz of night, so that even three rooms away they wake me.

I wait for more tapping. I will know he is still by the fireplace if he taps again. She will be in the armchair facing him. Now it is murmurs. His. On and on. Droning. Then hers, high, sharp, bold and insistent. He answering, commanding in an animal voice that rushes me to my door.

I spin the iron latch. I run. Something in the growl. Something in his loudness pushes me. I race across the brick porch, over the cobbles of the entrance, across more bricks to the open door of the living room. The flames rise high in the fireplace. The back of her red head is towards me. The light of the fire flares up in her hair. His eyes are wide, his eyebrows high in anger, his black mustache puffed out over his teeth like the hood of a cobra. He does not see me. She looks up at him, her daring self sitting up straight in the chair, full of challenge, full of certainty. She says one more word. He whirls to the fireplace, grabs a brass poker and raises it fast with both hands up over his head. She raises her arms, white in the firelight, a square of white skin framing the red blaze of her head.

I scream "STOP IT!" The two words pump out into the room as if someone behind me had shoved them right through my sternum.

He glares at me, throws the poker across the tile floor and shoves past me. He stomps down the cobble corridor. I can hear the iron key turn in the front door. It doesn't turn again. He has not taken the key. He has not locked the door. I am relieved that he's gone and I wish he would never come back.

Mama is crying. "It's all right," she says.

She always says "It's all right" when the worst is happening. I think she said it the day Negrita the Doberman stole chickens from the neighbor who is mad at Mama anyway because before we came she had the only little business for men and women in the village. We scolded the dog, but I don't think she remembered what she had done. She stole some more chickens and Mr.-I-Know-What-To-Do caught one of the dead chickens and tied it tight around her neck.

"That'll teach her," he said. He yanked her by the rope and tied her up to the brick pillar of the well. He brushed feathers from his hands and went for a walk. We didn't say anything, but we waited for him to come back to see what he would do when he saw shiny, beautiful Negrita asleep against the well. A few red feathers were still around her snout but the chicken was gone.

23 de diciembre
Dear Daddy,

This morning Mami rushed around. She was going to
Guadalajara. I wanted to talk to her for a minute but
she said she didn't have any minutes. I am scared when
she is like that. She says Right now about everything: I can't talk to you Right Now. I have to finish
this letter Right Now. I have to leave Right Now.

First I am writing to you. Then I think I'll take Rojo
for a ride through the acacia trees of the potrero,
past the camposanto with the baby graves and the rich
people's chapels.

I'm going to eat at someone's house so I don't have to
eat with Mr. I'm-Also-a-Painter. I don't like him. Do
you?

I came home before dark but Mami is not back. I don't
like the wait. I have to be in my room. I can't be in
the living room because He's there. Then he comes to
my room and knocks too hard and tells me it is time
for me to make dinner. There was only rice and eggs
so I fried them together with that good rough salt.

But the doctor said you can't have too much. See? I
didn't forget. I always take salt from the very bottom of the glass jar. Pilar told me that is where the
leche is, the salt-milk with the minerals.

Finally Primo and Amado came home. Amado loves Mami's
husband. Is Amado going to forget you, Daddy? That
man doesn't love Primo. And he doesn't like me either.
When Mami came home we ran to the car. On top of it
was a long, green fir tree. Mami was so happy and we
touched the tree and pushed our faces into the per-
fumed needles. Mami said "It came all the way to Mexico from Oregon!" I don't know why they were fighting so
terrible last night. Maybe about the money. Her husband hates Christmas, but he has a present for Amado
and it's a big secret.

love, Choli

28

Scorpion Club

Scor·pi·on n. A nocturnal arachnid of warm dry regions that has a long body with pincers in front and a thin segmented upturned tail tipped with a venomous sting.

Mama and her husband have made up again. He's all melty. He's even having good manners these days. She probably told him how much I want to write, that I am making stories in my diary. He has a writing studio two blocks away, in a little house that used to be a nightclub called The Scorpion Club. So, he has it all figured out how to make Mama happy again and not mad at him. She shouldn't be angry or happy. She should be scared of him. But she's not thinking about that.

"You can use it every afternoon, well, when I'm not using it," he says through the pipe stem in his teeth. "You can use my typewriter and my yellow onionskin paper, on certain days, when I'm not there, like today."

Mama sees that she found another father for me and smiles.

I can't look at him, but I do know that to make a real story you have to type so I want to go. I want everything he said. I want it more than the piano lessons I wanted in Mexico City. So I nod.

I go to my room and get the diary I bought at "La Violeta" with the money Daddy sent me for my birthday Nº 10. The cover is cardboard with black and white paper glued onto it. The spine is a strip of red ribbon. The pages are printed so faintly you can hardly see the lavender lines. I know it is a lie of time and wanting, but it feels as if I have waited for this writing studio for my whole life.

On the lines of the diary I have started something, something I want to finish.

"My skin is white, but my soul is brown, thought Rosario, then she whispered it out loud into the night, her hands holding on to the bars they had put on her window."

I don't have a whole idea. Maybe it's a poem, maybe a thought, or maybe really a story. The ink is splotched because I wrote with liquid ink and the Esterbrook pen Daddy gave me. Even though I want to write with brown ink, or even purple, I always write with Sheaffer's blue-black ink just like my father Leo Paz. No matter what I do, it is the beginning of being a reporter, like Daddy, a writer, a teller of secrets. "The air stirred itself for a night ride." There's a lot in the diary about the dark. "Dark takes little children and holds them when they don't want him to." Words are blurred and crossed out even though Gustav said that first you can write and afterwards you can think about it.

After lunch I take the iron key he gave me and walk to The Scorpion Club. When it was a club there was music and dancing and drinks. The painter who owned it was thrown out of the country. Thirty-threed, Mama said, which meant he had done something against the constitution of the country. You could 33 anyone if you knew someone to do it for you. They say it wasn't because he was black. No one minded that. He was safer here than in the United States. It wasn't because he was married to a white woman and had a beautiful caramel candy baby, because no one minded that either. But her other husband was let out of prison from the island of Las Tres Marías where the big criminals go. So maybe it was him. Maybe not. With those things no one knows for sure, and Mama says if you know you keep your mouth shut, or you disappear too, with a 33 or without one.

So now the club is empty and Mama's husband rents it for himself so he can write his novel. It's a small adobe on the corner of the Camino Real and the church street. I unlock the door and smell the damp courtyard. Green moss grows on the walls. Opposite the door is the well. Coral vines grow up the two brick pillars that hold the wood beam for the pulley that lowers the bucket to the water. The wooden lid, like a giant barrel-head, has a hinge in the middle and half is tilted open. I look into the well. It smells of soaked bricks, sour wet rope, and of the galvanized bucket, half-filled, balanced on the edge. I lean further over looking for my reflection. They say your reflection bounces off the bottom, so when you see your face you can guess how deep the water is. The cool air from the wet bricks seems to pull me in and down. Though I look into our well at home every day with the same strange feelings, this well will have to stay covered. If I leave it open, everything in me that I want to say, everything I want to write, will be drawn down to the cold air, to the perfectly painted, flat reflection. I close the lid fast.

Beyond the well is the kitchen with two holes in the counter for cooking with charcoal. A tray holds a large white enameled coffee pot, a bottle of Nescafé, and two topaz jars with sugar and powdered milk.

On the counter is a *cántaro*, a red, clay egg-shaped jug like the one we carry on our shoulders to the plaza for drinking water. A rough clay mug covers its mouth. For washing your hands or bathing there's a metal stand with a white enameled pitcher and ewer on it. The pitcher is covered with a cross-stitched cloth.

I lock the door to the street. My mother and her husband are taking a nap down the street at our house. This is my world for the afternoon.

I find matches in a cabinet covered with a screen and locked with a piece of wood that turns on a nail. There is no food behind the screen. Only matchboxes are kept safe there from mice. The

Clásicos matchbox is like the ones I hide in an old purse in my room. On the cover is the Venus de Milo. Her hair is drawn back. She looks serene even though her robe has fallen below her belly button, and both her arms are broken off so she has no hands.

On a shelf I find some pieces of *ocote,* the resin wood for starting fires. I pile a few pieces of charcoal over the *ocote* and light it. I fill the coffee pot with good water and set it over the coals.

In the living room rough mesquite beams hold up the cane roof. On top of the cane are the red tiles still made on men's thighs, forming a half curve smaller on the side of the man's knee and larger on the side of his upper thigh. On the new tiles we put on our house you can see the finger marks as they shaped and pulled the clay on their legs.

The house got its name from the dozens of scorpions that had dropped from the cane onto beds, onto sleepers and drinkers and now maybe even onto writers. I hope a scorpion is not above me waiting to drop down into my blouse to grab my skin in its lobster claws and sink its stinger into me the way one did to my mother. It walked right up her leg and stung her three times. They say one cure is to drink half a glass of tequila. Mama doesn't drink but the pain was so terrible we were all glad when she drank it down, turned red and passed out.

The top half of the thick wooden window is open and the sun shines in. I can see through into a small bedroom with a simple rope bed and a thin cotton mattress. A beautiful sarape from Jocotepec lies on it, with the special flowers and designs from that town. They use the colors of real sheep, browns and grays and white, and no dyes.

Under the window of the living room is a narrow table. On it is an old black Corona typewriter with silver surrounding each key, and a bright chrome handle for the carriage return. Next to it is an open box full of a ream of pale yellow paper just like he promised.

I go back to the kitchen and pick a huge flowered mug painted in Tlaquepaque. It is covered with birds and flowers. Making a cup of coffee is special. It means I am not just a girl. It means I am a writer. You have to have coffee when you write your book. I also want the cigarettes I keep hidden in my room. The cigarettes are called Belmont. They come in a bright red wrapper printed with a gold jockey on a gold horse. Next time I'll bring my cigarettes flattened into my jean pockets, hidden by my shirt.

I spoon Nescafé, sugar and powdered milk into the mug and stir them together with water from the boiling pot. The church bells near the house start ringing. I expect them to ring for four o'clock. But they don't. A single bell with a different, lower tone rings. It sounds as if it's broken. It's not a true note. It tolls with a long sad silence between each stroke. Someone has paid the bell man to ring for a long time. The coffin will be coming out of the huge church door. I know the black shapes around it and men with sombreros held with both hands in front of them. I stand motionless in the kitchen trying to feel who died. The coffin will be tilting down the brick steps now, carried across the courtyard and through the iron gates. I can't tell. Maybe it's La Güera Ester who had a grocery store. I saw her from the street. She was propped up, large and white, overflowing the chair they had rolled near the window to give her air. Bad smells came from her room. That day I crossed the street away from her window.

It feels as if the bell will ring two kilometers all the way to the graveyard. But it stops. Probably there are other sounds, but I only hear the hard silence when the bells stop.

I go back into the writing room and sit down in the straight chair. In front of me are the things I love most—paper, pencils, and the typewriter keys like on Daddy's Underwood that can make a letter, a dream, a world. When I was six my father taught me to type with two fingers like he did. My fingers loved the keys, ached for them, wanted the pain of hitting the edge of the metal on the cuticle, longed for the clack and making of words as the thin metal arms of the letters leapt over to the ribbon to leave their mark.

Now I can put ten fingers on the space bar and the keys. The left hand is ready to roll the carriage back with a finger against the cold scoop of the return. I sit staring as if my eyes could make the keys jump to the paper, as if telepathy could tap out my thoughts. The roll would scroll up, the carriage would reel back and forth like a shuttle, the weaving would emerge, the pattern would fall out on yellow sheets covering the brown glow of the table with my signals, my heart cross-stitched onto onionskin.

I put two sheets in the way my father taught me to do to protect the rubber roller, although it already bears the imprint of a million stamps of the letter shafts. I start.

"Rosario...."

When I write her name it's as if she's named herself. She rejected Rosa, Rosaura, Rosalía and Rocío. She wants to be Rosario, with bead after bead of prayer in her name. Her nickname is Chayo which is like Choli, so we are like sisters. She'll move about her life as if nothing is happening. There will be signs of contradiction, of longing for what is withheld, and for what was taken away. Rosario will show no grief or pain. She will not speak of things she doesn't understand. Nothing will be what it seems. She'll show herself doing, taking care of horses, coming home in time for meals. She'll talk to the step-man's face that dislikes her, while with his same mouth he speaks words that fool her mother. Rosario will speak in full sentences because that's what her real father likes. I start the story, here in the man's writing house, in the studio he speaks of so much, but in which he spends so little time.

When I am done with the first chapter, I sit for a few minutes holding the pages. One sheet alone is floppy, but propped up in my hands they are something alive, real, almost able to stand alone. I tap their new self against the table, and cover the pages with a plain piece of paper with no words on it, as if I were dressing the chapter to go out. I slip the sheets into my journal.

I go to the kitchen and wash my cup, find another starched napkin, with the folds ironed in to make sharp creases. It's embroidered with dogs running for their lives. I use it to cover the coffee pot so cockroaches won't crawl down the spout for a drink. I put everything back where I found it. I am thirsty for cool water that tastes of clay as if it had breathed in the mud used to make the pot, as if it had drunk in the life of the dark, old roots, the feet of the mango trees that shaded the single clear eye of the spring, the *ojo de agua*. I uncover the egg-shaped *cántaro* and tilt it to fill the clay mug. This drink brings me back into the Club. It brings the bricks of the kitchen floor pressing up against my feet. It prepares me for the squeak of the iron key in the lock as I say goodbye to my first day of life as a writer. It steadies me for the cobbles outside, and for the walk down the street, toward the lake, toward the afternoon mountains. An evening wind blows over the water waking me from the dream of living with words.

When I get home I go straight to my room. I don't want a cigarette any more. I don't want to read what I've written. I want to see my mother. No one else is home. She's in her study, bent over her desk, her thin arm resting on a letter. The last light of sunset comes in over the edge of the window and burns in her red hair.

"Would you like to read what I wrote?"

She looks at me with relief in her eyes.

"May I?"

"Yes."

"Should I read it now?

"No. Read it later. Then give it back."

"I'm so proud of you," she says, giving me one of her gentle hugs.

It's almost sundown. I have time before dark to go across the street and take one of the horses for a ride, look after their food and their stalls, make sure their hooves are clean and dry for the night, and to give them water and corn leaves. I take Rojo out. He's the one most in need of a run even though he resists the bit. He gets in the way of our getting ready, but once on the beach I can't hold him back. It's good to ride bareback near the water. I'm glad I don't have to be home until it's time for me to make supper. Mama's husband makes me cook because my mother works all day and sometimes he does too. But he sniffs at my choices.

On the other hand I'm not yet eleven. I collect recipes from a magazine called *Children's Activities* that a relative sends from the United States. It has recipes by 10-year olds and 12-year olds like Mucky Milky Cookie and Lazy Daze Cake. They're foreign. I try to remember how Pilar made her delicious angel hair soup of *fideos* with onions, tomatoes, and chicken broth. I remember that her secret was to break up the fine pasta and toast it with the onions and garlic till it was the color of honey before she added the tomatoes, and that she let them fry and then added hot broth. I remember that if I don't burn the skin off the tomatoes on hot coals, the soup is no good. Sometimes I make her special pie she learned from the French people she worked with before us. It's layers of fresh homemade bitter chocolate pudding, between French *Marie* cookies and topped with fresh cream. I put recipes into my diary so I don't make rice and eggs all the time. Pilar's best recipe I practiced alone and I made it when he was in New York, so I didn't have to look at his face, and he never tasted the most magical dish Pilar had ever made. I made twenty crêpes, then a thin spaghetti sauce with meat. I chopped spinach and poached it and drained it. Just before dinner I made the elegant "cake"—crêpes layered with sauce, topped with all of the spinach and the spinach topped with an inch of thick sour cream from the market, the kind of cream Mama knew was not pasteurized but which on this dish she let us eat without saying a word.

I can't make spaghetti for dinner because he's the only one allowed to do that. It takes him hours and nobody can do anything else in the tiny kitchen. We all have to pay attention to something about olive oil and special things about lettuce leaves and on and on about garlic and sourdough bread till you feel full by the time he's done and dinner is served. When you taste it, you have to say Mmm and Ahhh and practically faint and die in your chair to make him happy.

I never imagined that my mother would show her husband what I had written. I would never have shown it to him myself even though he let me use his writing house. I would have known better. She must want to convince him of something about me. I don't understand.

He laughs at it and snorts, "This is what you are writing? THIS? About this silly little girl?" He flutters the yellow sheets in my face. As the paper bird shudders in front of me, my hands burn. The burn starts at the nails where the keys struck the edges of my fingers. The ache moves up past my elbows and cuts me off at the shoulders. I no longer have hands. I stand like the Venus de Milo.

My mother looks shocked, so maybe like me she can't speak. She doesn't seem to recognize the words he uses. I recognize them. They are variations of the way he talks to me, the way he steps on me when she's not around, things like, "Who do you think you are? You're nobody!"

This time he chooses two new words I don't understand, but I record them in my memory the way you remember the weapons of the enemy. "You are an inveterate romantic," he says.

I can feel, that whatever he means by them, they are what my teacher calls ten-dollar words used to make someone feel small and ignorant. Even though I don't know what they mean, they hurt because of the arrows in his eyes.

The worst thing is that he squeals the name "Rosario," making fun of it, the name that carries inside it the long string of my world as I want to write it.

Mama is smart and daring, but sometimes she's blind. She doesn't know who he is. She wants him to be what she thinks I want.

It's how they play house.

She sleeps in his bed and lives with his loud, selfish self, but she doesn't want to believe his cruelty. She doesn't want to count the ways he loves to bully and destroy.

I will never show another story to my mother, even if I want to. I will never use his typewriter again. Not a single sheet of his paper. I don't have to worry about the scuttle along the cane or that something will fall on me from the beams.

The scorpion has already landed.

25 de septiembre and it's Primo's birthday!

Dear Daddy,

I found something that I never showed you. Last
year Gustav and his wife came to live in Ajijic and
Gustav told me to come at nine o'clock in the mornings
and he would type my life story with my words. That
was when I was nine. At the top he called it "My Life
of Nine Years."

He knew I could type. Why did he do that? Why did
he type it for me, and take time from his work each
morning till we were done? Why do some people who
even don't live with my family do that? Do you know?

Here is the first story I told him:

"Once I went on a trip to the United States to see
my grandmother, my aunt and my uncle and it was snow
and Christmas. I got a box of sea shells. They were
tiny shells for making necklaces. I got a ball and a
pencil and a pen so suddenly thought I should write
my story. Then I went home over the mountains with
woods of high trees. I heard the birds and saw squir-
rels. The night of that day we entered a hotel near
the railway station. It had a pond with a statue frog
in the middle of it that spat water. There were some
men where they give out the keys. I was only seven
then. A key got lost in the hotel. My little brother
Amado had thrown the key down the frog's mouth and
someone had to put his hand inside the frog and get
the key back. It was still there in the stomach of
the frog."

Later I will send you another story that I said to
him.

                    Love,
                        Choli

29

Blood in the Air

Sometimes there is no way to ask.

Soledad Paz

Serena, Juliana, Micaela and I are eleven years old, though we say we are almost twelve. We have small new breasts. My mother can't see them, though they bounce when I run, and the boys laugh. She doesn't take me to buy a bra. I have to ask again and again.

Then Serena and Juliana and I, we all have the blood. I get it before they do and I don't know what's happening. I don't tell my mother. If I told her I was dying, bleeding from there, I would find out if she loved me. I don't tell her that it came little by little and then more like Doña Trini when they took her to the hospital and they said the blood was black. Black and then she died. I didn't tell Mama it came like La Matraca's, the old sister of the priest, the one who sold honey, the one who never stopped talking so they called her The Racket. First she smelled. Then there was the blood. They wouldn't let anyone near her except the crones who wash the dead because they said the air carried the blood and the blood carried the canker and if you had even a little sore or a cut anywhere on your body you would get it and die. I wanted to see what the old crow women did with her, so I went down the long narrow trap of the path to her room, past her honey jars, that I never bought because

they smelled of her fingers. I walked silently past the lemon tree
that never gave fruit. Through the dusty gauze of the curtain I saw
them there in the dark room washing her, though it didn't look
to me as if she was really dead yet. Her head turned from side to
side in their hands. The old women had covered their heads with
cloths so only their eyes looked out. Candles and incense burned
thick. I heard them mutter "Santa María. Look how she's scratched
herself. Look how she's opened the wound. She didn't feel any pain
any more. It was the end."

When the wind blew the stained curtain up into my face, I ran,
and sure enough that's when my blood came. I cried at night in the
old bathroom. Finally, it seemed as if I was dying faster and faster
because more and more blood came on each day. I decided it would
be better to warn my mother so that I didn't just wake up dead one
morning. I didn't think it would be the same as when my breasts
came, when night by night, day by day I had watched the terrible
lumps grow on my chest. They had always talked about Father's
mother, Grandmama, dying of the tumor. And they talked about
Mama's mother and how they had taken off both her breasts but
all they found was clumps of black milk. They left her flat as a shirt
in the front. Finally one night, the fear got so big it dragged me up
and, even though Mama had guests, I knocked on the living room
door and told her that I had things on my chest and that they were
growing fast. Mama said how happy she was and she laughed and
hugged me and walked me back to my room. She said she was so
proud, and then she never mentioned my breasts again.

But now I had to tell her about the blood. I wanted to wait till
her guests left, but they stayed and stayed. I finally knocked on the
living room door and when she came out I told her the bad news,
Again she hugged me and laughed. In her bedroom she pulled out
a special drawer of underwear and soaps, stockings and evening
purses, and showed me tubes and gauzes she called pads and a little
elastic belt for holding them on. She gave me everything I needed
and told me to be clean. Little by little, by myself, I learned how to

use them. She never mentioned the blood again either. But I hated it that when she went back to her guests it seemed to me that she was telling them and that was why I could hear them laughing behind the door.

Micaela is already beautiful, and brown all over because her mother was from an island of people with gold skin. Her father knows everything—French, astronomy, how to use a ham radio. He was a concert violinist before he shot off the pointer finger on his left hand. He plays Mozart while he walks back and forth on their long porch, his boots clicking on the tiles, his eyes closed. We all close our eyes because how he plays is too beautiful to mix with what you see. Micaela's father wants to give her away as a wife to his friend, but only if he can watch. We don't want her to say yes.

In the end, he did give her away, but she came home. I thought she would not look like a gleaming, glowing mermaid any more, but she did, because she was not gone long enough to become part of another life.

Serena is thin and white and comes from England. Her eyes have blue rings under them on either side of her hook nose as if she never sleeps. It makes her look very sad. She is like someone in the Dickens stories Daddy reads to us, but I can't guess what she has lost or what is hurting her. I see the old woman who lives inside her. Both of us are old ones who ride the horse with Juliana, who is another old one. She has a father, but she thinks she's nobody, even though she's English. We giggle and swim, and sometimes Tacho comes with us to the lake, and suddenly things happen under the silty yellow water where you can't see his hands. He is the man who sold Rojo to Juliana's father, and also a mare I call Mambo. She had never had a colt and was too old to have babies, but she made a colt with Tacho's stallion anyway. Tacho is twenty-eight and he likes to work the horses with us, and dance with us at parties, and swim.

What does her father The Fergus see, or what does Juliana do, or does she lie, so that once in a while her father takes her rawhide quirt off her wrist and hauls her out of our sight into his hotel, and then from the walls of the bathroom covered in dark blue tiles we hear her scream and he yells and she screams and we can hear the whip on her skin. The sounds spin up and over the walls and out of the small window where steam comes when we shower because I don't have a shower at my house. We wait on the steps. When Juliana comes out, the quirt is back on her wrist. Her nose is large and red. Her face is white and obedient. She never says anything. Juliana's father walks away. I can see his pants moving up and down even from the back because he is scratching his front and you can tell he doesn't wear underwear. He always has his hand in his pocket, scratching, scratching. Then he takes peanuts from his pockets and opens them with his teeth. The Fergus has never offered anyone a peanut, and I wouldn't want one anyway, all warm from his scratchy pocket. "The" goes in front of his name because he is not like anyone else. Sometimes "the" is a good thing, but not with him. It's to pretend they respect him when they don't. I don't want to be called La Soledad, but maybe someday people will call me a name with "La" because I am neither *fu* nor *fa,* because maybe my village will like me and respect me and let me belong, and maybe it won't.

We don't ask Juliana why her father beats her. Maybe he saw the way Tacho is with us and thinks it's her fault. She never tells. We don't even know if she knows why.

On this day, Serena walks home with Micaela, and Juliana and I take Rojo and ride away along the lake. We don't want to know if anyone is waiting for us in the stone streets at home.

Daddy,

When we came home from visiting you in Mexico City my cats were gone. The woman said she loved animals and she promised to take care of the cats but they are gone. Mama's husband picked that woman to stay in our house. He picked her.

Tacho says he saw her on the way to Chapala when he was driving the bus. He saw her with a big cloth bag and he saw her stop on the bridge where it is narrow and only one car can go through. Tacho says she threw away my cats.

Daddy. I am so sad. They're gone and I don't know what to do and I hate her. She's there on the pier sunning herself all covered with coconut oil frying to get beautiful for Ernesto and he doesn't even like women is what Tacho says, and even Tacho is sometimes not very nice.

But, Daddy, can you buy me a book as old as Malinche so I can read about her?

Love

Soledad

Choli

30

Horseback

Aquellos ojos verdes, serenos como un lago....
Green eyes, calm as a lake....

—Mexican love song

My room is in the west end of the adobe. It is easy to sneak out along the corridors, through the garden and down to the back wall that divides our house from Lorena's next door. In the village they call her Doña Lorena, which is supposed to be a sign of respect, but for her it is an invisible joke. No one respects her because of the things she does when she's drunk. At night I have seen her haul in the fat musician with the big belly, dragging him in over her windowsill into her bedroom as if she were landing a whale into a boat. I think they call her Doña so she won't know they know what their husbands know, and the carpenter and the mason know. When she is over her drunk, she warns Mama never to trust any of these men because they are so bad they would do certain things to a hole in the wall or even to a bottle filled with raw liver. Mama always looks disgusted and later she reminds me that Lorena doesn't just drink Pepsi Cola even though that's how she made her money.

Lorena has a pomegranate tree and I know the corner where it shades the rock wall between my house and her house.

When I cut pomegranates to mix with avocados and grapefruit, I stay under the tree alone eating one of the fruits, the painted skin cracked, open, ripe, ready, the glossy, faceted grains fitted into the thin skin like a hive of blood-red jewels. I eat it compartment by compartment, peeling away the thin parchment separations, rolling the red beads off into my palm, one by one, trying not to burst the shine of their fragile skin until they break their juice on my tongue, sour and sweet, then bitter when I chew their seeds.

It is a secret place. It is the place I say to Tacho when he asks me to pick a place where I can meet him alone at night. The corner wall is made of whole, rough, melon-sized rocks stuck together crudely with cement. I wait for the noises to die in my house. My mother's husband shuts the chessboard with a bang. He must have lost. My brothers start snoring in the next room.

Once Mama asked Chona's daughter Chata to take care of us when she and her husband went away for the night. Now I am scared of the dark and of Chata's dead grandmother who appeared that night out of the dark cane grove by the well. Under her white lace dress she had no legs. Chata said she saw her ride over the well on a horse, but the horse didn't have any legs either. Chata ran screaming back to my room. My brothers and I held her. She was the one who was supposed to be taking care of us.

Now, waiting to walk past the same well, I think I see the old lady, floating on her legless horse over the cane brake. She is an amputated torso in a white dress, her gray hair flying wild like Doña Lorena's when she's drunk. But Tacho is coming, so I open my eyes wide to see only the bushes, the trees, the two brick pillars of the well, the machete-edged leaves of the cane, the lime tree on our side of the corner, and, in the moonlight, the delicate feathering of the pomegranate tree with its top branches falling over our wall.

I climb the wall slowly, using the bulging rocks as steps, then slip down the other side to wait for him under the tree.

For months my friends and I have done everything together, Juliana and Micaela and I, and Serena too. We are eleven years old or almost twelve. Micaela's father was going to teach me French, but Mama knows too much about what he does at night, so he only teaches Micaela and her brother.

Tonight I will be alone with Tacho. His skin glows and he trims his black mustache, narrow and perfect, to the exact line of his upper lip. His real name is Anastasio but everyone uses his nickname. Tonight I don't have to share him. He only asked me.

"All English girls have horses," Juliana said when her father bought Tacho's favorite horse Rojo for her. Rojo is a solid little red with high spirits mixed with obedience. Tacho sold him because he wanted a wilder animal, a stallion, one to tame and train, one to show off in parades under his wide hat.

Months ago Juliana begged her father to let Tacho teach all of us to ride and to train Rojo to do English tricks like jumping. We could hardly wait for our riding lessons with him.

The first day he showed up in his *charro* hat. He was dressed top to toe in gleaming, breathtaking white. His olive face was smooth and shiny. He had pulled a few dark curls onto his forehead. At the outside of his black eyes there was a sad fold of skin, just like my father's, and his mouth, shiny and wet, was barely open in a sweet smile. His teeth were small, white and perfect. He didn't have to speak. I only wanted to see his lips under the sad, glowing eyes. I wanted to see the wordless whiteness of his smile, curved up and open like the mouths of my dolls, like the mouths of the plaster saints in the church. He was more interested in Juliana and Micaela than in me, so I watched with my back eye, the eye deep in my head which sees even when I am not really looking. With that eye I looked as much as I wanted at his tongue-wet mouth, at his eyes that made me feel sorry.

We roped Rojo with Tacho, learning to make Rojo obey and turn in circles. We taught him to rear and back and to bow like a proud horse, which Rojo hated to do, but which Tacho loved. He would slap his whip against his own thigh and snap his orders to Rojo. Then, when Rojo was down, bowing and fidgeting with being cut down to size, Tacho would rest his boot on Rojo's withers and hold his arms up like the master of ceremonies at the circus. After we worked training Rojo, Tacho helped the three of us get on the horse. Hot froth gathered between Rojo's flanks, his coat was wet and slippery, his nostrils were flared and he snorted wet on our legs. Then, laughing and holding on tight, we rode him into the lake. We swam on him, just his head above the surface, the water filling his coat and making us float lightly on his body which was invisible under our wet, slippery thighs.

When Rojo got tired he plunged through the waves back up to the beach. As soon as he got to the small gray sand bank, we all flew off him before he went down on his knees and rolled in the sand. When he got up, we let the rope hang loose so he could graze in the short mossy grass at the edge of the lake. We three went back into the shallows and Tacho took off his clothes down to a tight white bathing suit to swim with us. His hands ran into us like fish. They darted into places where we had never been touched. None of us said anything. We squealed and dove and swam and ran for the beach, all of us sleek and bright with water, the colors of the sand and grass and sky mixing with lavenders and silver as we ran laughing, away from Tacho's fishes. Then we would catch Rojo, run to our pile of dry clothes and put them on right over our wet suits.

Juliana laughed on the sand. "Did you hear about María?" she asked Micaela. I pretended not to care what she was saying. "Did you hear why they wouldn't let her ride in the parade with us?"

"Why?"

"'Cause she's having a baby by Tacho. That's why."

"She is not," I said, giving away that I cared.

"Is too. He did it again. Poor Lara, remember? And now María. I heard it. That's why she didn't ride with us. He's like a dog."

"And you even like him," muttered Micaela.

"Do not." Juliana rode away down the beach on Rojo, leaving Micaela and me to walk to Serena's.

One afternoon I borrowed Rojo and rode to meet the bus coming back from the city. It left every day at dawn and returned every evening at sunset, its roof loaded with chickens, boxes, and supplies for the neighborhood stores. It came lumbering along the old road, before they paved the new road with the ground-up insides of the mountain where they used to find real gold. Tacho was on the bus. He got off when he saw me and stood looking up at me, holding Rojo's bridle. When the bus had turned a curve in the road he jumped up behind me, reaching around me for the reins, taking control. I was small and obedient in the middle of the surprise, in the middle of being special. He was choosing me for something.

"I have something to show you," he said. We rode down through the corn fields, through the acacia arches of *guamúchil* trees, past the low green tents of the *chayote* arbors down to the lake, to the high green *tule* weeds at the edge. We got off Rojo and tied him up to a mesquite fence post with high grass around it. Rojo dropped his head to nibble and Tacho led me to a place where the weeds were already pressed down, making a damp green cave of soft, long shadows. A secret place.

"Lie down," he said. "Do you like my surprise?"

"Yes."

I wanted to speak green. I wanted to say what floated away inside of me. I wanted to say the story books of damsels and princes. I wanted to say magic. I wanted to say words for all the colors that came through the sunset tules onto him all in white, words for the last light of the day and the beginning of gray, which took the words away.

I lay down. He lay next to me up on one elbow looking at my face, and I thought he could understand the words of the light because they seemed to come through his eyes. I looked at Rojo, but now he was a mythic horse from a story. He had wings and might rise up in a moment to fly to another patch of grass or into the sky. He might grow one single silver horn and nudge the clouds.

Next to me, too close, Tacho looked and looked with his soft wet smile, with my father's sad eyes. The look poured something into me which I didn't understand but which I liked.

"Let's go." Suddenly he was up, moving quickly to get me on my feet, as if something had happened. I didn't do anything. Why were we going. I was sorry to go. It was nice in the green cave. He cupped his hands and gave me a leg up onto Rojo, then he jumped on behind and stuck his hands under his buttocks. He did not hold onto me. I steered Rojo myself. Before we came to the cobbled streets of Ajijic, he slipped off. No one saw us. He tipped his hand up in the air as if to touch a wide ranchero hat, the sombrero he was not wearing, and walked away. I rode into town a princess, the winner, tall in the saddle, breathless, excited. He had chosen me to lie beside him in the green cave. We had a secret, even though I wasn't sure what it was. I wouldn't say anything to Juliana or Micaela.

I had something which was mine.

That night Juliana, Serena and Micaela came to my house. My mother and her husband were not home. We made hot drinks with a small triangle of Ibarra chocolate melted in boiling water. We could have used the whole circle but Juliana made us use only a small section, even though it was my chocolate and we were in my house. She would only use a thin stream of milk even though it was my milk. Juliana made thin wartime pancakes for us, full of water and with just one egg as if she still had no food, as if she were still in London, as if the war had followed her to Mexico and might bomb our little roofs leaving us with nothing. Micaela looked up over the brown cup of watery chocolate and said that the other day behind the church Tacho had kissed her and with his whole tongue too.

Serena's eyes opened wide. Not from surprise. She looked sad and old.

"That's nothing," said Juliana. "The other day when we were swimming he took my hand and held it right on his thing."

I couldn't run home to hide because I was already home. I couldn't run to my room because then they would know something had happened. I was second-best after all. My broken heart filled my whole body. Even my ankles ached. He had not chosen me.

The next day was my day to learn to iron with Tacho's older sister. Her name was Dolores but everyone used her nickname Lola. She ironed all his white clothes. I liked standing opposite her, learning how to start a shirt at the collar without pressing wrinkles into it, how to sprinkle and wrap and unwrap and push or turn the iron. I liked the damp air that rose from the table, smelling of him in different ways and in different places. In the front it smelled of yellow soap, in the armpit of his sweat, in the collar of orange water and smoke. The irons were piled on the charcoal, all the points facing in. I learned the clockwise order of picking them up, holding the hot handle with a folded cloth, touching my tongue with two fingers and testing the black iron bottom for sizzle. If it spat back, I cleaned the ashes from it on another cloth, burned and yellow, shiny from the wipe of the irons hot from the coals. I learned the order for knowing when the white shirts no longer gleamed with smoothness and it was time to set the iron back on the coals and get a hotter iron from the coals.

I learned to make quince jelly with Lola too, going at dawn on the bus to Ixtlahuacán de los Membrillos, the mountain orchards of quinces, where that is all they grow, quinces from hill to hill to hill, then picked and piled by the road in yellow pyramids of fruit covered with a soft white down. She showed me how to peel them and cut them, plunging them into the water like apples so they wouldn't rust in the air. We cut and plunged till the clay vat was full. Then we poured in bags of rough raw sugar, stirring with a long wood paddle like the butcher used for lard from his buckets. Stirring and stirring, we listened to the radio and gossiped about her friends, about the times when she was young. She was much older than I. But we worked along as if we were schoolmates or friends.

I never knew why she let me. I never knew why a child could stand with a woman, ironing, and boiling quinces, talking of things for hours. I think no one else listened to her. I think she was young like me but living in the body of a woman. Or I was very old and filled with lives, living in the body of a girl. I think maybe no one spoke to her because six years ago she made a baby with an important man who going to marry her, but he abandoned her, so her mother Blanca didn't have the new life she had planned on with his money. Lola's little girl went with her everywhere. Blanca never let either of them go out alone. She turned her granddaughter into a tiny chaperone. She turned Lola into a maid. This was the way her mother punished her. But what about the stories about Lola's mother? Where was her husband? And who were the fathers of her three children? No one said. She too had been left. She learned to be a nurse to feed them, but her own daughter she kept to the chores, to the house, with no companions except me, an eleven-year old girl.

Tacho came home as we boiled and stirred, fixing the long oblong molds to receive the quince paste, the *ate,* the *cajeta de membrillo*, cutting the wax paper to cover it later against bees and flies. We stood stirring and waiting for the color in the boiling pot to turn deeper than orange blossom honey and to form thin transparent ribbons at the top of the clay vat. He came home and called me into his room just when we were going to pour the jelly into the molds, so that day Lola had to do it by herself.

"Come in and close the door." He lay down on his bed and turned toward the Victrola on the night table. He wound it up awkwardly from the side. This is going to be our song."

"You kissed Micaela and...."

"This song 'Green Eyes.' See? *Aquellos ojos verdes.* Green eyes serene as a lake."

"And Juliana said you put her...."

"Oh, that's all just so they won't know I love you," he interrupted. "I want you to meet me tomorrow."

"Tomorrow?"

"Yes. But at night. Any place you want. Just for a little while. Just for a few minutes. Just so I can be with you alone."

"No." I don't know why I said No. I didn't know how to say No. I barely knew how to say Yes.

"Like maybe in the back of Doña Lorena's garden."

"No," I said, which meant Yes, but I had not forgotten about Micaela and Juliana.

Lola knocked softly on the door. "Choli. It's time to cover the *membrillo.*"

Tacho said, "Listen. This is our song. It is about your green eyes and how I want to be with your eyes. You know why? Because you stare at me as if you are looking for something. I want to know what you want. Meet me tomorrow. Listen for the church bells. At ten."

"Everyone will be awake."

"At twelve, then. After the bells. And you know what?"

"What?"

"It'll be a full moon." He leaned back on his bed and closed his eyes. His mouth was always wet. I watched him lick it again.

I went back to his sister. We covered pan after pan with waxed paper. I could hear the song in his room. I didn't know I had green eyes. He loved me after all.

Now here I am waiting. I sit against the pomegranate tree in the dark. I try to look toward Doña Lorena's to be sure there are no lights. I am afraid I will see the grandmother on her horse. I close my eyes to keep from throwing myself over the wall and running back to my room. Instead I see the afternoons—Tacho fishing for us under water, darting between my legs with his hands, licking his mouth, meeting me in the rushes by the lake, jumping up on Rojo behind me.

I think about that day at sunset when I went to the hotel to groom the horses. I picked red Mambo to go for a run. We were going along the cobblestone street waiting for a sandy path to run on when Tacho galloped up behind me on his black stallion and then lost control of him.

The stallion's hooves clung to my mare, thudding up near my thighs and down again, flashing in the air, pawing for a hold and entry, over and over. I ducked low and looked back while Tacho, laughing, all in white, stayed on him, the stallion rearing and rising, his long black rubber penis landing on this side and that, and my Mambo tucking and bucking. I held on to the pummel, to the rope, to the reins. I hugged her sides with my knees and held my head down close to her withers. Her head flung and tossed as if in fight, then surrender, then in fear as the stallion rose up on her again from behind, his head biting at wind near my face, his shoes gouging her sides as he slipped, drawing blood. I had not noticed that she was in heat, and now we were riding the storm of her scent. The stallion's iron heels, climbing the air, nearly struck my back. He could tear me, break me, pull me off of her with his teeth. I could see Tacho on top of him, in the fling and twirl as Mambo both evaded and came to him. Tacho was laughing under the black mustache, his small white teeth shining. Then his face hid from me as I fell. When I woke up he was holding me. He was sitting on the sidewalk with half of me on his thighs and my legs on the cobbles. He was waiting for me to wake up. He had a mocking look as if I had picked an odd time for a nap.

The stallion and Mambo, free of riders, were dancing, dancing. Suddenly she stopped and seemed to back up to him. He swam up on her and she stood her ground as his teeth bit into her mane and held her. She was damp with white strings of his foam, damp and foamy on her chest from tossing in the flames of confusion. And the long black penis slid into her as he reared up onto her, his tail and their manes black and gold in the sun. I wanted to sleep there in Tacho's lap. His arms were not too tight and not too loose. They were just right. The arms that hold you after a scare.

I can hear him coming through the garden. Where is Doña Lorena? I wonder how he can get into her house and walk right through it to the garden.

"She's asleep," he says as if he had heard me. He holds my chin and looks into my eyes, just like in the movies. Then he kisses me lightly on the mouth. No one has ever kissed me on the mouth.

"Lie down here under the tree."

So I lie down on the bed of leaves and he stretches out right beside me touching my body with parts of his body all the way down. He touches my lips with one finger and then my eyelids which makes me close my eyes for a moment before I blink them open again quickly. He lays one hand lightly, like a cup, warm and damp, on my poached egg breast. He starts to unbutton my shirt, the shirt with man|woman, man|woman, man|woman embroidered in stiff little figures down one side and up the other. I tremble and I'm afraid but I don't know why.

"Why are you shaking?"

"I don't know."

"Are you afraid?"

"I am trying not to shake but I can't stop."

"I'll show you how."

I shake more.

He says, "Are you afraid we'll have a baby?"

It seems stupid to say yes, because how does that happen anyway? Why is he asking? And what about Lara and María?

I say, "Yes."

Then, he kisses me the way Micaela said, with his tongue, and I pull my head back tasting orange blossoms.

"Stand up," he says.

He holds me tight and leans me against the rock wall. He presses into me so hard I want to scream with the pain of the rock pushing into my spine. I try to tell him how much it hurts, but he is kissing me again, one hand holding my throat. My head is against a rock. He kisses me harder and the pain of the rocks pushing into my head, my neck and into my back scares me more. I think he will snap my bones. I turn my head away hard, rolling it on the rock that already seems to be halfway inside my head.

"It hurts," I say. Suddenly the tears come and I can't see or talk.

"Let me do what I'm doing," he said. "Don't make me stop. There are things I have to do or it will hurt me down here. Look. Feel." He put my hand where Juliana said. "Here. It will hurt me so much for a long time if you don't let me do everything. Do you want to hurt me. Let me do everything and then I won't hurt any more."

He pushes his tongue into my mouth and with his hands he starts to undo my jeans and to unbutton more of my shirt. He uses his head and his hips to keep me against the rocks.

I start crying so hard it shakes both of us. He lets go. He touches my cheek. I cry harder, without any noise, shaking. He wipes my tears with his handkerchief.

"Come," he says. "Lie down here for a moment. Lie down."

"I want to go home."

"Then why do you look at me with those eyes. You want me. But I don't want to hurt you. I want to love you."

"I want to go home."

I turn to face the wall and try to find the right rock for my foot so I can climb up. He comes close to me like a little boy, his head bent to the ground, his hands clasped in a stirrup to give me a leg up just like he does when I mount Rojo. I swing my leg over the top of the wall, sit astride it, and hold on to the crest of back-breaking stones. I stare down at him, legs, his stomach, his shoulders piled together like white rocks in the moonlight. He holds my foot. He smiles. He pouts with his mouth to make a kiss. It looks like a dark, wet, wrinkled belly button.

I slide down my side of the wall and tiptoe to the old bathroom by the well. I slip down into a corner in the dark. I want to throw up. I shake, sobbing without a sound so Mama won't wake up and find me. I cry until I can no longer open my eyes. I stand up to the old mirror with its speckled mercury running behind the glass. Moonlight comes through the skylight. I try to look at myself. I don't know the girl who looks at me with a swollen face and red slits of eyes. I don't recognize her body that trembles and shakes like a puppet. She is scared of something I don't know. She is the one who knows I wanted something with him. She is the one who knows that her body wanted something which is different from what I know in my mind. He's wrong, or I am wrong. I have done something or nothing. The body knows for sure, but it has no words. It knows to shake, to shudder out the sharp pieces of desire and fear. Harsh breathing knows where it comes from but has no way to tell. Animal eyes stare back at the eye in the back of my mind. And that eye looks without love at the strange face in the glass.

                              Calle Morelos
                              Ajijic

Dear Daddy,
   The mare kicked her baby. She acts as if her colt
is a strange animal. Mambo attacked little Bamba. Now
the colt has only one eye. No one could save it. It is
turning white and blue and looks yucky.

   I am sad for her life. No one will want her. She
won't know why.
   But I can't write about that.

   I can't write about any really things. It is better
if everything is just about horses.

   I went with the horse doctor to take care of Rojo
and Mambo. They grew big tumors like blisters and the
old man who knows about horses built a fire and put in
branding irons and burned their blisters off. I didn't
think I could watch but I had to be brave because I
take care of them and if I am not brave they will be
more scared. Now I have to put black paste on them
every day. Like tar. It works so they are better now.

   Some tourists say the name of our village so
wrong. They say Ahaheek. They should say Aheeheek.
Even some who have lived here for years say it wrong.

   When are you coming to tell us some stories?

                              Your,

                              Choli

31

More Men in White

White like light
turns black, they say.
One has no colors—
the other has them all.
What if
bright white and black night
both made you blind?

Soledad Paz

There are three Englishmen in Ajijic. Mama says that the two, Fergus and Philip, who bought the hotel across the street, left England for reasons so secret or so silly that no one has been able to figure them out. I don't care because Fergus is the father of Juliana, and Philip is the father of Serena, so now I have friends who are not from my town and I have my local friends too. With the new girls we do things like exploring the caves in the hills behind us, and riding to the next town to shoe the horses. We also do things with my friends from the village, like comb our hair with linseed oil, curl it in rags on Saturday night, so that on Sunday night we can walk around the plaza and our curls will bounce, stiff and shiny. We make hollow eggs with confetti for fiesta days, and ride in parades. When other girls our age turn up from Guadalajara or the United States for vacation, Mama has taught me how to invite them, absorb them, get along with all of them. Mama made me into a hinge.

There are very few hinges like me. Micaela is one because she was born in Tahiti and she speaks English and Spanish. She is brown and beautiful and walks like a mermaid on land. They say her father is part goat because he has a red beard, narrow yellow teeth, has a violin that plays gypsy magic, and because too many women come in and out of his house. They even say the heels on his boots are really split in half so that his split hooves can fit into them. They say a lot of things about him. Some of them are true.

The third Englishman is Herbert Johnson. He doesn't have children. He wears white from top to toe. Wide, white, flowing linen. The jacket and the pants are way too big for him, but that is how he has them made in Guadalajara. He wears a white plantation hat as if he had always been master of a vast domain, but really he was an engineer in England. He invented something priceless, got lots of money and came to this lake, to this little village to live his life of growing food and flowers, and the exotic foods Mama misses because she used to buy them in Mexico City. I think he grows them just for her, not for his wife who might not even know what they are, and who picks up a whistle from her flat breasts to call him from his garden to sit down with her for tea and crumpets. Once a month we go to their house at night. He has the only stereo in town. Mama says he's tone deaf and doesn't know Beethoven from broccoli, but he loves it that Mama is desperate for this beautiful music, so he orders hundreds of records from the States. They stand alphabetically in giant shelves on his verandah. Each month he picks records from one letter of the alphabet. We sit in the dream house that Mama wants, and on the verandah that Mama loves, looking over the lake to Mount García. She is happy to come to the musicale, to listen to whatever letter he picks, Prokofief, Rachmaninoff, Schubert, and to drink the single glass of Orange Crush his wife hands each of us in the middle of the evening. We sit on a long bench covered with a hand woven sarape from Jocotepec. The bench is his coffin. He had it made because he's so tall. He doesn't want to be stuffed into the ordinary little coffins the mortuaries send. He says he's heard the stories. No need to break his bones to make him fit, he says.

At eight in the morning, when Johnson knows we are eating breakfast, when he knows he will not miss Mama, he bangs with his iron key on our street door. We all jump even though we know who it is, and Chona says *JesusMariayJosé* to throw out her fear. Mama walks down the cobbles and opens one side of the tall door.

"Eliana, my dear, I've just had success with some endive and asparagus, a few other things, lettuce, tomatoes," he says. "And there is some orange marmalade—Seville orange, of course, with the pips in, you know. There, there. Must be off."

That's it. He's gone. Mama comes back up the entrance with the basket which some afternoon at teatime she will return. And we finish breakfast.

At ten in the morning the Welshman Creighton comes to start our English lessons. Creighton is in his usual whites, top to toe. His shirt flawless, rolled up and folded neatly just a few inches above the wrist. The white cotton pants are spotless with a crease running from his waist down to his tan feet in narrow brown huaraches. His feet are small and perfect. He is so clean. He smells of soap. Soap and tobacco. Primo will learn biology and mathematics and maybe other things because they are sending him to the United States to school. It is not mentioned what will happen to me. While Creighton and Primo start, I have to go to another room and teach myself to type fast and the right way, with all the fingers, not looking at the keys, copying things like a secretary from an old black Gregg book that stands up by itself beside me. On Fridays Mama puts adhesive tape on all the keys and I take my test alone. I can't be there looking at Creighton's black wavy hair and his beautiful hazel eyes. Later in the morning, Creighton will teach me French. I won't look at him then either.

On the typewriter I mimic what the book says letter by letter, line by line, cutting out the words with the rhythmic and exasperating clack, the boring and repetitive clack clack, that drones out the ideas, the lessons, the glossy books, and even the questions that Primo asks Creighton. I clack while Creighton answers about things I am not asked to learn. Clack. But sometimes I have to hear and I stop.

"Here, let me explain the diagram. Let's look it up in the Britannica." Then the mutter of phylum, pin worm, tape worm, segments, intestine.

Clack, clack.

"The Phoenicians. Tyre... Mediterranean... dead language. Pyramids... The Inca... the Maya."

I want to ask him things. Do I have to wait till next year? Does he know if it's true that Cortés had a son in Spain and that he called him Martín, just like the baby he had with Malintzin? Creighton always says to Primo, "You explain it to me. You be the teacher."

I want to ask more questions. Can I just ask? They aren't doing Mexico history right now. That was last month. But does Creighton know that Cortés also gave Malinche away? I thought he would always need her, but he gave her away to Juan Jaramillo, and she had a baby and she baptized her María, almost just like Marina. That's what they say. But did Creighton read it?

Then it is time for French. I can join them. I sit next to Creighton on the crust of the morning that is left before he leaves and it is time for lunch.

He sits at the head of the long table and I am near him. Primo sits at the foot of the table and starts his homework. He doesn't do French.

Last night I heard Creighton and one of his girlfriends. Chairs flew across the room in the hotel across the street. It was his voice, but it was slurred, and it bobbled insults, accusations at the woman he visited. She answered him in a deep tequila-soaked voice that came up out of the room like bubbles from something that had sunk to the bottom but still held life. His volume rose up against her volume and the chairs crashed again above them. Glass shattered. The lights went out. They brought the noise out into the street. I looked out through my lace curtain. He stumbled at her and she stumbled at him. Then they pushed away and they both stumbled backwards but their chewed and gargled words pulled them into each other again.

"Oops," he said, "I'm sorry." He had stepped on her tiny foot.

"You're sweet," she said, starting to cry. They pushed and leaned into each other and went back into the hotel.

Then, who is this Creighton who is here right at ten, in spotless white, quiet, patient, even-tempered, doling out infinite knowledge sentence by sentence, never mocking, never challenging, just finding information in the material, in his memory, in the reference books, and handing it out in a thin constant line? Who is the Creighton who at the end of the session puts everything neatly away, his white oval Delicados cigarettes into his white pocket, who, after three hours, rises with everything about him intact. Even where he crossed his legs there is no wrinkle. His thick black hair lies perfectly in place above his tan face. Not a hair in his mustache and trimmed goatee is disturbed by his stroking them in thought.

I learn the French verbs from his fingers, turning away from his blinding shirt to the black conjugations he writes on soft gray newsprint. I learn the language from the neat columns growing on the page in his clear script with no flourishes, no broken leads, no erasures.

I listen to the sweetness of his French, his mouth making no contortions, his voice making no dramatization, never scaring me with wild foreign gestures. I watch the black he makes on the page and I eat every word with part of my sight while part of me watches the sheen on his fingers, the squareness of his wrist. I eat every sound with part of my ears while part of me only listens to the low rumble in his throat. I am calmed by his arrangement of things, by the gentleness of his body in the chair and the simple economical movements, breaking nothing, threatening nothing, quietly, logically, truthfully transferring his knowing to my knowing, his information to my paper, his French and his order to my mind.

But he is another man in white, and it hurts my eyes.

It is not enough that when I was eleven Tacho pressed me into the rocks while I cried, terrified of what I didn't know and of what he wanted. It is not enough that Tacho pulled me from my horse and showed me the secret bed in the flattened tules. It is not enough that Tacho laughed when his stallion rose up on my mare.

Now Beto, Tacho's younger brother, is here beneath my window, before dawn. Did Tacho tell him to try his ways? Were they going to share when they found out how to get me?

Standing on the brick ledge of my window I reach for the iron latch, the *aldaba* nailed with horseshoe nails into the thick wood of the long window. Slowly I lift the iron hook out of the iron eye and pull on the frame till I can look through the chink, and through the iron bars to slices of the musicians and to Beto standing, all in white, just like his brother, in the moonlight on the cobbled street. The night light shines on the *guitarrón* held up on the musician's stomach like a wood tub with strings. The moon gleams on the trumpet and the violins. I tip this way and that to look through the long thin opening in the window, through the black bars, to look at them all and then at him in front of the singers. He is looking up at the window, smiling.

Behind him the mariachis start a song and accompany him softly while he sings just to me, the lines I know. *"Este amor que yo siento, es como un niño."* His love's like a little boy. *"Que se siente perdido."* Only God knows how, but he's lost and alone, *"sin tu cariño,"* without my love.

This brother has something different in the mouth. He is not wet and shiny with spit. He is dry and firm and his eyes don't hang down sad at the outside corners like an animal's. They are the eyes of a man, though both of the brothers have the soft voice, and both of them swing their legs as they walk, like women, but also like men. They enjoy the slow whip of their hips and their loose pants moving in the wide space between their legs around something I haven't seen, at least not on them, although I see it everywhere else—on my brothers, on my father as he shaved, on the stallion, on the donkey touching the ground with his long black hose and then rearing up, holding the she-donkey between his stiff forelegs, nipping at her, his black, speckled hose missing the place, slipping from side to side. We were sure he couldn't get it in since he didn't seem to own it, but just when we weren't looking it disappeared into her. The same with the dog that finally got unstuck and stood there with his long pink banging against his stomach as he still humped and humped alone while the bitch lay panting, squinting into the sun, her tongue hanging out, looking as if she had forgotten why she was there.

This brother has brought me mariachis. No one in my house will wake up and come to see why there is music under my window. Even if they hear it, they will turn over and go back to sleep because they'll think the music is for someone else.

So maybe Beto thinks I am like a real woman, not a girl almost twelve. He can tell who's inside. I have seen these serenades in the movies. They bring a band of mariachis to a girlfriend, the *novia*. She has to stand nearly hidden in the casement, her eyes shining and flirting, the curtain hiding half of her body, a *rebozo* falling partly open over the thin white gown on her breasts. I want to open the window wider to see him. And them. The eyes of the musicians. He has brought me mariachis. Just like they do to women. So he knows that inside I am tall and serious. He knows that inside I love, and I want, and that I know everything and nothing. Maybe he even knows I have never been a child, that

I was born by mistake into this small being, waiting to be seen. Maybe he knows what I don't know for sure, that something comes at night into the dreams of a woman and which I hold all day in the heart of a girl.

"Even if you're not with me...." Now he is singing louder and the musicians more softly behind him.

The iron bars are cold. I hold on with both hands. Mama put the bars on after I ran each full moon to the beach to dance with my friends in the large rings that opened into larger and larger rounds till everyone arrived and we laughed, holding hands, singing songs we learned as we danced on the flowery short-moss of the beach, near the bank of gray sand, near the rising breasts of the lilac-brown lake.

"I am with you."

I am glad there are iron bars, and I am not. When the song finishes, he comes away from the group. He's calling my whole name. "Soledad."

He comes to me, toward the lip of the window where the bricks stick out. I have seen this in the movies too. He looks up and walks, his hips softly swinging. I sink down, my forehead sliding slowly along the iron bars till I am kneeling on my floor. My elbows hold me on the ledge, my hands, on either side of my face, never move from the bars. I watch him come to me out of the moonlight into my near dark, to my face, to my mouth, where his lips hold mine in a soft kiss as if my own lips closed on my mouth, with no hand, no hold, no grasp, no force, his mouth so gentle I can't breathe, and my body is kissed inside, my eyes, my hair. His hands holding the bars are not holding my hands, so I can and I cannot open my eyes because the sweetness that fills me with his kiss does not reach for me. No hands pull at me or twist my clothes. My legs kneeling are pressed against each other so the gentleness does not kill me. If the musicians are playing and singing without him I don't know. My new breasts hide in my arms, my hands are safe holding the reins of the bars, his lips are gently moving my lips, his breath is breathing my breath and I learn what is a kiss.

If his brother kissed me that other night, with his wet mouth, it's gone. How he nearly broke me against the rocks is gone. Now there is this. I am the girl in the window. I am the one whose skin is my mouth and his hands come through the bars with his eyes.

He whispers, "Go to the door and let me in."

"No."

"Let me in."

"No."

                              Dom. Con., Ajijic, Jalisco

Dear Daddy,

First I made the envelope for you. I wrote the street
that used to be our house.

Malintzin # 19   Coyoacán, Mexico, DF.

Daddy, if Malinche was so bad a woman why did they
call our street that way with her name? And also why
did Miss Galindo call her Doña Marina as if she was
a dama and important. Mama says the streets in Guadalajara are named for heroes of the revolution, not
from the time of Cortez. Maybe Mama forgot about
our street in Coyoacán. Maybe she forgot we lived in
the mango house on the street called Colón for that
Christopher Colón.

Sometimes I want to write her name "Malintzin" and
sometimes "Malinche" like the Spaniards called her.
You showed me the house he made for her. Remember?
Near our house. Near the church. It is all blood red
with big squares all over her walls. Which was her
window? Did her window have bars on it? Where did her
guards stand? Did she sit in the sun of her patio to
meet with Cortés to interpret for the big chiefs that
came? They call it Casa Malinche, but it is not like
a house. It is like a little castle or maybe a fort. I
don't know. What do you call it, Daddy?

I dream that Casa Malinche is my house. You know
about dreams. In my dream I am asking "Who stole the
saint from the niche high up on the street corner
of my Malinche house?" I look in all the rooms for
Cortés, upstairs and downstairs, but he's gone. I am
always alone in the red house. I call and call but no
one comes. I don't want to go out any more because
the niche is empty. Anyone near me could have taken
it. That is the dream.

Love from your Choli

32

Talisman

Tardo, pero no olvido.
I may be late, but I have not forgotten.

—Mexican saying

Once or twice a year, my brother Primo and I take the bus down to visit Daddy in Coyoacán. It's the same bus Daddy takes north to visit us—Tres Estrellas de Oro, the three gold stars. It's not second class with chickens stuck in the racks. It's first class, *directo*, between Guadalajara and Mexico City.

When we go there, Daddy mostly does things with Primo. I spend my days and evenings with Pilar, who keeps house for him like she did for us when we were a family. I can look at things on his desk, letters I know how to write, addresses I know to put on packages. I look near his typewriter for the real pieces of him. There's a letter to his best friend.

"My dear Harrington, Such sullen sorrow at this new phase. The aviary empty. The chirping silent. My chicks all gone."

I cover it with his copy of a letter to the Huntington Library, but my heart is all feathers, cries, as if flutters could bring us all back home, and him back to my cage to hold me in his hand.

Daddy takes Primo downtown, to the Post Office with marble walls and cell after cell of shiny brass, one for buying stamps, and one special shiny window where Daddy can push his packages of books through and get them mailed at any time of night. Beyond them are the golden banisters that scroll up the marble steps to floors we never get to see. Daddy takes Primo to the bookbinder, the printer and to certain places he says he wants Primo to see so he will never go to them on his own. It worked. Primo doesn't like nightclubs. The salve of the father is not the salve of the son.

We lost Daddy when Mama took us away and he lost part of us and part of himself. So when we visit him in the City he begins to call himself Father. With this new formality he is trying to make us a gift—from his childhood, from the man he called Father, remembered, unknown, mad, institutionalized, sick, or not.

We still call him Daddy. We never call him Father. That way we don't have to pronounce it right either.

On one of these visits to Coyoacán, Daddy suddenly notices me. I am about eleven. It's as if he woke up after his cigarette and coffee and found me. He calls me to the part of the dining-room table that he uses as a desk. He says, "Come, Soledad. Fathah wants to show you something special. It will be yours one day. It was my grandmother's and my mother's. I once gave it to your mother. Now I am keeping it for you. Here. Sit in my chair."

I sit down in the deep brown well of his wooden swivel chair with wide oak arms. He leans over me and pulls out the drawer where we used to keep the silver that my mother took north with us to the village. The drawer is full of pencils and erasers, the poisonous-smelling eradicator for cleaning the foxing in his rare books, bottles of paste and shavings, and razor blades for sharpening the yellow pencils with soft black leads. Far at the back is a small blue leather box. Father doesn't seem to want to get to it too soon.

"Have you ever seen what's in here, Soledad?"

I shake my head. No. It's so small it could hold a coin, a marble, a pebble, half a walnut.

He doesn't bring the box all the way out of the drawer. He only slides it to the front. With his cigarette-stained fingers he gently lifts the lid. From the open mouth of the black box four stones pick up the light from the window. On a band of gold a ruby flickers, an emerald, a sapphire and a diamond—lined up, brilliant—shining from all of their facets.

"It was re-set at Tiffany's," he says. "The stones have been in the family for... oh, more than a hundred years. I'm saving it for you. When you're a woman, it will be yours. Of course, it's worth a great deal of money, and you'll have to be very careful with it. That's why Fathah is keeping it for you."

He takes the box out and opens it wide so we can both look into the blue leather mouth lined with dull black velvet. Inside my skull I hear the far-off sound of running water. The jeweled ring of gold whispers stories I long for.

Daddy takes the ring out and holds it for me to see between his thumb and forefinger. Then he leans over and takes my left hand. "Would you like to wear it for a moment?"

I stand next to him like a little bride in the newspaper pictures. He slides the ring over my finger. He lets the tips of my fingers rest in his palm, my hand barely in his as if waiting for benediction. We look down at the ring together. It must be talking to him too because he doesn't move. I don't move an eyelash, not a hair. Far away the water falls on him from the last shining pieces of secrets and lies, on me for the fragments of stories and myths that weave themselves into a fabric at the back of my mind.

The stones are round and simple, cut uniformly. They are elegant and perfect. Though I have never seen jewels nor cared about them except in stories and fables like "Gigi and the Magic Ring," I love this ring. It binds me to my father. It binds me to the woman, his mother, whom I never knew. It binds me to his grandmother whom he seldom mentions but whose name I wear. It binds me to my mother who left my father and disowned the ring. My father has returned me to the lineage, to continuity and family. He has given me the promise of my patrimony to wear the ring of the women of the house of Paz. It is my talisman, a blazon, the sign of coming of age with the four stones of four women.

My mother is the emerald. My grandmother is the sapphire, and before her is the diamond—white, pure, distant, the dame, the elder, the first of the four, my dead great-grandmother. I am the ruby. The sense of it pours in with the lights, the pink, the white, blue and green shining into me. We belong together after all, though we came apart, though we live far from him, though the family has died or separated and scattered.

My father is the ring of gold glinting at me from the teeth at the back of his smile. The gold is his father, and his father's father—ore, *or*, veins, *aurum,* nuggets, the shine in the night cave of the mind, the mystery of my father's being, hidden away with dark, gleaming jewels, like the secrets I know of him, that he never tells me, but which I carry anyway, protecting them whether he reveals himself or not.

Father slowly takes the ring off my finger and sets it at an angle in the gash of velvet.

I don't want him to close the box. The ring is speaking to me in fables of the old ones. It's giving him and his people to me. It's giving me to the generations of his women, and they are saying themselves to me through their colors.

My great-grandmother the diamond lies deep in the earth shining and perfect, a distant legend of the untouchable, rewarding and reproaching, reminding and regretting, the bright dispassionate eyes never closing on my father's name, on his heritage, on everything rigid and patriarchal, bigoted and defended, on everything that he abandoned because they broke his heart with their intolerance, judgments, racism and lies.

My grandmother the sapphire is dying. The candles are lit. Relatives from miles away hover like dark messengers of death in the hallway, muttering things she can't hear, looking at her, sending in the priest, and then impatiently gathering in the dark corners of the room as if their presence will give her the last push. The priest nods sadly as if to say that she has already started her departure. More candles are lit. She opens one blue eye and looks at each person in turn. The candlelight beams back out of the bright stone she turns on them one by one. Finally, she opens both eyes, looks at the people in the open door, and says, "A watched pot doesn't boil."

My mother, the emerald, lay by my father's side, captured in a net of wild, red and green fishes that turned and swept on themselves into braids and flashes, their fins dotted by jewels and chains, all gleaming in her large green eyes, daring, charming, weeping, challenging, darting, swimming, changing. She lay there long before I was born and then for the space of my child life. Then the net emptied and the light died. He was the love of her life, but she could no longer bear to live with his nighttown desires, his will to save and redeem the fallen, obsessions that he tried and failed to tame.

I am his ruby, ripening, one last pomegranate seed, willing to do his work, to know his mind, to spell well. His ruby, wanting to drink in the wine of the words of his antiquarian trade, thirsting for the names of Durán, Sahagún, the Codex Zumárraga, the Codex Nuttall, the Library of Congress, Chiapas, Cornell, Purdue, folios, Florentine, first editions and facsimiles.

He closes the little box, pushes it back to the deepest, darkest corner and closes the drawer. He pats me on the head, which I usually hate. This time I don't care. I am new. I am his and theirs. I sit quietly in the stories of the ring that still come to me through the closed leather, through the closed wood, that come to me like the whistle talk of whales in the deep, the high cry of coyotes biting at the moon, the trolley bell ringing over the screech of brakes at the corner. I know what it was to see the cut of the jewel and to feel his family of women bound to my hands by the gift of the ring.

My father is already absorbed in a project with Primo. They are learning special knots, turning and tying large packages. They are packing piles of catalogs printed for him, that Primo and I folded. Silently I thank him. He is absorbed. He is no longer thinking of me.

It doesn't matter. I thank him from my heart.

The ring is mine. And I am his.

8 de marzo

Dear Daddy,
    I got your letter with the stamps and that you are
proud that I did not misspell too much.

    It is six months that the cats were taken away by
that woman. Her mouth smells bad but she thinks she
is so beautiful. It is six months, and today when I
went to the kitchen guess what I saw? I know you told
me not to ask questions in letters because you can't
answer. But guess what I saw?

    Cenizas! Up on the highest shelf in the closed
kitchen! She looked wild and dirty grey. I purred and
she came down slowly to hide her head right where my
elbow bends when I hug her. We purred and purred.

    Mama says cats know how to come home like Lass-
ie. And Laddie. You took me to see Laddie the son of
Lassie and I cried so hard. Remember? And you said do
you want me to take you out. and I said no I want to
see. so we stayed with me crying and Primo thought I
was stupid.

    And tonight? When I went to the kitchen because I
am supposed to make something for dinner, black Agüilote was sitting in the chair waiting for me. My cats
came home. They came home.

    Bye. I know. I'm not supposed to say bye in a
letter.

                love,

            Choli

33

Copper Coin from Coyoacán

There are some coins you can never spend.

Soledad Paz

My father is coming. He canceled and canceled but now he is coming. He likes to ride from Mexico City on the line of the Tres Estrellas de Oro, the express bus with three gold stars that makes the trip in one night. He gets off in Guadalajara in the morning and waits to transfer to our town bus, Tacho's red and white *Venado,* which comes straight into town each afternoon. The mountains are gold with dry grasses and mesquite. It is a kind of winter. Mama's husband wanted vacation without my Daddy, so now he is coming at least near Christmas, and I don't care anymore that Someone did not "allow" him to be with us on the real day.

The red and white bus comes wobbling down the main street, the Camino Real, with tied-up cardboard boxes, twig cages filled with chickens, belted suitcases, and the empty crates for the farmers who will pick them up and fill them with *chayotes* and papayas to send to market.

I am always afraid that Daddy won't be on the bus. Primo and I wait at the corner. I was going to wear my jeans and embroidered shirt, but I decide to wear the dress Daddy bought me in Mexico

City for my eleventh birthday, the blue and white checked taffeta that Mama doesn't like. I can tell she thinks it's ordinary. It's nothing she would have designed and made for me. I want to wear it for him. Primo and I stand on the cobbled street that cuts the village in half, running between the long range of mountains and the edge of the lake. We don't talk to each other. He is almost fourteen and he doesn't like to talk to me. I am almost twelve and I don't want to talk to him. We just wait. The bus stops at the corner. I can see Daddy walking through to the front. He is the only one with a dark brown hat. When he starts to get off the bus with the small, scratched leather suitcase, I look away while he starts down the steps. I don't want to watch his limp. I don't want to see how he spares the leg, holding on to the long chrome bar and easing himself along it so the leg will come down easy. I don't want to watch, but I see it.

That is the leg that tried to catch me when I was bad in Coyo-acán, before Mama took us away. That was the leg I stopped for so he would not have to hobble after me to spank me with the silver brush. It is the leg of the story we want to hear over and over, how he built a bird house on the roof of the third floor, how his hammer fell over the edge and caught in some wire so he thought that he could reach it, how he fell three stories to the courtyard. We always wanted to hear the part about the doctor taking the brick dust off his brain with a chicken feather. I didn't like the part of how they kept breaking and re-setting his leg, finally screwing a silver plate into the bone.

He has seen us. The whitewashed house behind him blinds me. He is crossing the street, everything dark about him under the felt hat, his brown suit, the black worn shoes, polished and polished, his coat and tie black and brown. His black eyes have a look to them as if he is waiting, judging and checking, and at the same time, under the black mustache, he is smiling a small sweet smile. He kisses Primo and then me. There is no real hug. An arm comes out, and then the quick dry kiss on the cheek.

"So-So-Soledad. Have you been good?"

I don't have to answer. It's always the same. It's part of the greeting. I can look down at my toes sticking out of my *huaraches* and smile because his voice will go to Primo and I don't have to answer. He has not said anything about the dress.

We go with him up the hill away from our house, away from the lake, up a few blocks to the center square where the yellow primavera tree is blooming, where the jacaranda tree drops a pool of purple blossoms on the cobbles and on the benches around it. We go with Daddy like little tour guides up to the Posada La Trinidad where he will stay. I limp with him to keep the same pace, rocking as he does, over to one side, every other step. Primo doesn't pay any attention. He walks ahead, turning, walking backwards, walking forwards, stepping down from the sidewalk and up again, talking and talking to Daddy.

Doña Trini shows us his room. Her two long braids start in a black helmet, go down either side of her head and fall straight down the back to her shoes. She is as long as her hair.

Slowly we go up the stairs, down the yellow hall and into one of the doors, all identical. We got him the best room. The one that faces out on the street. There is a sink in every room because it used to be a whorehouse. Everyone knows, but no one remembers when. When I tell someone my father is staying at the Trinidad, they laugh, but they don't tell me the stories. I imagine the women going from the bed to the sink and from the sink to the bed. I don't see them in the bed and I don't see them at the window. I only see them with a cloth at the sink, in red garters and red panties, like in the movies, bending over the soap and water and then leaning over the bed.

Daddy hangs his tie over the wardrobe door covered with bubbles of chipping varnish. He takes off his hat and sets it on top of the armoire. I go to the window and look out. The edge is smeared with dirt, painted in coat after coat. I wait while he changes. I don't want to see his white legs with the small round brown spots on them like the marks on an over-ripe mango. He says they are from the screws that hold the plate into his shin. I don't want to see the black socks with garters up to his knees where they strangle the white skin.

In Coyoacán, on Malintzin, in Mexico City, he used to let Primo and me stand in the bathroom with him to watch him shave. I was little. My head did not reach the bottom of his shirt and he wore nothing under his shirt. Before he shaved he reached into the sink with a shaving brush, then turned it round and around in the wooden soap cup. I watched his pink penis bobbing and turning under his shirt, sticking out now and then between the shirttails. Then he brushed the soap in little circles all over his face, making a white beard, over his lips, around his chin and down his neck to the chest hairs that rose up out of the collar. Daddy stuck his tongue into one cheek and looked down, pleased with us for being with him in the afternoon as he got ready for his errands in the night city. After shaving, he swished the razor in the sink, brushed his teeth and gargled loudly with the red liquid he poured into his mouth from a magical bubble of glass that looked like Aladdin's lamp. He put on striped undershorts, socks, his suit and tie, and sat down to tie his shoes, the shoes Primo and I polished. Then our time was over. He put on his hat and left for *el centro*, downtown, the parts of the city where one post office, a binder, a printer, and his other special places did not sleep.

I stand looking out of the window of the Posada Trinidad, down into the street, with my back to him, hearing him. He takes off his coat and hangs it up and then I hear him take off his pants. He has a way of dropping the waist fast upside down on the hanger so nothing falls out of the pockets, then the hanger clicks over the wood rod in the wardrobe. He is talking to Primo. I can turn around now. He is in khaki and a white shirt. He is in the clothes of outings. Mama told him in one of her letters that he could not come visit in the country with his dark city clothes. His hat on top of the wardrobe reminds me that in two days he'll be gone.

He takes three books from his suitcase and puts them on the tiny bedside table. There are three little packages at the bottom of the suitcase wrapped in brown paper. He looks around at us mischievously and we know they are our Christmas. I don't care. He's the present. The day on the calendar isn't, especially if Mr. Puff Pipe thinks he controls when Daddy can come and when he can't. Daddy takes out his bright green pack of Bohemios and lights a cigarette. He has to smoke and he has stories he is going to write. We go back down the hall, down the yellow stairs and walk home.

In the living room near the tall brick pyramid of the fireplace is Mama's tree. It is not like Mexico City. It is a tree loaded with tinsel and glass balls. No doves with branch clips on their feet. No real candles. I am glad. We all eat supper with Mama and her new husband. I don't listen. Everyone is polite. My father is kind. My mother is neutral so she doesn't upset the husband who eats fast and then leans far back in his chair and makes a big production of rolling out his tobacco pouch, filling and pressing the tobacco into his pipe, his eyes always on what he is doing with an odd quick glance at the rest of us as if to catch us at leaving him out, or at knowing something he can never know. There is nothing special to listen to. Everyone is too careful. We all know he's spying for what we have with Daddy, for what Daddy, who some call "civilized," who is intelligent and educated, had had with my mother. He's looking for the past, looking at me as if something were my fault. There is nothing to say at this table because his eyes over the pipe are too sharp.

Daddy hands each of us, Primo, Amado and me, a brown wrapped package—presents for this not quite Christmas, not quite Three Kings Day. We watch Amado rip his first. He laughs and starts to tell each adventure from the pictures. And points to Pinocchio sitting on Geppeto's knee. Mr. Pipe is not amused. He doesn't read children's stories to Amado. He reads to him from his own books, even Plato, because, he says, there is nothing wrong with being self-educated.

Primo opens *The Oregon Trail* and shouts, "Daddy, you remembered! Wow! Look at that illustrated cover. Thank you!"

I open *Little Women*. I have one but it is from the library and has parts cut out. This one is red leather and has all the words. I leaf through the engravings of the girls. "I love it Daddy. This one I can read over and over on my bed. And I don't have to give it back to the library. When I finish it, I'll read the next one and the next one. Thank you." I lean on Daddy and give him a kiss, and it's over. Daddy gets up to leave. He says his thank yous and goodnights.

Primo and I wait. We like our presents but we don't care about this time at Mama's house. We want the night to be over so we can get up in the morning, gobble breakfast, run up to the Trinidad, knock on the door and go into his room. That's when we are really with Daddy.

Daddy likes to sleep late in the morning because he reads and writes all night. Primo and I go late to wake him. Mr. I-Have-a-New-Car has already taken Amado away for a ride. It is nearly noon. We knock. Daddy's room door is not locked. We go in. The bed is rumpled. He lies in the middle of it, reading, his black-rimmed glasses halfway down his nose so he can look up at us with that mixed look of curiosity and affection. He is smoking. On the table are the green Bohemios and a pile of gray and brown cigarette stubs.

"Well, what shall I read to you?" he says. "Want to hear *Tom Sawyer* or *Swiss Family Robinson?*" He always reads to us in English. He never reads to us in Spanish. He wants us to know Huck Finn and Oliver Twist and Crusoe. He wants us to know his best friends.

Primo wants *Kidnapped*.

I slip off my *huaraches* and get into bed beside him. Primo runs around the bed, takes off his *huaraches*, and gets in on the other side. My head is on one shoulder, and Primo's head is on the other, our heads held up stiff on the shoulder bones as if we were propped up on rocks. Daddy holds the book with both hands, reaching around us to read then getting us to hold the book in the middle of his chest while his arms rest. I don't know if he reads to me or if it is his joy to read to his son. I don't know if he knows we are together, but then he says, "You are my little axilar family."

"What's *axilar,*" says Primo.

"Well, it actually comes from Latin and refers to your armpit."

"Oh."

We are a family, lying in his arms, bound by a soft, brown book.

When he doesn't read to us, he tells us stories. Stories and stories and stories. About jumping ship from the merchant marine. How he and best friend ran through the bayous in some southern part of the United States and were caught and thrown into a chain gang and how they escaped.

Mama used to listen to him tell the stories. She knew them, but she didn't look as if she believed all of them, especially not the one about jumping ship and being put in a chain gang. There was a miraculous escape, but I forgot how it went because by the end Mama's face would really look funny.

We had three favorites. One was about the Eight-Foot-Long Woman. One was about The Book From The London Fire, and the third was about how he started his collection when he bought The Dictionary with his very own work money.

The story of the eight-foot-long woman was scary each time he told it. He was working the graveyard shift for a newspaper. It was his favorite shift. He could write his own stories before the shift, do his work, and then go home and sleep the morning away. One night he followed a police call to a very rundown neighborhood. It was a summer night with a full moon. Boys had been playing in the street with balls and bats. Late in the evening a ball went through a basement window. The police were called on account of the smell. He used to remind us that the street was on his "beat," so it would be his story. He stood on the street, and he said it was true—the smell was dreadful—a smell you couldn't quite name.

The police went down the stone steps and broke down the basement door. They tried to turn on a light, but there was no power. They shone a flashlight around the room. Nothing. There were pots on the stove and the oven was open. They all started to choke. The gas was on. Someone quickly turned it off and ran across the room to open windows, but the windows stuck and the men had to break out more glass and then run out into the street. My father covered his mouth with his handkerchief and looked carefully around. In the corner he saw her. She was hanging from a water pipe with a rope around her neck. She had been there so long she had stretched out to eight feet long. Her neck, pulled thin by her weight, was about to snap like a thread.

He ran out for air and then came back for pictures. They ran his story the next day about the woman found strangely preserved, The Eight-Foot-Long Woman.

Daddy reads bits of *Kidnapped* but he is not paying attention. He keeps losing his place. This is a day for his stories. My favorite is the one about the book from The Great Fire of London.

"Daddy, tell about the greasy book," I say.

"Oh, my dear. That story makes me so sad."

"I know, but it was the best book you ever found. You said it was the book of a lifetime."

"I did, and it was."

"Tell," says Primo. "Tell it again."

"Well, I was visiting my sister, your Aunt Soledad, in the States. I was on a long book trip and I was so tired. I had been away from you for a long time and I wanted to go home to Coyoacán."

"Is that the trip when you were sick with your thick blood?" I ask.

"No. I was just tired from going from city to city. I had just been to Chicago to evaluate a man's private collection. He said he might let me buy some volumes from him, but in the end he mostly used me to satisfy himself that he had a prize collection."

"That's not fair," says Primo.

"I know. I know. But as a consolation he sent me to a friend of his in New York who was having money troubles but who had some good books. So something came of it. When I got to New York I found the man. He was very nervous. He was perspiring and kept wiping his forehead and making his handkerchief into a ball and stuffing it into his coat pocket. He showed me this and that. It turned out that I could use one or two of his books for orders I wanted to fill back in Mexico. We made up a little package, but as I was about to write him a check, he said that he had something quite special. Well, you know what that reminded me of. Remember the man who specialized in antiquities and wanted to sell me the skull of Don Benito Juárez?"

"Yeah, he tried to trick you," I say.

"Don't say 'yeah,' Choli. Say 'yes'. Anyway, you remember that I told him I was not interested, so he pulled out a much smaller skull insisting that THIS skull would surely win me over. I said 'What's that?' and he said 'It's the skull of Don Benito Juárez when he was a baby.' So I thought that perhaps something like that was going to happen here with this nervous man.

"He said, 'Well, Paz, I never wanted to part with this book, but you're just the man to own it, I can see that. This is something I would pass on to my son, my grandson. This is the book of a lifetime. I swore I would never part with it.'

"I said to him, 'I am also the man to know that if you love this book so much you must not sell it.' But when I said that to him, it gave him a fresh bath of perspiration, so I said no more.

"He said, 'Wait here.'

"He came back with a parcel. It was surely just one book and no bigger than a cheap paperback. I asked him what it was.

"He said, 'Well, Paz, it is the rarest book in Kingdom Come.'

"I started to perspire too at the thought of an inconceivable treasure coming into my possession.

"He asked me, 'Do you remember the Great Fire of London of 1666 which ended the plague and destroyed the City?'

"I told him, 'Indeed I do. I also remember what Samuel Johnson said. The stones in St. Paul's Cathedral burst, and the Cathedral's leaded windows all melted into rivers of lead that ran in the streets. The city was like a volcano.'

"He paused for a second as if remembering the fire. 'Well, Paz....' He always called me Paz. He never once called me Leo, but you know? He wrote a book about us treasure hunters, and he said I knew more about Mexicana, Latinamericana, and Americana than anyone in the world. That was nice."

Those three big words were under his name on the onionskin stationery I rolled into his typewriter.

"Daddy! The book!" Primo said.

"Yes. Yes. The book. 'Paz,' he said, 'You probably remember that some rogues found certain unclaimed bodies, and people said that they made lampshades out of their skin.'

"I told him, 'I've heard that, but I've also heard that it was not true because so few people died from the fire.'

" 'Be that as it may,' he said. 'Some people did as I have indicated. One man was about to be found out and punished, so he turned the contraband of the lampshade, which was such an obvious possession, into the binding for this book which could stand unnoticed in his library.' "

Daddy looked from left to right at Primo and at me. He liked to check to see if we were still interested. Then he went on.

"The hair stood up on the back of my neck. I watched him unwrap it as if I were watching someone take the hood off a falcon or the rope off a poisonous snake ready to place it in my hands. For a moment he just let it lie in the paper. The color was like old butter. The texture appeared to be exceedingly fine. He picked it up and handed it to me. The first thing I sensed was that it was not only the color of butter, but that it had a peculiar feel of fat. Parchment was always smooth but dry. Not this book. This book lay in my palm like the fat hand of a man. Of course, it was not made from the skin of hands. It would have been made from a larger piece of skin, maybe from a back or a buttock. There were no patches, no stitches. I touched it with my other hand. It was colder than other leather books, and you know I have hundreds of those. It had that particular feel of exuding oil.

"I asked what he wanted for it, and although it was a steep sum and more than I had expected to pay for all the books I found on this trip, I could not let it go. I had to have it. He understood. I wrote him a check. He rewrapped the little book in its own paper and added it to the parcel he was making of the other books I had chosen.

"I left his house and went to rest at my sister's before going to Washington to get an order from the Library of Congress. I always slept on the third floor in a tiny guest room with two narrow beds, a bedside table between them and a lamp. I often read many hours into the night by that lamp. The night I arrived back there, the only book I wanted to look at was the special book. I knew the contents were somewhat ordinary, but the binding was a story all to itself.

"When I returned from Washington I went up to my room. The book was not on the bedside table. I threw open the bedclothes, looked under everything, opened every drawer. I moved the chest of drawers away from the wall. I hoisted the curtains up from the carpet. I even looked under the Persian carpet. When I was done I looked everywhere again. I wondered if I had at the last minute taken it with me to Washington. I emptied my briefcase and my suitcase on the bed and looked in every pocket. I could not find it. I ran down to my sister.

" 'Have you seen the book that I left by my bedside?'

"She answered rather vaguely, I thought. 'A book?'

" 'Yes. I left a book on the nightstand. A very special and valuable book.'

"She said, 'Oh, it could not have been very valuable. 'There was no printing on the front and nothing on the spine, and it was so dirty. It must have been handled by a thousand people. I picked it up and the oily filth practically stuck to my hands.'

"Now I was upset. I asked her, 'Where is it?'

" 'Don't you dare raise your voice to me, Leo.'

" 'Where is it?' My voice clearly told her that I was more upset than she had ever seen me in forty years. She actually looked afraid.

" 'Where?' I repeated.

"She backed away some distance from me and started to leave the room as if fearing for her life. 'Well, if you must know, I can't see why you would bring such a book into my house. I threw that soiled little volume down the garbage chute.'

"That meant that it had gone straight into the trash bin. I ran down to the basement to look for it, but the bin was empty. The trash had already been picked up."

This is the part when it is always hard to look at Daddy. He told the story, but at the end his loss seems just as terrible as on the day it happened.

Primo says, "Read, Daddy. Read to us."

Daddy opens *Kidnapped* again, and suddenly I can feel he is diving and taking us with him into the pages of this old adventure, flying to a world safe from the pain of his memories. I don't listen. I am trying to fit into the body and head of my aunt, into the act of taking something that was not hers and upsetting my father for a lifetime. I can't fit into her and I don't like what she did.

Through the years he read to us about pirates, explorers and mythology. He read us mysteries and epics, adventures and history. In Mexico City he used to read aloud to my mother and she read aloud to him.

Now here he is in this odd tall room reading aloud to us again. His voice is soft and low. I like his southern accent. It sounds almost English. He tries to get us to say "mother," the way he does, "mo-thah," but we can't. "Not firrrst," he says, correcting us. "Say 'fuhst.'"

When he reads to us in English, I try to follow the stories, but the words have too much magic. He rolls the dialects of Huck Finn and Tom Sawyer like the juices coming from the steamed okra we grow in our garden. The words flow like maple syrup over corn fritters, like gravy over hush puppies, like *atole* over *tamales*. And if the words stop, it's so he can turn to look at us, one at a time, with his brown-black eyes turned golden from the pleasure of stories. His eyes stop to look at us over the rims of his round black glasses, measuring us without words, seeing that we understand and that we are happy to return to those safe worlds.

I want to ask him why Cortés gave Malintzin away like a thing when he made her marry Jaramillo. Didn't he love her any more? Did he hate her? Was she useless all of a sudden? Why? I can't ask, because Daddy is on the Mississippi with Huck or on a desert island with Friday. He is in another land. When he reads he is not really in Mexico.

After the last story, we get ready to go to lunch at our house. At the door of his room Daddy reaches into his pocket and brings out a leather coin purse. He takes out two large copper *veintes* and gives one to Primo and one to me. Then we start down the hill toward our house near the lake. Lunch will be waiting, and my mother's husband, with his flicking serpent eyes, smoking his pipe and sending gray puffs of indifference out of his large wet lips. I walk close to the wall. The heat of the coin and the worry about having to go back home turns into the serpent god Quetzalcóatl, his shadow walking down the steps of his temple. I hold my *veinte* tight between my thumb and first finger and push the coin deep into the soft skin of the wall. As I walk I raise and lower my arm, making tall waves and deep dips in the whitewashed adobe. The powder flakes up on my fingers and the viper comes out of my heart and down my arm, rising and falling in its progress down the street. Behind me a small trail of powder sails down in clouds to where the wall meets the sidewalk.

Daddy suddenly notices and talks sharply to me. "Don't do that. You must never scrape other people's walls. And never scrape anything with coins. Money is hard to come by, and worth a great deal. Coins are not tools for scraping."

He is angry. But he has spoken to me.

After lunch Daddy talks to Primo about going to the beach. Even though he is here to see the three of us, Primo, Amado and me, he pays the most attention to Primo. He told Mama we are all too young, that he'll talk to us when we are older. That made her mad. Is Daddy just giving Amado to my mother? Is he just going to let my mother's husband keep hiding Amado? Daddy and Primo don't invite me to the beach. Also they don't tell me not to come, so I go along with them down the cobblestones to the lake. I want to be with Daddy before he goes back to Mexico City. They start to undress, tossing socks and shoes and shirts on the straggly line of old rocks left over from building the pier. I look down at the moss with tiny white daisy flowers. I look down at the rocks bleached white with dead hair on them from when long water plants lay green and alive under water. I am standing by the water dressed in my long socks, in the new blue and white taffeta dress, my hair falling long, my arms flat at my sides.

I look up when Daddy and Primo have their bathing suits on.

I don't remember ever seeing Daddy's whole body. I have only seen his legs with the rusty spots, the yellow nicotine-stained knuckles that he rubbed, the back of his head balding, something under his shirttails, the top of his shoulders in the bath with back hairs that grew up towards his neck like sprouts towards the light. Now here is my entire father. I don't recognize him. He has on a tight black satiny bathing suit. He is no longer skinny and blue-white, tobacco stained, with splotchy legs. Where are the streaky black hairs that stuck to the bald spot? Even his hair looks healthier. Did he get well because we left him? Is it my eyes that have changed? No. The medicine worked. They cured him. The amoebas are not killing him any more and he has gained weight. His blood is balanced. Doctor Maldonado is taking good care of him, and the food Pilar makes for him is turning him into this new firm-fleshed man, the color of parchment, smooth and yellow, with legs of muscle in a very nice shape, standing healthy and strong beside his son, and looking as if he had swallowed a secret.

It does not belong to me and he is smiling, but not because he is about to share it. He stands on one of the large white rocks. Primo is balancing from one leg to another walking on the rocks to the edge of the water.

Daddy says, "Go on home, Soledad. We're going to have man talk."

Walking back up the street, I am like a sail—a sail filled with the black wind of shame pushing me up the street, tumbling me up and away from them. My eyes are open but I don't use them. I walk heavy-footed and clumsy in the dress I wore because he bought it for me. I decided to wear it as a thank you, as a sign that I was his daughter and that I would wear the dress he picked, but now I know he does not even remember, because he didn't really pick it. I picked it, and he paid the salesgirl for it after he said Yes, he liked it very much. It was supposed to remind him that I was his favorite daughter. He always said so. The dress feels cold against my legs and it is too tight around my chest. The collar is choking me. There is nothing special about it after all.

After Daddy takes the bus back to Coyoacán, I walk straight up to his room at Posada la Trinidad. I look in the wastebasket. Sheets of his newsprint are crumpled in the bottom.

"Harrington, my friend. Eliane says I must find a fine, intelligent, amusing wife. She has been disgusted with my choices. But I think I have finally done it. Elly said I should have a book-lover for wife. I met a librarian in New York. Maybe this is it. Much to do to make ready the house. It will be a few months before she comes, or I go to New York. Elly says I could be a bookman in the US as well as here. We'll see if...."

No more. On the way home I draw and scrape a different coin through the white, the yellow, the blue whitewash on the soft adobe walls. I draw the blood out of the walls into my hand, into my world. I draw and scrape the coin through the plaster till the scold of him comes out and falls to the sidewalk, and I can do what I want and not what he says. I don't use the coin he gave me for this. I use a coin I was saving. I hide the copper coin he gave me, the large red *veinte*, in the old navy-blue silk purse Mama threw away. I hoard the copper *veinte* with my cigarettes. In my room I make a ring of tinfoil from my pack of Belmonts. Then with the sharp edge of the *veinte*, I draw ring lines into my skin and dig X's into the inside of each of my fingers where no one will see the cuts. I cut one X for each of the stones on the ring Daddy will give me some day. I try to paint the tinfoil ring with blood and when it dries I put it on to cover the cuts.

The copper coin he gave me has not done what it came to do. It has not taken me home to him, and it has not really brought him back to me. But I can never spend it.

December 5

Dear Daddy,
     We are not going to Mexico City to see you before
Christmas comes. Mama says No. I think Mr. Scabby
Hands is the one with the big NO.
     If "You Know Who" says OK can you come here for
our really Christmas?
     We got presents in El Nuevo Mundo for Amado, and
books for Primo at the Librería Internacional. At Fa-
vier I got Mama her perfume Heure Intime. Your present is I am making a story just for you.
     Mama drove to the antique store at Morelos 888.
We looked through the boxes of tin paintings to the
saints. I wanted all of them. The Santo Niño de Atocha
in his red velvet gown. One of a woman on the rail-
road tracks and a picture of her in bed with Nuestra
Señora at her feet. I don't know if she died or didn't
die. I could only read Gracias -- 1908.
     We drove to the church of red cantera stone. Yel-
low lights were hanging from the wrought iron spears
of the church courtyard. Under them were dozens of
enormous green trees. I could feel part of Mama run
to the trees, throwing herself against them, as if she
were little in her summers in Michigan, her winters
at school, her Christmas in Albany. I saw her hide
her red hair and her white face in the trees, breathing in her other life in their branches. I was quiet
walking beside her, like walking with the dead, her
mother so far away, her father buried under a syca-
more, her world of El Norte lost. Everything changed
forever like it is with you in Coyoacán and us here
at the lake.
     ¿Y éste cuánto cuesta? she asked the man. He
couldn't get his price right because of her smile and
her green eyes, and her white hand pointing like a
wand to a jade fir. We tied it on the car. The cross
to support it hung out over the trunk. Mama opened
the boughs over the hood so she could see. We drove
through the night for an hour to Ajijic.
     Mama smiled.
     You know how she smiled all the way home!
                                        Choli

34

Bullfight: Permission

Only the right words can save you.

Soledad Paz

My mother does not look up from the chessboard. "Who's going to the bullfight tomorrow?" she asks, turning her body toward me but keeping her eyes on the board. I stand beside the table. I don't answer. She looks at me. Her eyes are dark green almonds. "Soledad?"

Her husband takes a deep puff on his pipe and the smoke slips across the little game table and winds like a small gray snake through Mama's hair.

"Serena is going," I say, "and her father, the English."

"Say The Englishman, or say Philip," she corrects me.

I can see out of the corner of my eye how the saliva gathers in white crusts around the stem of his pipe. Under the stuck-out mustache, his fat lips pop out smoke like puffs of unspeakable words.

He moves a piece. She must not have expected it. She looks hard at how it changes things.

He has a disease on his hands. They are painted with gentian violet. Flakes of skin look ready to fall off, shiny and purple with the gloss of the medicine. "Tincture," he calls it, his large lips rising up off his teeth and into his mustache to make the word. He is always talking about how no one can decide what causes it. "It's the turps," he says, never saying the whole word "turpentine," like that makes him a famous painter. Sometimes he says, "It's the typewriter ribbon," because that reminds everyone that he is a writer, especially since the day one of Hemingway's wives came to our house for lunch and said, "Oh, you look just like Ernie!"

"I am writing a book," he likes to say, spit sizzling in the mouthpiece of his pipe. Sometimes he blames the scabs on the loom business, "It could be the dye in our threads." Because of that, he works less and less. He lets my mother stand by the looms designing new fabrics. He lets her buy and sell and search for new textures and colors, unless, of course, the wife of the Governor is coming. Then suddenly he is an expert about everything.

My mother moves a chess piece. They have forgotten me.

"Serena's father, Philip," I say to her. "He's going,"

"Yes, you told me that. Who's driving?"

"Juliana's father, The Fergus." Mama doesn't like it when we put 'the' in front of people's names, but it's the custom in the village for those who are different. Sometimes you say La Lola or El Pepe when they have done something special and they are very respected. But at other times, like with The Fergus, it's because there is something wrong with them—nothing you can see—nothing you can say, just something.

"Who else is going?"

"When I gave Creighton my homework this morning, he said he was going."

People call him El Maestro or El Profe, and, for him, because he's a good teacher, the "el" is respectful.

Mother looks relieved. Three of her men are going, the men she trusts, one of them our tutor for English, and the two Englishmen, Philip and Fergus, because Englishmen would naturally be protection, especially Serena's father, Philip. He stands and walks so correctly, like a leader, his rear end out, his back soldier straight.

His clothes are filled with himself, his stomach ample, his corduroy pants gold and tight. He wears tweedy sweaters, and his beard lies full and flat against his chest. He holds his head high. His mouth is always red so that sometimes I wonder if his lips, glossy and puffed, are painted or bruised, so much so that I sometimes forget that his blue eyes are pale, unblinking and sweet. Mostly I see his mouth. When I visit his daughter Serena, I watch him holding his newborn son and I stare at his solid, glossy fingers. He took a picture of me with his baby in my arms. I look like a woman old enough to be the baby's mother, even though I am only twelve. His wife is much older than he is. She makes his babies, but she looks like his mother, fat and warm, large-breasted and disheveled, with gray corkscrew hair around her shoulders. Her dress, which she calls a frock, has large milk stains from nursing. She has worn, red hands and she smiles like a cherub.

"Do you want to go?" Mama asks.

"Yes."

"But you'll be coming home after dark." Mama is beginning to find reasons to doubt.

Her husband's eyes shoot up to the ceiling and back to the board. I can see he wants my mother back. He's itching to continue the attack he's planning. He hates to lose anything, even attention. I'm not his problem. Puffing and popping the smoke around the crusted mouthpiece of his pipe he says, "Oh, let her go."

The tincture has gathered under his nails. The cracked skin opens up under the flakes, black and lavender and loose. I stand far enough away so that he won't reach for me. I see anger and jealousy boiling under his skin.

Now I don't want to go to the bullfight. I see it will be convenient for him if I go, so I'll stay. Even though I want to go, I'll stay.

My mother suddenly looks at me with interest. He tried to take the decision away from her. She wants it back. She wants to decide.

The skin on his fingers is peeling off and I know it is not from anything he touches. It is from something inside him.

He reaches for her cheek. His eyes are all soft and brown and I think they will leak like caramel out of the sockets. She lets him pat her face with the fingers that are shedding from dyes and ink and tincture and turps. She looks at the chessboard coyly and quickly moves a piece. It's a good move. He's not happy. He looks at me out of the corner of his eye as if it were my fault.

Before they were married he changed for tennis in her room and then sat at lunch just in a towel. No one had ever sat at my mother's table without all of their clothes on. When I went around the table to serve the salad, I saw the pink helmet of his mushroom coming out from between his legs and resting on the edge of the leather chair with the lace trim of the towel lying right on its neck as if it had been covered up for a little nap. I was too angry to eat because I had seen it, because he had let it out. Then one day they just came home from Guadalajara and said, "We were married today. Aren't you happy?"

No.

They never asked us, her three children, about should they get married.

She said she got my father's blessing. Where is my father? St. Louis? Veracruz? Chiapas? He never went only with me to the bullfights. Mama took me. We went with her friend the Catalán who bought good tickets in the shade. Mama saw Armillita and Manolete with Daddy. I want to see Arruza. He became a full matador in a bullfight with Armillita. And Procuna became a matador with Arruza. Now I get to see Procuna and Arruza. Has Mama forgotten EVERYTHING?

"Let's see...." Mama is back to the question of my going. "The drive to the city is two hours. You'll need money because you'll stop to eat. The corrida ends around six, you'll go to dinner, then two more hours home. I don't like you on the highway after dark. There are cows and horses on the road. What if you hit something?"

Now she's going to take it away. "Mama?"

"Who's driving?" She answers me with a question. She never listens.

"The Fergus," I say again.

Her husband turns and stares at me. I see a fire in him that scares me. Deep down, below the bright brown glaze, something is burning, a pinprick of old heat, the stem-end smoking. I look at him, wanting to see what he sees—maybe my father, or my father and my mother in love, making my birth. Or is the burn his lack, no father, his mother with the thick accent, his black memories charring me.

I lower my eyes to hide my hatred, my pity—to shut out the scorn in his face, to shut out his greed to be alone with my mother.

Mama draws me to her. Standing inside her arm, our faces are close. Now there is a charmed excitement in her face. She tilts her head to one side as if she were going to get to know me, as if she were going to engage me like one of her guests in an exciting conversation. "Well, do you want to go?"

I want to escape. I want to go to the bullfight on Sunday and never come back.

"Yes."

With one arm still around my waist she reaches down into her large straw basket and rustles among the papers and skeins of wool. She pulls out shopping lists, a measuring tape, a flashlight battery and a pair of leather driving gloves with special holes in them so your hands can breathe. I don't like to look in her basket. Everything is there. Everything she asks me to look for, everything she loses, and everything she needs, even things she hides like snippets of letters to my grandmother, and beautiful, short, bits of crossed-out poetry that end up in her old address book wrapped with rubber bands. There are Band-Aids, hairpins, loose coins, a key to the car, envelopes of sugar, powdered milk and coffee in case of emergency, torn corners of envelopes with important addresses, stamps with lint and tobacco stuck to them, shopping lists, and the business cards of lawyers.

"Oh, for God's sake! Here!" My Mama's chess partner pulls out a wad of money. He keeps a large bill on the outside to show off, and lots of small bills folded inside. He gives me two small bills. "Here. And when your birthday rolls around remember what I gave you." He shoves the money into my hand and pushes me away at the same time. The dry skin on his fingers scratches my wrist.

I know what he expects, so I look him straight in the eye. Something shrinks in me and loses its juice at this obedience. My shoulders drop. Probably that pleases him. I have to say, "Thank you," so I do. I have to smile, so I do.

I run out into the sun and through the warm cobbled streets to Serena's house. She and Juliana are going to wear skirts. I forgot to ask Mama about a skirt for me.

35

Bullfight: La Lidia

Cuando el río hace ruido
es que lleva piedras.

*When the river rumbles
it is rocks it tumbles.*

—Mexican saying

I am going to the city. I always wear jeans because of riding and taking care of horses, but early in the morning Mama calls me and says I have to wear a skirt to the bullfight. I am afraid everyone will be able to see up my legs. She's a magician with scissors and cloth. Before breakfast she helps me cut the red cotton piqué into a skirt on the ping-pong table. She measures my waist with a tape and decides on the length. After a few slashes with chalk, she cuts a full circle boldly with huge scissors. She helps me sew it and adds a white button the size of a peso. After breakfast she makes me a white wraparound blouse with a belt that ties. It makes me feel safe. I'll be in a new outfit before the car honks at the door for me. Then she gives me a wide, soft scarf she wove for her store. It is red with gold threads.

"There you are," she says. "It's winter. You'll be cold on the way home. Use it on your head, drape it on your elbows or sit on it if you're too hot during the fight. Wave it at…. Who's fighting?"

"Procuna."

"Wave it at him when you yell '*Olé*'."

I can't imagine doing any of it, so I fold it up quick and hold it flat against my purse.

"Don't let the bull see your red skirt!" Mama says.

"Mama, you told me they don't see colors. They only see the cape move!"

"I know," and she gives me one of her light, quick kisses too close to my ear. "Have a good time."

We are going to the bullfight. It will start exactly at four. It's two o'clock. Everyone is waiting by the black bubble of The Fergus's car. He's driving. I get in the back seat behind him. Philip, Serena's father, is sitting very straight in the middle next to me. Juliana is on his other side, all in blue. She and I each get a window because we get carsick. In the front seat, Serena is in the middle trying to push her grey skirt and her crinoline under her thighs. She's between The Fergus and my tutor Creighton. He's all in white. He's so tall his left arm reaches all along the back of the seat and he has to hang his right arm out the window so all three of them fit.

Creighton has the long, bright tickets printed with a painting of the red and black bull with a spray of long feathery *banderillas* hanging from his withers. The black letters say the day, the hour of the bullfight and the names of the main matadors. Luis Procuna and Carlos Arruza. The kings of the bullfighting world.

Except for actors in the movies, Creighton is the most handsome man I have ever seen, with neatly shaped birdwing black eyebrows that meet in the middle over his brown-green eyes. I can hardly listen to him in our lessons. I even forgot to tell him my idea about the sons of Hernán Cortés. Pilar gave me incense the last time I was in Coyoacán. The rider on the cover of the packet smelling of copal is San Martín Caballero, the patron saint of soldiers. So that's why both of the sons of Cortés were called Martín. That was my question I didn't ask Creighton. San Martín

Caballero—he is also the patron saint of weavers. There are so many Marías. Maybe, like Her, there are many San Martins—one for the soldiers, one for Malinche the Embroiderer, and one, with his special incense, to protect my Mama, The Weaver.

I watch everything Creighton does but without really looking. I have to stare at my pencil and notebook while I watch him, trying at the same time to hear what he is teaching my brother and also to understand what he is repeating about my homework, or what he is saying about French. His thick black hair rides back in a full wavy mane, shiny with red and blue in it like the back of a crow, and though I don't know where my fingers would go, my hands think of being in his hair. When he laughs, you can see his perfect, white teeth. With me he is very gentle. Almost indifferent. Kind. But when my brother says something wrong in class, Creighton rocks back in his chair with his perfectly manicured fingers hooked in the loops of his belt. His long leg comes up from the hip, the white cotton smooth and tight, and his brown *huarache* comes up from the knee and pretends to attack my brother right in the middle of his chest for an answer that is off the mark. I know from when we all go swimming in the lake that Creighton's legs are covered with gleaming reddish hair, and that the veins around his ankles look like tiny, blue, affectionate snakes.

I look at the back of Serena's head. Her hair is thin and pale brown. It looks dirty. She doesn't take care of herself. There's something wrong, but I don't know what. She makes me sad, as if she were dying, or was very sick, but when we play and have fun and ride she's all right. She has fun. I look at Creighton's arm along the back of the seat with his sleeve rolled up and the shiny hair forcing my eyes to stare, making me look at his square clean hand. I want to look so much that I move my eyes back to Serena's head. Philip, Serena's father, sits straight between me and Juliana. I think he is asleep. But if he is asleep why is his thigh so hot and why does it press closer and closer to me? If I had on my jeans I would not feel the heat so much on my knee, but I am wearing a skirt. I close my legs tight and lean against the door. Philip opens his large legs more and the gold corduroy melts the side of my thigh. On the curves Philip leans into me, but I sit straight. Once Creighton looks into the back seat and says "Fergus has never seen a bullfight." I think Philip pretends to wake up and they all laugh.

The corrida always starts on time. After we park we have to go through the narrow arch of the entrance and up to our seats before the trumpet blares to start the corrida.

The Fergus says, "Did we leave in good time? I don't want to miss the damn thing. Only two things start on time in Mexico, church mass and the bullfights. No, three things. Banks open on time."

I'm happy. We're on the straight stretch so Philip's leg can't come any closer. I listen as they buzz and talk about the bullfighters.

"That Arruza," says Creighton. "He doesn't fight on foot any more. Switched to horseback like they do in Portugal. But someone said he'll kill on foot."

"Must be scared, tired of those beastly horned buggers on the ground."

Creighton is the expert. "It's no safer on horseback. He's lost a lot of horses."

After an hour of rumbling along the old road to Guadalajara, the engine boils over. We roll to a stop near a pond. Egrets are standing in it as if they had walked a long way across the world and had to rest on one leg.

Creighton opens the hood and the trunk. He moves things around and finds two small cans. The Fergus stands around with his hand in his pocket scratching.

I take the cans from Creighton. "Let's go. Serena, Juliana, come on!" We run to the water, our skirts, blue and red and grey, flying up around us. The white egrets rise legless into the sky, and we fill the cans over and over until the engine is cool.

Serena's father Philip is back in the middle. I am by the window again. I roll it down. I am hot and my legs are sweaty from running and my skirt is wet from the water cans. Philip has his hands along his thighs so now the back of his hand is between his thigh and mine. I sit as still as I can and watch how tree by tree the city comes nearer. I look at Creighton's arm. I can't see Juliana. Maybe she's asleep on the other side of Philip. Even from the back, Serena looks sad.

We get to Guadalajara and press past the crowd waiting for tickets. Through the iron bars the ticket taker tears off the bottom stub and gestures down a black corridor toward SOL, the sunny side. He looks disgusted as if why are these *gringos* too cheap, too *pinchi* to buy seats in the expensive section in the shade. We go through the cool black passage and out into the blaze of the sunny side of the ring. Cheap seats, but good ones, close to the cement barrier, and close to the wooden *barrera* between the bullfighters and the ring. Juliana sits between her father and Creighton. Behind them, one step up in the cement bleachers, I sit between Serena and Philip, the patriarch in his gold corduroy, his beard shining in the sun, his hands gleaming in the light, his pale eyes warm and interested, looking straight out to the arena.

I don't know how to sit. I hold the red shawl like a parcel, square on my lap. Mama said Cross your ankles, but when I do, my knees fall apart. Last year I wore a skirt while I was riding Rojo. The priest yanked on Rojo's reins from the sidewalk and jerked poor Rojo's head, then he grabbed my arm and pulled me off my horse.

"How dare you ride bareback like that with your legs open!"

I didn't know if the spit was coming from his eyes or from his mouth.

"Females don't do that!"

I stood on the sidewalk and waited till his fat black gown disappeared up the street to his church where the next Sunday he fell out of the pulpit drunk. And Mama said that in his apartment next to the church he had the only refrigerator in town. He made ice cream so little boys would come visit him. The bishop found out and sent him to the punishment church. They call it that because its narrow windows suck in the stink of the garbage from the Libertad market in Guadalajara. Now here I am in a skirt again. It's as if I am waiting for *el padre* to come along from his garbage apartment and punish me.

The arena is like a large moon, half dark where the shade makes a slice on the yellow flesh of the sand. In the sunny part, the sand has dried to a pale cream, marked in circular tracks from the wide rake drawn by mules. After the bulls are killed, they are dragged away. All the splashes of dung and clumps of sandy blood are collected. Then there is more raking and smoothing to make it look as if nothing happened. Trumpets and bugles blast the first notes. It is exactly four o'clock. My legs are sweating. I don't want to get up at the end with a wet spot on my skirt. I pull part of the cloth out from under me and to one side. Then I pull on the other side and sit on that. Later I'll have to sit on my *rebozo*.

The mayor rides out and salutes the judges. Like tribes, the matadors and their team stream out. Procuna walks like a man on fire in his flickering, sequined sky-blue suit of lights. I thought Arruza would ride out, but he is walking. He wears a flat black flamenco hat, a short black jacket held at his throat with his famous three-part pin of silver. His white shirt comes out in lace at the cuffs. He takes his hat off. The crowd must have been waiting for this. They go mad, as if fireworks had gone off. I thought Creighton was handsome, but I was wrong. Arruza is the handsomest man in the world.

I watch as the *paseo* starts around the arena with the lowest members, the cleaners, the *monosabios* in red and white. The fat old picadors are stuffed into dull suits under the battered dishes of their hats. Their horses are as skinny as old dogs, wobbly and blindfolded. The horses' noses flare and snort with the stink of fear. Their ears flick back and forth above the blindfolds. Their tails are chopped square and short and flop from side to side at their Rocinante flanks. The picadors' nags are protected on one side by thick, gray quilted rags, torn, patched and blood-stained. On the other side, their dull skin, stretched over old bones, has no protection.

The matadors strut, tight and bright, glittering with twists of metallic braid, buttons, rivers of silver, their satiny legs so stiff and hard they bow out backwards at the knees and their stomachs stick out. Their calves are covered with pink stockings and their little feet toe sharply in, pounding down on the damp sand in black ballerina shoes. In the small of their backs there is a deep dip. At the top of their legs, along one thigh are those long bulges of their soft selves, where with a wrong turn the horn could gouge them out. Their waists are bound with wide satin belts. Procuna is in blue silk covered with silver braid. Arruza is in black with silver buttons and trims so bright they are nearly white. His wide belt, pulled as tight as a brace, has large silver coins on it.

Procuna takes off the little black hat with two round black ears on it. He turns in all directions and bows. At the back of his head the knot of hair looks like a disk of black brocade. On his right temple the sun shines for a moment on a patch of white hair.

"See the morgue mark?" Creighton asks.

Philip pretends to jump with surprise. "What's that, Creighton?"

"That's what they call it, the white patch on the right side of his head. It is his *seña particular*. Got it from a horn years ago. The hair grew in white. They say that if the bull chews him up and only his head is left, the coroner will still know it's Procuna."

Procuna holds his hat up to the crowd like a gift, like a black cup of honor from which we will sip his bravery and his fame. I drink from it. I feel like a queen. He looks our way, and Arruza does too, offering his flat, black flamenco hat like his chalice to the crowd. The crowd goes insane again as Carlos "El Ciclón" Arruza salutes them. The bullfighters look our way. I look down at them, wanting to bless them, so I wave the red folded square with gold threads, like a princess at King Arthur's court. I wish I were wearing their colors. I whisper, "I wish you well. I wish you well." They end their salute to the poor in *Sol.*

The parade is over. The pawns and principals have all lined up just like the little clay and wire replicas I play with at home, gray and white for the old picadors, red and white for the sandmen of the arena, blue and yellow for the bullfighters.

"Who goes first?" Philip wants to know. "They toss a coin?"

"There's a lottery for which bulls they'll fight," Creighton says, "but Arruza is a *rejoneador,* and the matador on horseback goes first."

A trumpet announces the release of the bull. The sign on the bull's door says "Curioso ~ 490 Kg."

Arruza looks even more noble, handsome and dignified on his pale grey horse.

"What kind of horse is that," the Fergus wants to know. "He's no English racer!"

The man in front of Creighton turns around with a grin. "Es un Lusitano. From Portugal. He use three horse. One now to see how bull horns left or right, one for *banderillas,* one to kill. Other two horse are Andaluz."

"Gracias, amigo," Creighton says.

Arruza tucks and turns, never once using his hands, all with squeezes of his thighs, the slide of his knees forward and back. He is wearing thick leather chaps. The stirrups are like boxes. His boots are thick. They look as if they are made of metal. He tips his torso to send signals through his hips, maybe even through his shoulders, maybe even from his jaw down to the intelligence and instinct of the horse that he protects from the horns.

Juliana turns around and says, "Do you like him, Soledad?"

"I love him. He's like a centaur."

Serena says, "It's scary. Riding is one thing. But against a bull, no. In Minos they just leapt over the bulls."

Juliana looks back at Serena and snaps, "That doesn't mean they didn't get killed!"

After Arruza's assistants read the bull, Arruza takes over again, managing the charges of the bull in large, elegant and difficult turns on the sand. When the bull charges, the white horse seems to leap with all four feet into the air to escape.

"Pegasus!" whispers Serena. It feels as if she is alone, calling out to her mythical world.

"I don't know how many horses he owns," drawls Creighton, "but each of them is worth a fortune."

I am glad that he and his horse are too quick to let the bull catch them. While Arruza's hands are free to do the passes, the horse rears, doubles back, stops. If the bull chases them, the horse seems to see the sharp points aimed at his sweat-flecked rump. The horse shrinks gracefully under his rider. Suddenly the hind legs get small like a rabbit's, and the horse shoots away.

From a dark gray horse, the one the man says is an Andaluz, Arruza puts in his own *banderillas*, the horse pausing for an instant, almost like a dog playing, freezing, then scooting sideways after the *rejoneador* reaches from the waist and places the *banderillas* perfectly into the bull's hump.

From the beautiful brown-black Andaluz , Arruza begins the last section.

"This is the faena," says Creighton. "Getting ready for the kill. He'll make his last moves and then have the horse taken away. Watch. He's going to drop to the sand with the red *muleta*. The horse vanishes behind the barrier.

The kill is perfect, as if Arruza had arranged every bone in the bull's feet—its feet planted for an instant together—ready for the bullfighter's stretch over the horns so that the sword might pull straight down into its heart.

The next bull is for Procuna. His name is Fly and he weighs more than a thousand pounds. The strip of wood over the door says "Mosco ~ Kg 510." Mosco blasts into the sun out of the black hole of the tunnel, his rear legs almost ahead of him, the long horns hauling his head left and right. Ribbons of mucus and saliva spin from his snout. His nostrils snort and flare as if the hot sunny air had stuck in his throat. His head rears up. His feet move with little quick struts and gallops. He is perfect, powerful, massive. For a moment he stands head high, solid as a statue, examining his strange new kingdom, ready and royal, a Brave Bull.

The assistants to Procuna swing the light capes this way and that, drawing the bull forward. He lowers his head and charges. They run backwards and disappear behind the wood guardrail. "What are they doing?" Serena asks.

Creighton says, "They have to see which horn he favors, if he hooks left or right. Their lives depend on it."

"Why are they wetting those capes and dragging them in the sand?" Serena wants to know.

"They are weighing them down. You don't want the capes to blow against your legs and bring the bull into you."

The Fergus is watching without any expression. "Why aren't the main blokes out there doing the work?"

"The main blokes are watching, getting advice, seeing if the bull is obedient or if he has a mind of his own. *"El capote manda,"* he says. "The cape is supposed to be the boss, not the bull, at least you hope so. Right now they're calculating how far they have to lower the bull's head before the kill, using the picadors and the *banderillas* to do that. They have to bring the head down before the last act when the matador goes in over the horns for the kill."

Philip asks, "What does it mean—the bull scraping his front feet like that?"

"I'm surprised. The way he came roaring out I didn't think he would end up scraping. It means the bull's indecisive, unpredictable, or a coward. Matadors hate that. When the bull delays and paws at the ground, the matador has to work closer to him. Some bulls pick a safe spot. They call it *la querencia.* Maybe backed up against the barrier. The bullfighter has to use his cape work to get him into the center, where there's room for the great passes."

"You know what?" says Serena.

"What?" I answer.

"I want a house with a big wall around me and a sign that says La Querencia."

"Me too!" I say.

"Oh, shush!" says The Fergus. "I want to know why the matador is in danger when the bull isn't even moving."

Creighton doesn't take his eyes off the bull. He watches Procuna's every move. I wish Creighton would wait for me to grow up so I can marry him.

"Look. There goes Procuna. If the bull doesn't charge, Procuna has to go into the most dangerous spot in the ring, the bull's safe place."

"What's wrong with that?" says The Fergus.

"The matador won't have room for making choices... like keeping the horns out of his gut! In the center you can move the bull around, get him where you want him, make him look good, make your passes look good. In his fear spot, in *la querencia,* the bull is actually in charge. He can stall then dart out unpredictably. If the matador is not in command he can't show his noblest work with a noble animal. He can't get a long charge from the bull and he can't fight close in with style."

Philip bends toward Creighton. "You told me the bulls respond to movement, so if the matador is still while shaking and twirling cape, the matador is safe?"

"Well, safer. They are not statues. Except the great Manolete! He perfected the art of being practically motionless. They called him the Vertical to the bull's Horizontal. Anyway, yes, you are right, they study to move as smooth as dancers. Like skaters." Creighton's eyes never leave the ring when he answers, so I can look at him as he talks. "They use the capes to advance but the bull can hardly tell that they're coming towards him. The bull watches the jerking cape. When the bullfighter is approaching *and* the cape is dancing the bull is a little confused. His eyes go from one to the other. But you don't want the bull too aware of the man.

Of course, if he's been ruined, if kids have jumped fences into the ranches where they raise the bulls and practice with them, then you're in trouble. That's a deadly bull. If a bull has wet his horn on the blood of a man, the matador will be his target, no matter how many flourishes he makes with the cape."

We are quiet. Creighton says, "They pray that the bull's horns are virgin. You can bet on it. That's what they pray for on their knees in the *capilla* right before the fight."

A great roar breaks out in the crowd as the bull charges and Procuna wraps him like a long black river around his body. The yellow and magenta cape catches on a horn and a corner of it sticks to Procuna's legs.

"*¡Al molino, Procuna!*"

"What are they saying?"

"They're warning him that the horns can catch the cape and spin the bullfighter when it blows against his legs. And he'll be gored!" Creighton says.

The bull turns and comes back as if he has forgotten something. Procuna twirls the black tonnage around his small, stiff self as if they had rehearsed and rehearsed, the cape swirling out like a dish, a wave, a flamenco dancer's skirt. He's a Brave Bull after all.

Again and again the matador draws him, turns him. Procuna is planted in one spot, his arms and the cape in a *chicuelina* pass bring the bull in right up past Procuna's heart, doubling the bull on himself and turning him around. We are close enough to hear him talking to the bull in a low voice just before the charge. "*'ora, toro... toro, 'ora.*" Each time he calls to the bull "Now... now," Procuna's buttocks tighten, the arch in his back deepens, his long bulge shows clearly down one leg. Then the bull charges. In the wrap and swim of the cape the two connect for an instant, drawn together by the lure, the line, the pull of the cloth, then they explode apart. Procuna strides slowly away, taut and arched like a bow. He makes a sign and the trumpets announce the picador. The crowd boos.

"What's wrong?" Philip asks.

Creighton mutters, "They're mad because they want to see Procuna work with a whole bull. They don't want him broken yet. He's powerful and he's dangerous. That's how the crowd likes it."

"What do you mean broken?" asks Serena.

I answer Serena. "The point on the lance of the picador weakens the withers so the bull lowers his head. The crowd doesn't like it if they weaken him too much. The matador doesn't like it either. He'll look like a coward if the bull is ruined."

The picadors trot out on their old nags blindfolded on the side of the open ring so they can't see the bull. One picador goes left along the *barrera* and one goes right. The fat dish-headed old rider spurs his horse. It hobbles closer to what he can smell is danger. There is obedience and fear in the old horse's head trembling and ready to turn away. As the picador spurs him on, leaning forward in his saddle into the high wall of the pummel, the horse seems to scrabble on the sand as if he's going forward and backward at the same time.

"That one's ready for the glue factory," says Creighton.

The riders keep the quilt side toward the bull. Suddenly the bull sees one of the horses. He charges and lowers his head under the quilt to the underbelly of the horse. The picador leans with all his weight, with all his strength on the long pole, shoving the sharp metal point into the black shoulder of the bull. The picador looks as if he has run aground, trying to pole off a large underwater rock before shipwreck. The bull lifts and gores under the quilt as if he had practiced. The horse's head tosses up and down as he tries to keep his balance. The pole bends as it passes into the shoulder, past the sheath that is supposed to keep it from going into the bones and center of the bull.

The crowd boos louder. You can tell Procuna didn't want the bull done that way. He tells the assistants to distract the bull, but it's too late. The pole has gone in too deep. The horse falls, and the stiff fat man has one leg trapped underneath. The long pole pops out of the shoulder of the bull and blood, bright against the black, pours down his side and drips onto the sand. While others cape the bull away, the ring lackeys roll the horse and pull the picador out. On foot he stomps angrily over to the barrier. The dying horse is dragged away, to be butchered and sold before the sun goes down.

Procuna waves away the next picador. He's saving part of a good bull. His Mosco looks at him now from a lowered head, but he still tosses it in rage and fear, trying to gore at the pain that surrounds him from neck to shoulders. Pink saliva swirls over his shoulders as he jerks his head. El Mosco follows the call of the cape and charges. Procuna works him. As the bull charges and doubles back, the blood in his shoulder pours up, then stills as he stands waiting. Procuna starts a new strut. He can dare some new steps. He can come closer. As the bull passes, Procuna runs his hand over the spine, over the rump. Close to the barrier, he turns his back on the bull and drags the cape in a dramatic swirl on the sand as if he were beginning to undress. At the last minute he flicks the cape and hangs it over the wood barrier. Then he signals again.

"Now what, Soledad?" asks Serena, half hiding her face.

"He's going to put in the first set of *banderillas*. Remember the pair that's in my room?"

My brother brought me a set from his first bullfight in Mexico City. They're covered with bright furls of cut paper like the paper on piñatas. At the end are sharp jagged iron arrows that hook into the flesh and hang from the shoulders of the bull, a decoration of spears, a bouquet of pain to weaken the neck muscle.

Procuna starts toward the bull. He's like a conductor, holding the *banderillas* high, plucking them up together in the air. His legs glide over the sand. His knees seem not to bend. His pigeon-toed black ballerina shoes balance out one step at a time. The bull looks from the man to the jerking sticks that peck at the air like iron beaks of frilly birds. The bull lowers his head and raises it, then lowers and charges. Procuna stands in the line of the charge. His feet seem to be stuck in place, but at the last instant his hips and his torso swing out of the way of the horns as he drives the *banderillas* into the blood-soaked shoulders. Seductively and slowly Procuna ambles back to the barrera knowing that the bull, caught in his own propulsion, can't stop or turn.

Procuna reaches for another pair of *banderillas* in a new color.

Serena says, "How many, Soledad?"

"Three pairs."

She's been watching horrified. The deep circles under her eyes are deeper and her hook nose looks white. But she also has the look I have seen when she is counting money or looking at a map in her schoolbooks when Philip helps her with her studies. She is looking for the main point here, for the center of this fight, just the way she looks, myopically and persistently, for the capital cities of small countries.

"He's still trying to bring the head down," Creighton says. "He needs to be able to sight down the sword over the bull's head into the heart so the kill is clean."

"Clean? What do you mean clean? I want to kill all of them and let the bulls go!" says Juliana.

"I mean quick," says Creighton. "Out of respect for the bull. He doesn't want to have to try over and over. Besides, the moment of the kill is the most dangerous for the man."

"Surely you mean for the bull," says The Fergus.

"You know," says Creighton, "the bull is sure to die. For the matador nothing is certain. He might get gored and die a horrible death rotting from the dung and filth punched into his gut with the horn. He could lie paralyzed in a hospital somewhere. He won't be any hero then. His girl-friend, or his mistress, she'll disappear. Maybe he'll have his mother and maiden aunts to watch over him and his gangrene. If he recovers and doesn't have part of himself amputated, he'll go to the next *lidia*, the next gore, the next afternoon of glory. Or he'll drink himself to death from fear and shame. You should see some of these guys. Their bodies look like railway lines full of long scars with hundreds of crooked stitches jabbed into them in a hurry in some bullring infirmary."

"What's the prize if they do a really good job?" says Serena.

"Hah! Good question. Flowers, ladies' scarves. Even underwear. Lots of Olé's. Permission to walk around the arena. Super job would earn him an ear. Better than that, an ear and a tail. Best, two ears and two tails—just kidding!—but, yes two ears, a tail and a walk around the ring holding them up to the crowd. But you know what? Manolete, the greatest of them all, got two ears, a tail and the two front feet."

"No!"

"Yup. Those can be the prizes. And your picture in the paper."

I remember when Manolete came to Mexico City. I stood with Mama under the gigantic statue of a bull. Everyone wanted two tickets, ten tickets, a hundred tickets. There weren't any. You had to buy them from people in the street. Mama got two for a very bad price. She couldn't get any more. It was too expensive, so she went with Daddy and I had to stay home. The next day they showed me the paper that described how elegantly he had fought. When Manolete died in Spain, all of Mexico City cried. We even cried at home for his sad long face, for his thin tender feet in dance shoes, planted for the last time in the ring of Linares, a village covered with sun.

Procuna puts in the last *banderillas*. The colors wave almost gaily from side to side, the long barbs eating into the flesh, as the bull charges and turns,. His blood is spread down both shoulders. For a moment Mosco stands stupefied with his tongue hanging out long. He swings his head from side to side as if to dislodge some enormous bloodsucker from his hide, but as he does, the *banderillas* flail, the paper flowers on them flip stiffly up and down in pink and green and blue. His haunches convulse as he makes a short bellow. A shot of urine squirts into the sand. But he is a Brave Bull.

Procuna comes into the ring with the red flannel cape, the special cape for the kill.

"This is the faena," says Creighton. "The last dance. The moment of truth. Some say it's when the man and the bull are one heart."

Juliana says, "Can't there be a time they don't kill the bull?"

"Yes, in some countries. Rare in Mexico. But it happens. When he has a supremely brave bull the *espada*, the matador, asks the judges for permission to spare him."

"What happens to him, then?"

"He is treated for his wounds and sent to a breeder to make more brave bulls."

For a few passes a wooden sword is in the red cape, the point set in to hold it out like a small red crooked sail. Then Procuna calls for the real sword. At the barrier he pours water on the red lip of the muleta and draws it through the sand. He looks up at the judges and gets the sign telling him he has permission to kill. Procuna raises one arm. He turns in a small circle and salutes the entire ring with the back of his hand. He is dedicating the bull to his public. There is a roar as if he had blown each of them a private and individual kiss.

Procuna calls the bull to him with the cloth. The red muleta seems to jump off the ground at each word until the bull lowers his head and runs into it, a straight black train with hoofs thudding on the sand. He follows the muleta sweep upwards, pulled up into the *pase de la muerte*, the horns drawing up past Procuna's neck, the bull's front feet right off the ground, a lumbering rise into the Pass of Death.

Procuna turns his back on the bull, twitching the red muleta behind him, turning around suddenly as the bull charges, drawing Mosco around in a long graceful circle, a circle so tight the bull steps and stumbles across his own front feet, falling to his knees. Creighton and I stand up and shout "*Olé*" with the wild crowd. Procuna is theirs. He is fighting the bull but he is in love with them. Thousands in the stands shout *Olé* in one voice because they know what is a brave pass. He's in love too, with the blood-red roses that fall at his feet, with the satin panties that land like butterflies on the sand. He is in love with the *Olé* that comes from one round, giant throat.

Procuna draws the bull to him with jerks on the muleta. Closer and closer, he designs a new path and prepares for the next close pass. He struts head-on into Mosco. The bull charges and swerves. His horn is buried, caught in the full scarlet weight of the muleta. The bouquet of *banderillas* is hidden for an instant under the cloth. To lift the bull up out of the pass with the red cape Procuna rises high on his toes, then he is off the ground, caught on the huge head, strung up along a horn, his back arched, his head dropped back toward the bloody hump, borne up like a trophy, twisting in the air as the bull raises his head and turns a large black circle on the sand, as if they had rehearsed and rehearsed.

The assistants rush from the barriers. Magenta and yellow capes fly and circle like enormous birds dancing and attacking. The bull's head rises and falls but Procuna is not released. Procuna folds forward over his own leg, then back again, opening up like a rag doll while his helpers sway in and play out, yelling at the bull, pushing into him, kicking him, covering his eyes with their capes, covering the other horn. Finally Mosco's head goes down. He backs up as if to unload the enemy. Procuna slides off the horn, and in one motion two groups of men swoop down on him. Others draw the bull away. The rescuers lift Procuna like a human log bleeding on their shoulders. They run from the ring carrying him high. They disappear down the dark alley to the infirmary. We all stand up and stare into the black hole.

Arruza watches from the barrier. The bull is slowly, gently worked around the arena, without flair, buying time, distracting him, tiring him. Everyone is waiting for a sign.

"Now what?"

We all want to know. I can hardly breathe.

"I don't know," Creighton says. "Maybe Arruza will finish him off. Strange, because Arruza is sort of Procuna's godfather. Procuna earned his place as a matador in a fight with Arruza. Strange if Arruza had to kill this one for 'his boy'."

"Could this be a time the bull doesn't die?" asks Juliana.

"Maybe. But there is no one to ask that he be spared. They might just bring in the oxen to lead the bull out. They'll shoot him and sell his meat outside the bullring. Men line up in droves if he's a brave bull to buy the meat, especially certain parts they think turn them into bulls!"

Suddenly there is a stutter from the trumpets. Part of the crowd looks up wondering what kind of signal this is. There is a triumphant blare. Creighton and I leap up with those who never took their eyes off the black passage to the infirmary. We roar—hundreds of people, shouting and yelling. My red *rebozo* is flying out like a flag. Procuna's leg is wrapped stiff as a cast in bandages from ankle to groin. His blue suit of lights is covered with blood. He comes limping through, supported on the shoulders of two of his men. Around his stomach is a thick waistband of gauze. Blood is already oozing through it. For a moment he stands tall and tight on his good leg. With his right hand raised to the sky, he holds up a piece of his suit. He flings it behind him and signals for the red muleta and the sword.

This is his bull.

He is alone with him.

Limping, Procuna moves to the center of the ring. The bull, head down, breathing heavily, watches. The ring is utterly silent. We can hear Procuna.

"*Eje, toro*," he says softly. "*Eje, toro*." Each time he speaks, he yanks on the red muleta. The bull charges. Procuna leans away on his good leg, whipping and twisting the cape so fast the horns are in it and the bull is turning even before he completes his charge. It looks as if the pass breaks the bull in half. Procuna does this three times, not changing his place, only turning his feet to call the bull back to him.

Then the matador stands perfectly still. He holds the muleta tight in his left hand and arranges his hold on the hidden sword. His right hand hangs high above his shoulder, like a dancer's.

"What's he doing?"

"He's lining up his bull."

"What do you mean?"

"For the perfect kill the bull's front feet will be together. Even more perfect, all four feet will land in a rectangle as the sword goes in. When you see the sword fly out in bad kills, it's because the feet were placed wrong and the sword hit a bone. In a good kill, the sword hits the aorta and that's that. Watch. He's ready."

Procuna jerks his wrist on the muleta. The bull shifts his weight. Procuna gets ready to draw the silver blade up out of the red flannel to deliver it down into his Mosco. The muleta dances rhythmically on the sand and Procuna's low growl of "*Eh, toro, ahora sí, eje, toro, toro torito,*" goes with it. El Mosco charges and Procuna pulls the sword out high. The bull goes for the cloth that swings out across the stiff and bandaged leg. Procuna stands on the tip of his good foot and sights down the sword. With his left hand he pulls the muleta across his body. As the bull comes at him, Procuna leans into the line of charge ready to swivel as he delivers. He falls into the bull, driving the point down to the hilt in the blood-red withers, the man and bull one, the whole arm seeming to follow deep into the heart. The red cloth draws up off the horns and over the dung-smeared rump, pulling the bull past Procuna. The bull turns. Procuna limps slowly toward him, the large white bandaged leg stiff as a crutch and already soaked in blood. He waves the red muleta wide left and wide right. Wide left. Wide right. The bull's head obeys. Follows it. The handle of the sword rises and falls out of his withers as if floating on an inner lake. The curved end of the sword turns and cuts inside, slowly finishing the kill with each sweep of the head. Blood comes down his tongue. Procuna limps closer, straight and slow with the red cloth weaving wide left, wide right. The bull sinks to his knees still staring at the cloth. Then for an instant he rises and stands again. Procuna stops on one leg in front of him and reaches out to rest one hand on the black curly mat between the horns. The bull falls to his knees as if the weight of one hand were too much for him. Procuna tucks the muleta under one arm. Raising his white bandaged leg out behind him, he bends down. He opens his arms and lightly holds the point of each horn. He bends further and puts his forehead on the forehead of the bull.

Procuna straightens up, steps to one side, and takes a tiny dagger, the *puntilla,* from his belt. Leaning forward, his wounded leg out stiff, he thrusts quickly at the back of the bull's head. Head and horns fall hard into the sand.

36

Bullfight: Home

They said the *curandero*
would boil an egg on my skin.
But he only opened my mouth
and made me spit out
the words.

Soledad Paz

On the way home I want to stay awake, but I lean against the window and doze off. In my dream I see, Serena's father, Philip, in gold corduroy and a blue suit of lights. His bulge is showing along one thigh. He is walking with Procuna who is wearing Philip's beard. Philip is straight and handsome with his rear end sticking out and blood on him in that place on the blue satin. There is blood on my hands from trying to carry first one man and then the other away from the bull. There is blood on my face as I turn, like the bull, wide left, wide right, from Arruza to Creighton, from Philip to Procuna.

I wake up and sit up straight because in the dark of the back seat of the car Philip's long hot hand is cupped over my breast. His fingers barely move, touching an electric place I didn't know, a small heart-stopping button in the middle of the mound. He must be pretending to be asleep but his hand is awake and I am frozen with its heat.

The car stops in front of my house.

Philip gets out. "Drive on. Take my daughter home. I'll walk back in a minute after they let Soledad in," he says. The car moves off. The door to the hall and courtyard of my house is not locked. I open it quietly. It's late. I don't want to wake anyone. Quietly Philip comes up the dark cobbled entrance with me. There is one kerosene lamp turned down to a small half-moon of flame on a far post. At the brick pillar near the top of the incline he leans into me gently, barely touching me with anything but the heat from him. He leans down to my face and puts his round lips, his full red lips softly over my mouth.

His hands cover the small swellings on my chest. On each he touches that center he found in the car. A map line runs fast and jagged to my stomach, then like a shock to that place between my legs that I press closed because I am wearing a skirt. His hand goes there too. Then his mouth is lightly on the outside of my blouse and circling my breasts. The pillar behind me is cool. I think it will go hard into my spine, but the brick pillar is soft because Philip is hot and gentle at the front, his tall full tweed jacket burning against me and everything about him barely touching so that I am dazed. Softened when the rolls of his lips touch me. Lulled when his hands move softer than cloth, unbuttoning one by one the shell buttons. Surprised at his hand behind me now, like the lift of water, a small warm wave under my skirt, lifting me up, pulling nothing, pushing nothing, taking nothing, not frightening, his fingers long and flat and hot, under and over and then up to my face to my forehead to my mouth and I am shaking so hard I can't tell are they his lips or are they his fingers.

In the dark corridor I forget that my mother could come out, that her husband could come out. My body forgets who is sleeping behind doors a few yards away. I don't open my eyes. I don't open my eyes because he kisses them. I don't open my eyes because I can't breathe. I move my hand to the back of his hand. I want to feel the gloss, the shine that my eyes see in daytime. He shivers. For the first time I open my eyes. His eyes fill with tears.

He settles slowly to his knees, then he curls all the way down to the stones. He holds my feet between his hands. He rests his forehead on my feet, tapping his head lightly on the tops of my arches, the way the *penitentes* hit their heads at the stations of the cross, the way the old dancer tapped her head into the mud around her mother's grave, the way Procuna bowed into the curly forehead of his bull

Still kneeling, he puts his forehead against my stomach. His tears go hot right through my skirt. I look down at him, his body shaking with silent sobs.

He has remembered who he is. He is Serena's father, the father of my friend. The lamplight wobbles. I close my eyes. He stands up and closes my blouse, locking each little button one by one. He pulls at his jacket with one hand and with the other he flattens his beard down to his neck, closing his face. He kisses me lightly, his mouth barely touching mine. Then he turns and walks tall and straight down the cobbled entrance to the double door to the street. Without a sound he lifts the latch as if he knew it by heart. I feel the cold air coming up from the lake. I walk down to close the door. My joints are hot and stiff. I have trouble moving on the familiar slope of cobbles. My legs feel stuffed, as if extra blood had been pumped into them. Everything about me is strange, swollen and liquid. I close the door and turn the large iron key without even a squeak as if it too were heated and smoothed.

I lean against the iron latch. Its cold kiss, right between my eyebrows, brings a picture of tomorrow, when I'll see Serena and understand about the hollows under her sad eyes, when I will see her father Philip and forget everything about him except his mouth.

12 de diciembre   El día de la Virgen de Guadalupe

Did you tell me the goddess Tonantzin had stars like
La Virgen? Did Tepeyac belong to Tonantzin? Juan Diego
found the roses there to prove he saw La Virgen. Are
they the same goddess, just born different times for
new people like us? Sometimes the roses they grow for
her are too red. Too like blood.

Dear Daddy,

I have to write to you. Because. Oh, well. Maybe not.

Remember that when I was nine Gustav typed of the
story of my life? I stood by his typewriter and told
it and he listened and typed.

When we finished he made a top paper with the title
and gave me my life as a present.

Here is from another day I told him. I was only nine
so maybe it is not right in all things.

     "My brother Primo is eleven and Amado is 4. Primo
is always teasing, but if someone teases back he loses
his temper. He paints his chin with charcoal to make
himself a pirate, but he doesn't look like a pirate.
     A pirate must look rougher and tougher. He still
reads comics. He likes to play aviator. He protects
Amado. He doesn't like it if I boss Amado.
     Amado changes his clothes all the time. Sometimes
he thinks he is an Indian and sometimes a soldier.
He has much fantasy. He looks in the mirror. I think
he will be an actor some day. Everyone knows him. He
goes out by himself. He has a little guitarra and he
sings his own mariachi songs. He thinks he is much
older than he is and he behaves like it. He talks to
himself but nobody can hear him because he hides in
his room. He has often something mischievous in his
mind, but he is good in his heart and he is generous."

Love to you and to Pilar. And to Tigre.

                     Your Choli

37

Rabies in Yellow

Afraid that I am a hungry coyote
that I could be dangerous
that a shot could go off in my head.

Soledad Paz

Right outside our house they fire shots. I run down to the door that opens wide enough for two oxen wearing a yoke. Mother tells us to stay in the house so we won't get hurt. But we race out to see who is shooting. The *delegado* runs past with his huge fisherman's hat flopping up and down on his head. His pistol is up in the air and a brown leather holster flaps empty against his thigh. They take turns being deputies, the men in Ajijic and then their sons. When their time is up chasing *bandidos*, they go on with their lives running the feed store, fishing in the lake, and walking up the mountain to the acres they farm in corn and chickpeas.

Two or three young men run by, then a wild scattering of children. Deafened by Mama's warnings, my brother Primo and I fall out of the door and run with them down to the beach.

"Why did they shoot?" I ask. "Who are they killing?"

"A coyote."

"No, it's not."

"O.K. Maybe it's a dog."

"Why are they shooting a dog?"

"Bit someone. It's a yellow dog with yellow eyes."

"I saw him this morning, running and panting." I had seen him. He came by the house, long-legged, running crooked, dodging something I couldn't see, crossing the cobbled street then crossing back, his tongue hanging out, trotting, running with his hind end separate from his front end as if he ran two different ways, scared, but there was nothing else anywhere on the street.

"He bit a little boy. Now they have to shoot him," says Primo.

"Why?"

"You know why, stupid. They want his brain. He has *el mal*. They have to shoot him to get his brain to see the rabies. If he does, they have to shoot the little boy in the stomach."

"Shoot him?"

"Inject him, stoopid."

I can see him. Or me. The men in white will stretch him out on a steel table and hold him down on the four corners and they will shoot him in the stomach every day. No matter where I hide. No matter where he hides. Twenty-one days they will inject him.

There are gun shots on the beach. We run to the sound. The sheriff and his men are racing toward the sun and away from the sun, toward the hills and away from the hills, toward the lake and away from the lake. I see the yellow dog. He runs out of the bushes. They shoot. They miss him. The dog changes direction, running steady, as if he had a long way to go. Everyone circles back the way they came, following him, losing sight of him in a stand of *tule*, shooting and missing.

His yellow eyes are in my head. I run, fearing for my life, fearing the guns and the shots. His eyes, topaz and shining with no dog in them, turn in a place I know. Rottenvaler's dog bit my brother Primo in the hand, deep, like a bullet hole, so they had to pour sulfa powder into it, but they didn't shoot my brother and they didn't shoot the dog. I looked into the holes on both sides of his hand. I wasn't there when it happened. I didn't see the German shepherd, but I looked at the dry holes with no blood coming from them. The shepherd had bitten my brother for me. I didn't have to do it. The dog bit him for me. Primo wants to kill me but he can't because he doesn't even know he wants to. Daddy is looking for his mother in my face, but he can't find her. He is looking for his sister in my name, looking for her dark owning look with the penetrating black eyes that are like his but without the sadness, without his loss, without his suffering, without his search for a way out of a nightmare, out of the dream into the day. He looks for her in me, waiting for me to take something away from him, to push him and tell him and close off his air, boss him, trap him as he turns and tries to stay ahead of her chase, trying to stay alive, panting and hiding in his night. But he can't find her in my gold eyes. He names me for her, and he names me for his mother even though she had blue eyes so he can't find her in me, either. He looks for her as she hid his father from him in the asylum, and hid the truth, the illness and the madness, so he didn't know through the secrets would his children also be mad? Did his father really fall off a horse and hit his head? Or, because of the lies, is he not sure about the fall, about the men in white coats, the terrible illness from something forbidden running in his blood, and I run because he is looking, but when I turn toward him he dreams that he will kill me because of her, because of his sister my namesake, because his mother is dead, because I can't be his father, because of running from the boys stinging him with "Hey Big Ears, your daddy's in the loony bin," cracking shots of laughter at him, afraid of his crutches, while he turns, crooked on his broken leg that won't mend, that he broke falling from the roof fixing the birdhouse so the birds would come home, limping on the leg with the silver bar that shrank in the winter cold and swelled in the summer heat, limping and crossing the street for no reason, and back again to get away, thirsty for their games, for where they went indoors to each other's houses, for where they ran to baseball, and even though he could still catch and throw the best they didn't want him any more,

gimpy, loony, bookworm, so he ran, crooked and dying, down
the black stairs to the basement bookstore where their last shots
missed him in the dark, but my yellow eyes ask him why, why did
your sister, why did your mother, and he runs from me to Primo
his firstborn son who only asks him questions about real things
like the Spanish Armada, and who only wants answers with words,
like books, Primo who never chases him with looks, Primo who
runs here on the beach beside me wishing he had his gun, shouting
that if he had a gun he would shoot too, while I run like a coyote,
away from the water that could kill me, back through the rushes
and out again because they can't see me and when they see me
they don't see me, so I double back to be safe, wanting to kill them
because they won't protect me, because they held me down and
shot me in the stomach twenty-one days in a row when the rabid
cat bit me, because they won't take care of me, because they won't
choose me, when my mother won't let me even raise my voice and
even when someone hurts me she is distant, since, after all, white
coats are good, and my mother can't take sides and lose Daddy, or
lose her doctor, or lose, so I run, because someone doesn't know
what he is doing, so I run, a wild animal, invisible, looking back,
looking forward, waiting for someone to come for me, but not to
hurt me, running till I can swerve back to them, but everyone is
getting more and more excited and the sheriff yells orders no one
hears, saying that the children shouldn't be there because of the
guns, although they are still shooting at something I can see coming out of the bushes, yellow, low to the ground, the dog with the
yellow eyes flickering bright as his head swivels, cutting back to
the street, running fast, trotting, shearing this way and that, and I
slow down, lost, sick, pain firing out of my amber eyes, my mouth
dry and terrified of drink, too sick for fear, knowing I could bite
someone, knowing I could be dangerous, waiting for a bullet to
go off in my head.

30 de agosto

Dear Daddy,

Daddy?

Last week Amado took my coin collection and went
through the whole village and gave them all away. He
went from house to house and gave everything from
Magyar, Italy, England, France, Germany and so many
countries where your friends went and brought me pen-
nies and everything. Now I have no coin collection.

I am hiding my stamp collection from him.

He did not take the copper veinte you gave me because
I was mad, I mean angry, and I already hid it very
well all by itself. It lives in a special place with
the silver peso you gave me when we left Malintzin No.
19, because they are not really money, and it is not a
collection.

OK. I am very sad. But Mama says Amado thought he was
being nice because everyone is poor, and he's little
and doesn't understand about collections and that he's
too little to know he wasn't giving pesos.

I don't know. Love to you and to Pilar and to you,

Choli

38

Standing in the Coffin to Tell

In my dream, the world of shelves turns sideways.
Floor to ceiling, confines of narrow coffins
stack the volumes wrong. No way to pull books out.
The word-houses turned almost upside down.

Soledad Paz

Only the Englishman Herbert Johnson knocks this hard on our front door. He brings his own iron key from home and bangs it with full force. Mama loves eccentrics and Herbert is one of her special ones. I think he secretly wants to protect her. When she needed emergency surgery and there was no ambulance and her husband was away visiting his mother, Herbert drove her thirty-five miles to the hospital. In her way maybe she saved his life, too.

He knocks again hard. Didn't Mama or her husband hear him the first time? It's barely light. It's not time to get up. It's scary that he's here at dawn. He usually brings his asparagus or the bitter orange marmalade at breakfast time. But this is no time for vegetables. I curl up tighter in bed. I don't want to answer the door. Someone else has to go. I hear the door open. The voices curl around the corner of the cobblestone entrance and fade into the living room.

For some reason I don't know, I jump out of bed and get dressed fast and then I just stand there with my forehead against my closed bedroom door. I feel odd. On a string. The string pulls me to dress, and the string tells me to stand there without opening my door. When Mama raps fast on it, the string forgets to tell me not to jump.

"Go get Amado and come to the living room," Mama says. "I need to talk to you."

"Where's Primo?"

"He's in the living room."

How did she get Primo from the room next to mine without me? Why didn't she get Amado at the same time?

I wake up Amado and cuddle him into his clothes. He's eight, but when he is sleepy he is three or four again. When he is awake he seems older than I am. He takes my hand very seriously as if he is the one to lead me to the living room, helping me walk the length of the verandah to the other side of the house.

Primo is crying. He is trying to be big. He is trying to be old and responsible. I can tell he wishes he could stop crying, but he can't, so he punches a fist hard into the arm of the sofa. Amado settles in next to him and watches Mama. I stand by the door.

"Why did Señor Herbert knock so early this morning? What did he want?" I ask.

"That's why I need to talk to you. He heard something on the radio." She is bending over the sofa, as if that would pull me to the seat where she wants me to be. Her words sound too careful. She sits down and reaches for me to sit next to her.

"What?" The string is pulling me to wait but I want to fall fast into what is in my mother's face, in Primo's angry sobs.

Mama's husband is standing like a statue looking out of the window. The long veil of the curtain covers him. He glances at me but there is nothing to read on his face. He fades out of the curtain, goes into their bedroom and closes the door. I'm glad.

"Herbert heard about a fire in Mexico City, and he heard the man on the radio say some names. He said your father's name," Mama says.

"What happened? Is he all right? Is he hurt?" I ask.

Primo says, "Did he try to save someone?"

"No. Herbert heard his name, and then he called the radio station in Mexico City. He has a phone now, you know, and the man at the station said that your father was.... That they found your father. That he could not get out. That...."

The string is pulling at me to be quiet. Let her speak. Wait until it is all out.

Mama holds my shoulder. She looks over at Amado and then right into my face. "He called and they said that Daddy died in the fire."

"What if it's not true?" says Primo angrily, wiping his nose with his hand.

"I know," says Mama. "That's why Herbert waited before coming to talk to us when he heard it. He wanted to make sure. He said they were sure. That the report came from the Green Cross. They are the ones that go to accidents."

"Where was Daddy? Where was the fire?" asks Primo.

Mama does not answer.

"Where was he?" Primo asks again, louder.

"In a nightclub. They said on the radio that someone set off a firecracker inside the club to celebrate Independence Day. A curtain caught fire."

"Did he burn up?" Primo asks as if more horrible than dying would be to burn up, when there is no difference.

I want something not to be worse so I can figure out dead.

"No. The man at the Green Cross said No, he was not burned."

"Did they take him to the hospital?" I ask.

"Where did they take him?" says Primo. "To the morgue?"

"I didn't want to say that word," says Mama. "Yes. To the morgue. I am going there. Herbert is going to help me pay for everything. I am flying to Mexico City right now by myself. I will find Daddy and take care of everything."

"I want to go with you," says Primo.

"No. I can't take you with me."

"I want to go too," I say.

"I know, but I have to go alone."

"But I want to SEE him," says Primo.

I say, "I want to see him too."

We are both crying hard now. The string is letting me shake. I collapse on the couch.

"Herbert said that the ambulance man reported that Daddy was not burned. But it would be very painful for you to see him. It wouldn't be the same."

"We don't care. We WANT to see him," Primo says.

"Well, if he wasn't burned," I ask, "why did he die? Why is he dead? I want to see him."

"They said he was asphyxiated," Mama says. "Too much smoke. No air. It wouldn't be like seeing him the way he was. I don't want that to be your last memory." Now Mama is crying too. She is not supposed to. If her husband sees that he'll really be mad. She glances over at the window. He's gone. She sits down and puts her arms around all of us on the couch. "I am so sorry," she whispers. "He was my best friend. I have lost my best friend." For a moment it feels as if she is all alone in the room.

I want to ask, If he was your best friend, why don't you live with him. But I know I don't understand. We are all crying together, then we are all quiet.

"Maybe he's not really dead," I say. "Maybe they made a mistake."

Mama says, "When I get to Mexico City I am going to call you, so go to the phone when they send the messenger and I'll tell you everything so you know. I have a lot to do. I have to go to the place where he is and find a nice coffin. I need to go to the graveyard and find a plot. I have to...." She cries as hard as all of us for a few moments, then she suddenly makes herself fine, standing in front of us, ready to go, ready for work. In no time she is on her way to the airport.

I hear the husband leave the house. I don't have any other thoughts. The string inside me is the only thing I feel. It says Go out to the China plum tree and find a ripe plum high in the feathery boughs. One falls. I put the whole thing in my mouth. It has a huge pit like a peanut. I roll the flesh off in my mouth.

When the pit is still rolling around my tutor comes. Creighton says, "I'm sorry about your father, and, I think it would be best not to have lessons today. I'm sorry. And, uh, see you later."

He leaves really fast. How can he know who I am and what I feel about my Daddy if all he sees is a girl looking for green fruit in a green tree with a big stone in her mouth? I am mad that we are not having lessons. It would be better to have class. To change nothing. To open books and write words. To look things up. To learn something new. Something I would want to tell to Daddy even if now I can't. Creighton should have stayed. Primo is hiding somewhere. Amado says he is going to look for the stepfather because he promised him a trip to the next town for breakfast.

I go to my room and cry. I slide off the bed and open the bottom drawer of the wardrobe. There is the straw heart box with needles and thread, and there are all the socks with holes in them. I pick up the one with the wooden egg deep in the toe. "I didn't finish," I whisper. "I didn't finish." I dip the needle up and down and across the threads closing a toe hole. I sew faster and faster, as if something could be better, as if things could go backwards if I would get just one sock done, and it might not really be true that Daddy is dead.

I am trapped in the tall brown box with the telephone. Mama tells me everything and now I have to go home and tell Primo and Amado. I listen carefully. Inside me the string is saying things too in the secret language I hear in my bones. Mama talks and at the same time I am hearing Why didn't I know when it was happening? Why didn't I feel it when he was choking? When they were stepping on him, why didn't I rise up screaming in the night and go for my mother?

Mama's voice is back, louder than anything inside me. "Soledad, did you understand everything I told you?"

"Yes."

"Do you have any questions?"

"No."

"I have to go now. There's a lot to do, the house, the obituary, the notice, the mortuary, the gravestone, the book business. I'm sorry, Choli. It is too much. It's so hard. Now I have to go get him and take him to the funeral home."

"Why?"

"A few people will come to see him."

"To see him?"

"I mean to pay their respects."

I don't want to talk to her any more. I want to go home. Everything she says is strange. I haven't found a place for it. The street is longer going home from the telephone because I have to tell Primo everything, and it will have to be exactly what Mama said and perfect and clear so he won't get mad. He listens without looking at me. It's just the facts, but he's too angry to hear any more cold facts.

The moment I finish talking to Primo he runs out of the house.

Another little kid comes to the door with that little piece of paper that says, "Ocurra teléfono." It never says who's calling. Maybe Mama forgot something, so I run up the hill. I don't want to go to that tall stand-up coffin for the phone. But there's no one else to go. Where's Primo? Why can't he go to the phone? He's the first-born, and Amado is too young.

I am holding the black earpiece away from my ear. My father's sister is on the line. It's my aunt, my namesake, Aunt Soledad. I don't want to talk to her. I don't want to hear her crackling questions. I don't want to see the truth in my head before I say it. If I pretend I can't hear her, maybe she'll hang up and call again when my mother is back. There is a kind of scream in my aunt's voice. She is asking the same question over and over. It's like her letters: *Did you get my check? Did you get my check?* Yes, I got her check, but I won't cash it because the check is the present, not what I buy with it.

"I got your mother's telegram!" she yells, "What about his body? Did they tell you about his body?" Static fries in my ear.

"Yes." I stand on tiptoe and face the mouthpiece. I make noises back, but I don't want to make words. Her voice ignites sparks along the line. I stare at the black pocked mouthpiece. Slowly I lift my head and arch my neck. I get ready to spit out the answers, to shout them up to her hundreds of miles away.

"Is his body all right?" she asks.

"Yes." There is a burning in my ear. I hold the earpiece too tight. I want to pretend I am on Micaela's ham radio. I want to shout CQ... CQ–HE1UE calling CQ, CQ, and getting nothing but snaps and buzzes.

"Did they find his body?" She asks, yelling down from the north.

"Yes." Why does she keep asking about his body? What difference does it make? I am afraid of her intensity, of the terrible things she wants to know, that I don't want to say.

I say, "What?"

"What about his body? What happened to him?" Aunt Soledad is not blurred now. Her words suddenly come through perfectly crisp. They go right into my head before I can stop them. "Is he burned?"

"No." I look at my feet. She's too far away to hear my heart trying to work, my mouth trying to breathe. I stand up straight, but I am suffocating. "No, Mother says...."

The one word I have given her makes her voice hotter.

She doesn't hear. She speaks over me. "Is his body burned?" The line snaps like kindling. This must be the voice she used when she answered him about the book. The book that she threw down the transom. The book from the London Fire. The book covered in a soft, oily human skin—my father's treasure of a lifetime. She threw it away. Didn't she know who he was? Didn't she know what he loved? How he searched from country to country, from hamlet to hamlet, from shelf to shelf, from trunk to trunk? What happened to it? Into the trash, into an incinerator, to burn into smoke above her city.

"No," I say. "Mother says No, he did not burn."

"Is he dead?"

I don't want to answer.

She says, "What?"

I shout, "YES!" Yes.

"Yes, what?" She says from thousands of miles away.

"Yes, he did not burn," I say. The fire in my head is quiet. "Yes, they say he is dead."

"Is his body gone? "

"NO. Mama says it is black and blue," I yell into the black tulip. Mama doesn't have to explain to my aunt. I know they stepped on him. I know he got knocked down. I know they walked over him before he could get to the door. Mama doesn't say, but I know he could have been saved. Mama tells us he died from the smoke, that the owner of the cabaret wanted them to pay before they ran from the fire. The owner wouldn't open the door. He wanted his money. Someone broke the door down. Some ran out. Some ran over the others. Some were saved. Some died burning in their clothes. The owner lived. Daddy did not.

"What about his body?" she asks again, yelling in a rough voice I have never heard from her.

What can I tell her? I know he's lying on a metal table in a place. I know he's dressed. Mama went to the house and got him another suit. His face is black and blue where they stepped on him. She's going to bury him. She's coming home in a few days. We can't go. I want to see him. She didn't take us. They hit him in the head with their feet. They ran over him. They stood on him to try to get out. They buried him under the others. They buried him in the smoke. Mother will bury him in the cemetery and then she will come home.

I say, "His face has marks on it."

"What?"

"His body is fine but his face is black and blue."

"Where was he?" The telephone wires cool as she begins to hear me.

I am not going to tell her where he was. I would never tell her that. Even he wouldn't tell her. "I don't know."

"When is the funeral?"

"I don't know." I do know, but Mama is not taking us to the funeral. She's not taking us to see him either. It's too far, or something like that.

"Maybe in one day they will bury him," I say. The law says you have to be buried in twenty-four hours.

"I can't come, you know."

"I know." She has never come. She will never come.

"Are they sure it is your fathah?" She says the word the way he does, the way he wants me to say it.

"Mama saw him."

The line is crackling again to cover her voice. And I say, as I used to do when Daddy called, "Yes, I know. Yes," I nod my head, looking out of the tall brown box that holds only one person. I look out of the little glass window of the coffin and wait for her to say goodbye.

After the line is silent and turned to ash, I still stand there with the tulip ear piece against my cheek.

I stand there with my head bowed, and tell him, "I am your daughter. I am the daughter of my father. I am your favorite and only daughter."

Because I will never stand in this box waiting for his voice again, I tell him, right through the bone of my forehead pressed into the black mouthpiece. I tell him, "You are my Daddy. You are my favorite and only Daddy."

39

The Child in the Throat

In my dream
we are more alive than dead.

Soledad Paz

In my dream, Daddy and Primo and I are together. It feels like the
inside of a blue streetcar, but in Coyoacán they are all yellow. It
feels as if we are in Ajijic, but there is no trolley to the lake, only a red
and white bus. We are near a carousel, and only Primo is on a wild
wooden horse, going up and down. Daddy and I are standing on the
ground in the middle of the merry-go-round. We are watching Primo.

Daddy says, "You are my favorite daughter, you know that,
don't you?" He holds me quickly in a short hug.

I look down because it feels good. I look up. His eyes are twinkling with a joke. I think the joke is on me, but it might be on him.
He is twinkling at my brother Primo as if he has said something
very clever. He thinks he talked to me. He thinks he held me. But
he has only thrown me a bone. I am to slink off like a good little
dog and chew on that hard bone for a few years. I can see he wants
a lot of credit for finding the solution to memory.

"Go and play now. We have man things to do," Daddy says.
How can he say that to me in a dream, almost exactly the same
thing he said to me on the beach on his last visit?

I am going to be good. I am going to smile down at my shoes, obedient all through the shoulder bones. All through my gut and my knees. All through my nails that want to dig. Through my throat that wants to yell. My tonsils swell. A fever comes from the damp of night, from the damp bricks. My throat traps words, words that could kill if they were released, and stores them in two red, infected balls at the back of my throat, two colored eggs I will use for food. The tonsils bulge and close together. Nothing comes past them from the voice box. Nothing comes past them from the heart. Nothing goes past them from the tray of poached eggs and tea. Primo and Daddy don't walk away. They fade away and they take everything with them even the carrousel horse.

Mama wakes me. She is sitting on the bed. I am thirteen. I am sick and Daddy is dead. He will never see me when I am fifteen, or twenty-one, when he said he would really be able to talk to me. Mama wants to take us to Mexico City. She thinks we should see the house before she sells it, and bring things home that we want to keep, and maybe go out to the grave. But I am too sick to go. I sleep and cough and sleep.

It is not time for one of her visits. Usually, she comes to my room early in the morning and then at night. She comes when she has time, when she doesn't have to work designing fabric, buying gigantic boxes of threads, ordering dyes, teaching someone to cut and drape her cloth, measuring wood for another loom, being charming to customers who suddenly feel they have known her forever so she brings them home for lunch. This time she comes to my room in the middle of the day.

"I'll get the doctor to see you. He can give you an injection. You are very sick. I think it's your tonsils, don't you?"

I can't speak, so I nod. Nodding makes Mama happy. Mama likes it when you look at her and agree. She is relieved. If you disagree and look down, it's not the same. She is nervous. Eyes.

She wants to look into your eyes. She thinks she sees the truth. Even if she sees lies.

"You'll be better tomorrow and we can go."

I don't want to go. She has already buried him. She ordered the stone. And she paid for care for the grave in perpetuity, which means forever. She keeps reassuring us that he died of asphyxiation. He didn't die from burning. Smoke inhalation and asphyxiation. She says she read it. There's a certificate. Also she looked at him to be sure, so she could tell us. He would have been unconscious when it happened, she always adds. But when? Before the pain or after? Before the terror of trying to reach the door or after? Before the feet on his face or after? Does that mean that nothing hurt? Does she know when he knew he would be dead? He was unconscious, she says. But before that, Mama! BEFORE that, what?

He died in a fire but he didn't burn to death. September 15. The eve of Mexico's Independence Day. Daddy was celebrating. Who was he with in the cabaret? Mama said Call it a nightclub, it sounds better. The flames leap from a firecracker. The curtains flare. Smoke flattens out against the ceiling. The owner locks the door. Pay as you leave. They are falling and crawling over each other to get the owner out of the way. He opens the door and runs away down the street. Some are burned to death. Some are not, but anyway they die in the fire.

Mama wants to take us to Daddy's house. Our house. But it will be empty. He won't be there. Pilar will be there and Tigre. And the books, but not his hands. All of his children abandoned. What will they do without him? My room is there that I don't live in any more except when I go to see him.

Mama is standing beside my bed again. "The doctor is here. He's going to give you very strong medicine. You are going to be all right so we can go to Daddy's house."

How do I go to Daddy's house if he isn't there?

For two more days I can't speak. Mama doesn't even look at me. There is no looking and no nodding. Something is going on. I can't read the signals. I hear her whispering with the doctor. "Don't worry, this isn't the same as before," he says and then he leaves.

In the morning she comes to my room. She sits so gently on my bed that I don't recognize her. She is not impatient today. Maybe I died in the night. That's how she'll be to me now that I'm dead. Gently she puts the cold thermometer in my mouth. It tastes of alcohol. She doesn't look at me. She waits. It's a long time, one minute, to wait for the mercury. She waits without moving. I have never seen my mother sit for one minute without moving.

"You have a fever of a hundred and four."

I know that's high. It means I can slide down in the covers and wait for hibiscus tea and white rice with sweetened condensed milk. It means I can sleep all day. It means she'll leave me alone until the doctor comes again in the afternoon. It means I don't have to go. I don't have to get in the car. I don't have to drive and vomit along the thousand curves of Mil Cumbres. It means I don't have to arrive in Coyoacán where he is not.

"Get up," Mama says. "I am going to wrap you warmly. The car is outside. We are going."

"But I'm sick."

"I know. We're going anyway. Take your pillow, and your blanket. You can curl up in the car and sleep all the way."

I wander out to the car, feverish, deceived, unprepared. "I didn't brush my teeth."

"That's all right. You can brush them tomorrow."

When I had whooping cough the doctor said I would die. He stood tall in black in the long door. He thought I was asleep. He said "Her fever is too high. Many children have died this week." He said I could die when I had the mumps and tonsillitis and measles that made a bloody nose, and when the hernia fell like an egg out of my pink truss. And now she is going to take me anyway.

We drive away over the cobbles, down the gravel road to the highway, up through the mountain passes on our way to the city. In an hour my fever is gone and my throat is clear. The string is pulling at me inside, like on the day of the knocking on the door. The string says, You just had to be moved. You had to be on the way to the truth, with nothing to stop it, not even the fever. Now you know you can't make yourself die not to see the empty house. You are going to Coyoacán.

I sit with my face against the cold window. I look where we're going. I don't think back. I don't think ahead. Primo leans against the other side. Amado gets to sit in front with Mama. I look at the pines spinning past, at the telephone wires, joining and falling apart, joining and sagging, swinging up together to the pole and hanging away, swooping up to the black cross and looping separately down, up, and looping separately down.

He isn't really dead. I'll look for him. I'll find him.

40

The Fifth Stone of the Heart

I look for my patrimony—
in the thieves' market,
in the pawnshop.
Glass eyes and wigs
trophies and plaques
guns and sewing machines.
No four-stone rings.

Soledad Paz

We come for the last time to my father's house, Malinche #19, in Coyoacán, the town still named for hungry coyotes. I don't want to come. But I do.

First I stand under the fir tree. I walk behind the stable where we used to pile Caramelo's manure to let it "cool" and dry out before we put it around the broccoli. I walk to the tar-topped wall where I grabbed the rabid white cat. I go around the corner to the gate where my head got stuck and I waited terrified for the kidnappers. Back in the house, I find Pilar in the kitchen and she holds me. I am as tall as she is now. In the living room I stand on the carpet of Persian apples with green leaves on a ground of burgundy and blue. I smell Daddy's cigarettes and the bottles of tincture, the inks and pastes. I sniff the backs of his books and

I open them randomly to inhale him from the yellowed, musty leaves. I stroke shelf after shelf of leather bindings as if with one last touch I could prepare them for whatever is to come.

Why did Mama have to sell them? Why did they have to go to another house, to another business. I want a giant sign over the gate that says LEO PAZ, Sucesora. The heir to Leo Paz. I have never seen that. Male successors, yes. Juan Sánchez e Hijos. Why not LEO PAZ E HIJA? Yes, I would make it like that, with the daughter part. I wouldn't mention successor because it would be a reminder that he was dead. I would write all the correspondence and all the orders. I would save newspapers to wrap the books, and knot together all the broken ends of twine. I would sign my name, Soledad Paz, BIBLIÓFILA. I'd wrap packages and take them to the post office. I might even have a car, and not go on the bus at night the way he had. Guatemala is in me. And St. Louis and Washington, D.C.. Mama is keeping a few special books, but she and her husband are not in the book business. They have looms. They make textiles. They are going to send me to the States. They are not going to let me inherit my father.

I go to my room. Piles of books have migrated there, covering my bed and the dresser, covering the floor and the chairs, burying the low desk.

I walk down to the front garden by the white staircase where I used to hear his limp in the night. I press my face into the bunches of pale pink roses. Then I return to the long table in the dining room. I sit down where he sat me for the presentation of the ring. I open the drawer slowly to take my gift, to take the ring of belonging from which I will conjure memories, pieces of fantasy and dreams. Everything is there: A bright green flattened packet of Bohemios with a couple of cigarettes left in it. I take one out and light it. I wait for the smell to bring him back. It doesn't. The smoke smells different coming from my mouth. I leave it in his ashtray. There are matchboxes with the picture of Venus de Milo and the steam engine running beneath her feet.

Daddy's black Esterbrook ink pens. His blue-black ink in the bottle with side wells for filling his fountain pens. The special thin book paste. Tiny slips of aged and watermarked paper for mending pages. Pencils and shavings. Razors for trimming edges and sharpening points. A tiny box with two small bottles—black and white, before and after, positive and negative—magic, smelly liquids with their little glass sticks with knob ends that we used to dip and work around on the paper to bleach the fox-stained spots on pages.

My arm reaches deep into the black corner of his drawer. I move papers around. I reach into the other corner, waiting for my fingers to touch the box. I find it and open it. It's empty.

"She took it," says Pilar.

I jump. I hadn't heard her come up behind me.

"She took it," she says again.

I turn to her. I can't get out of his chair. My thirteen-year-old self, reaching and finding nothing, shrinks into an eleven-year-old again. I am emptied out. He is really gone.

"Who took it?"

"The street woman. *Esa. La maldita de la calle.*" Pilar holds a corner of white apron over her mouth, the way she does when she has toothache, the way she does when her heart breaks. The black stones of her eyes sparkle with tears of anger and at the same time with impotence.

"Who?"

"La Josefina. I couldn't stop her. What could I do? He let her in. He even made me cook for her that night. She wanted to go dancing. *¡Bruta!* How was the Señor to dance with that leg? She laughed at him, with her teeth in his face. He was holding her waist. She said, 'Well, if you can't dance like me, then do something special for me? What can you do, hmmm? What can you do for me this night?' I saw it. I stood behind the door in the kitchen."

She wipes both eyes hard with her apron.

"La Josefina took it," Pilar says. "*Perra*. A bitch in heat for something. He was blind. He asked her if she wanted to see something pretty. So he took it out of the drawer and opened the box and her eyes jumped like claws at the pretty thing. He held it back a little like this, then he said, 'Just look at it. I'm only going to show it to you.' She whined and twisted around him till he put it on her finger. Then she danced like a.... She danced with her hand like this up in the air. 'Let me wear it just tonight, just tonight, *Leoncito*,' she whined, as if 'little Lion' were his name! He let her. She wore it that night when they went out to the nightclub. The next day he told me she went to the bathroom and never came back. He cried when he told me. He cried because she never came back and he cried because he was so stupid to trust her. He trusted those street dogs. And me? From me he asked for accounts in writing, on a piece of paper, for each cucumber and fig, for every cheese and pin, for the sweet cream and the petroleum, for the chops from the butcher, for the breads from Chucho on the corner, for the cactus fruit he loved, for his Bohemios. He asked accounts from me, I who can barely write, I who loved him, who fed him. For twenty years I ironed his shirts. For twenty years I made the fires to heat water for his tub. Your father...."

The whole apron covers her face now and she shakes her sobs into it, the clutch of white in her fists filling with tears, pulled up like the large white sheets from the stone laundry tub, the lavadero where everything came clean.

I sit in the large wooden pool of his chair and cry for the stolen gift that carried away my grandmother and my mother and my father and which instructed my brain to remember a Josefina whom I don't even know. I find one of her letters in his desk. The address is Callejón de los Misterios #59. Just the address would have drawn him to her. It's a rambling letter in pencil on lined paper, with no sentences and no periods, saying she was sorry to deceive him, asking him, Leo, Leo, if he would take her back, could he please send money right away for her front teeth so she could work again. He must have sent her some because in another letter she tells him he didn't send enough and he should send more if he loved her because she was trying to better herself—just like he told her to.

I cry for the silver bar in his leg and for the limp that broke him when she laughed because he couldn't dance the way she wanted, the limp that made him pay with my ring for her promises, for a night on the town, for nights in her bed. I cry for the half of him that fell down and for the half that stood proud. I cry for the limp of the father that stole the gift of the child.

"It was mine," I say to Pilar.

"I know."

I hold Pilar's hand, brown and smooth, swollen with her silky fat. I hold it to my face, to my tears. She seems to know I don't want her to hug me. I hold her hand to my cheek, the hand that smoothed my ears and my hands and my heart. I hold it, the hand of onyx, of divination and healings, the hand that crushed herbs and fanned teas so they wouldn't burn my lips, the hand of the gods and the corn, of punishment and comfort. I hold the hand that rolled the pocked pestle and the long *mano* of stone she used to grind a fine *masa* on the metate. I hold the hand that turned tortillas on the *comal*, that held cactus *tunas* between their clusters of spiny hairs and peeled them cold from the ice—first for my father and then for us—the hand that smoothed my braids while my face was buried in her apron for solace, the hand that chopped *nopales* and missed all the spines, that drove a stick into a mango and peeled it without touching it, that suctioned soapsuds from our faces in the bath, that turned crêpes with her fingers to make my mother's favorite dish, the fingers that twisted her handkerchief into a point and took pieces of straw from my eye, the hand that batted my wrist when I dipped into the crab apple jelly falling in hot streams from her ladle, that held my chin so that I could feel in her skin how she loved me even if she scolded, the hand that knew where the pain was but touched it only with the soft cross she made on my forehead with her thumb. I hold the hand of the earth and the trees. I hold the hand of an ancient, holy, and translucent obsidian.

I hold the hand of the fifth stone of the heart.

41

Reading the Father

I have been seen
gathering snake skins.
I have been seen
shielding a hungry heart
with my hand in the hollow
of a yellow coyote
that has swallowed the moon.

Soledad Paz

MEXICO CITY

I have not been here for twenty years. I'm on a pilgrimage to my
birthplace, to the grave of my father. Next time I'll bring my
children. They must see the avalanches of jasmine, the mural-sized
walls of lava rock topped with broken glass, the tsunami waves of
purple bougainvillea, the thick wooden hacienda doors as mysterious as the locked portals of nunneries.

My taxi follows the tracks of the streetcar past beggars and
limos, past flower markets and fruit stalls. The thighs of the giant
bronzes of Salvador catch the sun. Cobblestone streets survive the
freeway overpass. I enter the crucigram of the city, its heart silent
and cool, my memories fragrant and tireless.

The cemetery is there and the marble covering my father. In my bag is the red leather volume of Antonio Peñafiel with the designs for place names of ancient Mexico. The page for Coyoacán is loose in the binding. The edges are split from being found so many times. On top of the Peñafiel is the heart-shaped basket my father gave me, with a small ring of woven straw for lifting the cover. I have taken out everything it held for fixing Daddy's socks. Inside, on the quilted satin like the inside of a coffin, are cards and packets of letters. Some have ribbons around them. Some have rubber bands. One has an old rusted spring clip that is stuck to the paper. Someone seeing me with the basket in my hand might think I had brought his ashes, but Mama put his whole body in the casket. The straw heart holds his letters to me, and they want to find him. They want to be read to him. They want to be heard.

We drive past the old convent of San Jerónimo, a letter-writing saint. Near the convent we are only a short distance from the open market I came to as a child. The architects of produce arrange stacks of blood oranges. The giant vulvas of the papayas are standing, split open to show their clutches of black shiny seeds. Life itself is stacked in pyramids of green *tunas*, orange mangos like young breasts, and near them, the spread of swollen fingers of the *plátano macho*, the long fat plantain with a purple tinge where it is not quite ripe. Leaning into them, saffron *mameyes* slashed open to their large private gleaming pits.

Mexico City is everything—tumult and color exuding a natural and necessary heat, and the inner knowing from the single cell of the solitary.

The taxi takes me back through the suburbs of Mexico City, through San Angel, past Barranca del Muerto, the gorge of the dead, past Águilas, to the Periférico, toward the hills of the cemeteries. We cross Rio Churubusco. We pass Nuestra Señora del Carmen and the Rotonda de los Niños Héroes. I have never driven here myself, but I can tell at Azcapotzalco that we are getting near. We cross México-Tacuba and I tell the driver which cemetery I want, and then I look out the window with false abstraction as if I did this every Sunday. Which I don't. This might be the last time. I am leaving Mexico. It won't be easy to come here when I go to live far away in The North.

The winding road to the American Cemetery goes up the hill crowded with flower vendors getting ready for the Days of the Dead. The stalls are filled with pansies, roses, zinnias, countless blooms—tuberoses, cannas and callas.

On the ground are cheap mortuary vases, painted to look like malachite, gray to match anything, pink and white for the graves of babies. The vases are narrow, tall and empty until they are filled by mourners who buy more flowers than the vases can hold.

We drive past the Jewish cemetery and the British.

Under the sheet-shaded stands are flowers arranged in tiers, in steps like a choir, their colors exuberant, the bunches enormous. Against the frail posts are wreaths with diagonal satin ribbons waiting for names. Wreaths around frames wait for a photo. Wreaths of pine, laurel and ivy punched by a hundred white carnations. Straw gilded with tinfoil, then neatly studded with everlasting flowers. Like the trophies at the hippodrome, the enormous wheels of blood red roses are ready to be placed on the necks of those who have won the race to the final destination.

I ask the driver to stop. Why? I meant to go straight there. I thought I hadn't wanted any of those flowers already dying as you buy them. I thought I didn't want any vases filled with lilies. No garlands of the bright dying eyes of sweet Williams. No flowers which would be snatched from his grave and put on someone else's as soon as I was out of the gate.

I get out. The thick pungency of the tuberose strangles me and buckles me at the knees with its perfume of incense, grief, graves, coffins, veils. Its delicate creamy buds, tinged with pale green, are for wakes, to cover the stink of failed surgeries and unwashable sores. "*Nardo*," Mama said, "the flower of the dead. Never, ever put spikenard in a house bouquet." I remember the *nardos* next to the half open eyes, the waxy fingers of laid-out babies, breathing itself out over the stench of Don Francisco's poorly shrouded wound. Spikenard, more penetrating than the scent of cinnamon, coffee or tequila served to the mourners. The ivory tuberose can't fool me with its tall, elegant grace. Surrounded by hectares of fragrant flowers, it stands out and coats my nose with the singular smell of death. Mama hated them. Now I know why.

I don't want to speak. Words would lighten me, make this like shopping for flowers for a party. I point and pick pink roses like the ones near the iron gate of Daddy's house, then callas like trumpets with their dangerous orange pistils, and huge, deep-red roses like the ones Daddy gave to his mother even though he had bought them for a woman who had thrown them in the trash. I need to fill my arms to have something to walk with as I get near him. The vendor adds asparagus fern and a leaf of baby palm. Before tying it and adding a funnel of clear cellophane to my bouquet, she stabs in a spike of *nardo* as if I have neglected the principal ingredient. Spikenard. The bloom of death that could break my mother's heart with its sadness. I shake my head. No. Not even to please this stranger. Not even as the gift which she intends. I pull it out and hand it back to her, but I hold her fingers for a moment. She seems to understand.

The taxi drops me at the white arches of the American Cemetery. It will wait till I am ready to return to the City from this maze, down the mountain, off Calgary.

I walk through and down the middle avenue. Suddenly I am lost. Which way did we turn, Mama and I? I walk straight away from the gates, passing by three then four, then five avenues of graves. Stone angels, crosses, family vaults, large plots with iron gates as if after dark there were a coming and going. Trees. I don't remember the pines and the firs.

Daddy, where are you? I want to run calling his name as if we have been separated at a picnic, in the mountains, in a park. I go farther from the gate, looking both ways, glancing at the names of everyone.

Deeper and deeper, thinking that since it was so long ago, there are new aisles. Maybe I have passed him. Maybe he is where I began, among the first.

Daddy, I have forgotten where Mama put you. I stop. The labyrinth of headstones has stolen my bearings. If I run, someone will be alarmed. But I want to run so that speed will take me to him, without mind, without thought, without memory which has deceived me.

I can barely see through the tears. I look at my feet, hardly noticing the edges of the graves. Empty rusty cans of tomatoes and chiles. More gloomy vases holding dead stems and black knobs of zinnias and asters. Flags and photos and brilliant fresh flowers. Neat lines of fake flowers stuck into a grave like windmills. Plastic flowers no one will steal.

At a crossroads I close my eyes. Daddy, tell me where to go. Lead me. Remind me. Forgive me. Slowly I weave back and forth. His thread pulls me as softly as a web back toward the entrance gates, then along the yellow wall of soft *tepetate*. I turn and bend low to fit under a pine bough. There he is.

I burst into tears. So plain. The gray marble. My father: Your name carved in capitals, in a formal font. Leo LeRoy Paz. Your mother's maiden name in the middle, not at the end in the Mexican way. You liked the English way better. I remember. "You wrote to me: *Soledad. Your name is not Soledad Paz O'Rohan. Use my last name, Paz, at the end. That way when you go to the United States to school no one will be confused.*"

A busyness takes me over since I don't remember the rules for this reunion. My hands sweep the stone and brush the pine needles off the name. To make up for lost time. To fix, to mend, to care, to tend. Crying. I am distraught that there are no plants, no green for you. What have they done? We paid in perpetuity for the care of the grave. Nothing. A neighbor has a green blanket of grass over him and empty tin cans at his feet. I borrow them and run along the wall to find a faucet. I am in a rush because I've been remiss. Because, Daddy, you are suddenly close. I have been truant and afraid. They didn't let me see you dead. They didn't let me come to bury you.

I quickly fill the tin cans with flowers. The stone is so empty. Quick. Color it. Grace it. Where are the succulents, the evergreens we had? We seldom come. The grave gardener knows it. We are not like the Sunday plots, where there is someone kneeling every week, weeding, watering, pinching, brushing, clearing, praying, crying, thanking the caretaker, tipping him. Why should he work for us in vain?

My heart aches for the years I have not been faithful. At the corner of the marble, I sit with my chin on my knees wanting to hear his voice, the tone of his postcards and letters.

I take the heart basket out of my bag. For a moment I want to dig deep like a dog and bury it in the dry dirt at the edge of the grave. But I can't. I want the letters with me because they are something I can touch. I open the box and pile up letters at your feet. The postcards I stand up along the edge. You never wrote the year on them, so I lay them out like an itinerary. Chiapas, Guatemala, Honduras, Bolivia, Peru. Then New Orleans, New York, St. Louis, Palo Alto, Mexico City.

One letter is to Primo. *If I should die, you will be the man in the family.* Daddy, did you know they sent him away to boarding school in the North when you died? He had to be a man all on his own, and he was only fifteen. I had to go too. They said it's what you wanted.

A letter for me. *Soledad, my darling daughter.* I don't remember that you called me Darling. Did you? I can't hear it. But you wrote it. It's like the life that is only in words, in books. *Dearest daughter, Your little brother Amado can't read or write yet. I am very worried about him. What are WE going to do about it? You must teach him. Don't you agree?*

You say "We." I didn't know we had a "we." Amado could write, at least in Spanish, but, you know, That Man would not let him write to you. Maybe today is the first time you know that. I'm sorry. Anyway, if Amado did write to you, that man wouldn't mail Amado's letters. He hoarded Amado, you know. He wanted him for himself because Amado was little when they met and Amado still believed that the man who lived with his mother was a good man. I know you wanted us to practice our English with Amado. We did.

Why do I have Primo's letters? Mama meant to give them to Primo later. Or do I have them because I wanted what you had with him? I don't know.

Primo, The jackknife I bought for you was very expensive. I work hard for you, often seven days a week, and often late into the night to make enough money to send to Mother. I can't afford to buy you another. You must learn to be more careful about your things. You must find it.

You laughed when I told you that I, a girl, wanted a jackknife. Now I have one. My son gave it to me. I take it with me everywhere. Because that's what you did, and that's what you wanted Primo to do.

Primo, Soledad spells better than you. Why can't you spell as well as she? Primo didn't like it when you said that, Daddy. Mama said you didn't know how to talk to children, that you were waiting till we were grown so you could talk to us like adults. I talk to my children a lot.

My dear Soledad, Do you know why I ask you to have good penmanship and to spell well? People are judged by these things. Your character and your mind are measured. If someone sees that you write poorly they will think you are lazy or slovenly. You wouldn't want that would you?

I didn't re-read your letters for many years. They made me itch. They made me squirm as if I had been called on the carpet but had forgotten both the rules and my crime. The word "slovenly" was a heavy, ugly word, like a slug, telling me a thing I should not be. Your expectations left me lonely for a simpler kind of love.

My dear daughter, You must always write your whole name, and not your nickname "Choli." It is Who you are and Who you were named for. Thank you for writing me so often. It makes me happy to receive your letters. Sometimes I am happy for days afterward.

Did you say that? "Happy for days after"? Like when you love someone?

But your dear old dad cannot always answer you. I have been working hard and I have been ill. I have had dysentery again since I returned from El Salvador. My friend Dr. Maldonado thinks they have found a cure. Perhaps I won't bleed any more. When I am better I can come to see you for one or two days.

I am in the hospital, but I am all right. I am going to Denver next. Write to me there. Write me at once so that I receive your letter when I get there.

"At once." I almost jump out of my skin. My marrow remembers that one. You always said "at once," just like Mama in a hurry always said "I don't have any minutes."

The last time I went back to Coyoacán after one of my buying trips hundreds of books got lost. Others were sent to the wrong people. Some were returned. That's why I don't have much money right now. It is so difficult when things go wrong. The customs people kept many of my books because they said they were national patrimony. They wanted exorbitant duty for them so I had to send them back. Now, I must return money to the libraries and the collectors who paid for them.

Daddy, I long to help you. I long to be in Mexico City receiving the books, marking them for the right owners. Fixing all those mistakes. Lifting your burden.

Write to me in San Antonio, but do it at once or your letter will not be there when I arrive. I know you haven't forgotten me.

I see that you knew I loved you, and that maybe you needed me or even really loved me.

You mislaid a letter once. Darling, mail is important, and order, and tidiness. Confusion is dirty, and, worse than that, it leads to opportunities lost forever. How many people have lost money, and addresses of friends, and business orders, and your father among them. You must learn to be orderly. Your typing is good. I can find only a few errors.

The words *dirty, confusion, tidiness, lost forever* made me want to throw up. You were confusing and your life was not tidy and you are lost forever. You meant well. You said "darling."

My dearest friend.

This one is to his friend Harrington.

This old house. So empty. I can tell no one of the anguish, the loneliness, the longing to hear their voices. Elly and the children are in Jalisco and it is for good. Such a failure. Regret and guilt. You will understand. You have gone through it all. If I can lean on you now and then, I can bear this and stand alone again. I thought I was heroic. I was Don Quixote with a noble mission. I would conquer the demons for the love of my DulceEliana. Now I am more like Dostoyevsky, fearing madness, possessed of a great deal of hell, and working, working. Also trying to write, looking for something of heaven.

Daddy's words throw me. I am suddenly inside of him. His letter to another man is nothing like the ones he wrote to me. What about the librarian he was going to marry? Who wrote to her? Who told her about the fire? Did she come and find him gone?

Soledad: Are you angry with me for picking out faults? Don't be, darling.

Darling. Again. If you ever said it out loud to me, it must have been buried next to a sharp sliver of criticism because I don't remember it.

You write very well and fluently in English. Train your eye and your ear to recognize clear expression in talking and in writing. <u>Your own expression is the most important thing.</u>

Get along with Primo, and don't tease Amado.

You must know, children, that I often feel so sad that we cannot live together. I miss and love all three of you dearly. I should like to be with you all the time to help and guide you in so many ways.

But we can help each other in letters can't we?

CHICAGO

An old bookman took me home with him for dinner. He buys books that look beautiful. But he gets things wrong. He says, "Oh, Spencer—Spenser—What's the difference!" and "Francis Bacon, Roger Bacon. Well, maybe I did send the wrong one!"

I thought you would like that story.

He has asked me to stay and work with him to turn his collection of rare <u>bindings</u> into a collection of rare <u>books</u>! Someday you will laugh with me. The other day he got a letter from the Bey of Egypt—at the command of the King of Egypt, so he rushed over to me at my desk. He needed my help to fill this order!

What's the Bey of Egypt? I know. You will say I must look it up. I see your letterhead, the long lines of universities and libraries that bought books and manuscripts from you: Dartmouth, Duke, Indiana, Berkeley, Library of Congress, Harvard. I hear you saying them like the names of friends, "I must write to Purdue; I must answer Yale."

This note is to Mama. *I am sorry about the ring. I got it out of pawn, but, as I told you, I then did a very stupid thing with that woman. Well, you were right about her.*

My ring. Even before that woman took it, the ring was in and out of pawn. I wish I were wearing it today. I look for it everywhere I go. A Tiffany setting with four stones in a row.

MEXICO CITY

I am home again. Did you like your heart-shaped sewing basket from Tequisquiapan? By mistake my secretary bought nail scissors instead of sewing scissors. Can you use them and not be angry with your poor old Dad? You must not say "mad" when you mean angry. Madness is a terrible thing. Insanity. Look up these words in the dictionary that I sent you. Don't break its back when you open it. Be careful with your books so that they last you your lifetime.

Your secretary. I always thought the basket was a treasure you chose and bought for me yourself. I didn't know you even had a "secretary" who worked away from the house. She probably wasn't one. You just took her with you for a week-end. Maybe you didn't even know her.

My socks are coming. You can darn them with the needle and thread in your new basket.... Mother will show you how to do it neatly so it won't hurt Father's heels.

The socks. The blue wardrobe. The bottom drawer. The day you died Mama found me crying, trying to finish at least one, even though it was too late. I didn't do what you asked. I put it off. The socks had arrived in the mail, batch after batch, and I just put them away.

The tears come again now, against my knees. I want to hold you. Because I am flesh and blood. It is hard to have you only in my mind. I remember your smell of tobacco, your thumb yellow with nicotine. I want to lie with my whole body flat on your marble slab as if then I could feel you.

I cry quietly and rub the pebbles at the edge of the grave, rubbing the dirt where you are, pressing my fingers, my palms, my ache into the ground.

When I look up, the air is graying. I pick up the cards and letters and pile them in the basket. They have changed. They are no longer letters. They are my father. I kneel with my hands flat against the slab.

Goodbye, Papá. Goodbye, Father, Daddy.

I am leaving Mexico. When will I come to be with you again?

I hear you. Your answer comes to my face in a cool air. "We will separate now. You will leave. But do not grieve. We will never be far apart."

Whispering, I answer you, "I will go now, but do not grieve. We will never be far apart."

I get up and stand at the foot of the grave. I hold the basket tight against my heart.

Acknowledgments

I would like to express my grateful thanks to colleagues within the Santa Barbara writing community, and to writers within the Santa Barbara Writers Conference including Barnaby Conrad (author of *The Death of Manolete*), who read the bullfight chapter for technical accuracy, Bill Downey and Grace Rachow.

Extraordinary thanks go to the writers, artists and professors who read early drafts: Cynthia Anderson, Toni Lorien Bixby, Carrie Chu Brown, John Daniel, Barbara Deal, Karin Finell, Christina Forsythe, Phyllis Gebauer, Azul and Hedy Goodridge, John Goodridge, Susan Gulbransen, Alexandra Ingram, Matthew Ingram, Janis Jennings, Jacqueline Noel Langley, Sara Norquay, Dean Pananides, Tom Price, Phyllis and Georg Rauch, Sheila Tenold, Dan Tingle, Jim Tremaine and Agustín Velarde.

Special thanks to Tony Burton and also to my sister-in-law Ingrid Goodridge for making the manuscript available to Tony in Mexico.

I am deeply grateful to a small group of writer friends who read and critiqued the manuscript and supported the final stages of its creation: Susan Chiavelli, Fran Davis, Grace Rachow and Linda Stewart-Oaten.

Glossary of Spanish language words

abuelita	*grandmother*
adoberos	*brick makers*
agüilote	*tree bearing bitter black berries*
ajo	*garlic*
ajonjolí	*sesame*
albóndiga	*meatball*
aldaba	*iron latch*
alemanes	*Germans*
amado	*loved (Also proper name "Amado")*
ámatl	*paper made from fig bark*
¡Ándale!	*Hurry up!*
angelitos	*angels; babies who die unbaptized*
arte	*art*
ate	*fruit paste*
atole	*sweet flavored drink of finely ground corn*
avena	*oatmeal*
avenidas	*wide avenues*
banderillas	*barbed, decorated sticks used to weaken bull's neck*
barranca	*gorge*
barrera	*wooden barrier*
bebé	*baby*
beso	*kiss*
bibliófilo	*book lover, bibliophile*
bibliophilos	*love of books*
birote	*French bread rolls*
bismuto	*bismuth*
bistec	*steak*

blanquillos	eggs (local word)
bobo	silly
bolillos	French bread rolls
bóveda	arched brick ceiling
bracero	Mexican worker in US
bruta	brutish woman
caja	box
cajeta	paste, jelly
calaca	skeleton figure
caldo michi	catfish stew
callejón	alley
¡Cállese!	Shut up!
Camino Real	main or "royal" road
camposanto	cemetery
cangrejo	crab
cántaro	clay water jug
capilla	chapel
capirotada	bread pudding
capote	large bullfighting cape
casa	house
catalán	person or language of Cataluña, Spain
cenizas	ashes
centavos	cents
chapopote	tar
chayote	green pear-shaped vegetable
chayotera	stand for chayote vine
chicle	gum
chicuelina	bullfight move where bullfighter wraps himself in the cape
chilango (a)	nickname for person from Mexico City
chingar	to f—k
chiquihuite	basket woven of cane
cielito	term of endearment; little sky
cilantro	coriander
codeína	codeine
codices	illustrated books painted on fig bark
cojera	limp
comadre	close female friend; godmother
comal	griddle
conquistadores	Spanish conquerors
consentida	favorite

corazón	*heart*
corazoncito	*term of endearment; "little heart"*
corrida	*bullfight*
crucigrama	*crossword; crucigram*
cruda (la cruda)	*hangover*
cuñado (a)	*brother-in-law; sister-in-law*
curandero	*healer, shaman*
curioso	*clever*
dama	*lady*
de pilón	*not necessary, extra*
delegado	*deputy*
Deténganla	*Hold her!*
Diosito mío	*my God*
directo	*non-stop*
domingo	*Sunday*
doña	*old lady; lady; term of respect*
el centro	*town center or downtown*
el mal	*rabies*
el norte	*US*
epazote	*herb for cooking beans*
equipal	*leather chair*
estropajo	*hemp dish scrubber*
feria	*fair*
fideos	*angel hair pasta*
fu-man-chu	*something like "Shazam!"*
gracias	*thanks*
Gracias a Dios	*Thank God*
gringicana	*word invented by Soledad Paz to describe herself as hybrid*
gringo (a)	*popular name in Mexico for person from US*
gripe	*flu*
guajolote	*based on Náhuatl for turkey: guajolotl*
guamuchil	*acacia*
güera	*white-skinned woman*
guerreros	*warriors*
guitarrón	*large-bellied bass guitar*
hacienda	*large house within a plantation*
Hazte	*"Out of my way!"*
hijastra	*stepdaughter*
hipódromo	*horse-racing arena; horsetrack*
huaraches	*woven leather sandals*

hueso	bone
incunabula	earliest books printed on moveable type
jamaica	hibiscus
jarabe	syrup
jinete	cowboy
kinderheim	place for child care
kinderkennel	invented word for bad place for child care
lavadero	wash tub
lidia	bullfight; struggle; combat
Lo siento.	I'm sorry.
lunes	Monday
maderos	carpenters
Madre de Dios	Mother of God
maldita	evil woman
mamacita	term of endearment for little girl; vulgar: connotes intimacy
mamey	orange-fleshed melon
manta	muslin
masa	corn prepared for tortillas or tamales
matraca	a noisy twirling child's wooden toy; noisemaker
membrillo	quince
metate	flat grinding stone usually of volcanic rock
metlapil	long stone pestle
mijita	term of endearment; my little daughter
molcajete	stone mortar
mole	complex chile and chocolate sauce
molino	mill
monosabios	arena cleaners
morir	to die
mosco	fly
muerte	death
muleta	small, red cape used for end of bullfight
nahuales	humans in animal form; shapeshifters
náhuatl	language of the Náhuatl people including the Aztecs
nalgas	buttocks
nana	nursemaid
Negrita (o)	Blackie; often name of black dogs
nena	baby girl or little girl
nopales	cactus leaves or "pads"; chopped cactus
noticiero policíaco	police news
novio; novia	boyfriend; girlfriend

ocote	fat wood to start fires
ocurra teléfono	go to the phone
ojo	eye
ojo de agua	natural spring
padre	priest; father
Padre nuestro	Our Father
pajarilla	caterpillar; slang for penis
paleta	popsicle
pan	bread, loaf, bun; vulgar: connotative for female genitals
pan dulce	sweet breakfast pastry or bread
panocha	old-fashioned cone of brown sugar; vulgar for female genitals
pantalones	pants
papelito	scrap of paper
pase de la muerte	the pass of death in bullfighting
pedernal	volcanic stone
pedregal	lava bed
pena	shame or sorrow
pendejo	s.o.b.
penitente	one doing penance
pensión	inn or hotel
pero	but
perra	female dog; bitch
pescuezo	throat
petate	mat made of woven reeds
picante	spicy
piñata	decorated clay jug broken at children's parties
pinchi	stingy
pinole	sugary powdered corn
plátano macho	plantain
posada	inn; Christmas event searching for inn for Jesus' birth
preciosa	dear one
Primo	name implying first or best; proper name; also cousin
pucha	a circular loaf of bread; vulgar: slang for female private parts
puntilla	small dagger
puta	whore
querencia	favored spot; safe spot
queso	cheese
queso fresco	pressed farmer cheese
quinceañera	girl's fifteenth birthday fiesta
raspado	drink made with syrup poured over crushed ice

rebozo	*shawl*
rejoneador	*matador on horseback*
remedio	*cure*
ribereña	*person living at water's edge (cf. riviera)*
robachicos	*kidnappers*
rojo	*red*
Santa María	*Blessed Mary*
sarape	*blanket or mantle*
seña particular	*identifying mark*
señor	*similar to "Sir" or "Mister"*
sí	*yes*
Si Dios quiere	*God willing.*
sol	*sun; cheap section*
soledad	*solitude, loneliness, isolation*
soplador	*fan for charcoal fire*
suero	*rehydration fluid*
taco	*food wrapped in a tortilla; slang for female private parts*
tamal	*ground corn wrapped in corn husks*
taquito	*small taco*
tejolote	*pestle*
tepetate	*soft yellow stone*
tilma	*mantle*
tlacuache	*possum*
tlacuilo	*scribe*
tlatolli	*pictographs for Náhuatl words*
toro	*bull*
tripas	*intestines*
tule	*rushes or tule reeds*
tuna	*cactus fruit*
veinte	*20; a coin worth 20 centavos*
viejito	*little old man*
volute	*a large comma representing speech*
xócotl	*crabapple*
zafada	*crazy*
zócalo	*main square or plaza in a city, esp. Mexico City*

Personae

This memoir is based on real life incidents and characters. Some names and identifying details have been changed to protect the privacy of individuals. Noteworthy people in this book, besides famous Mexican artists Frida Kahlo, Diego Rivera, Juan O'Gorman and José Clemente Orozco, include:

Helen Kirtland. Soledad's mother. Gifted designer.
E. Read Goodridge. Soledad's father. Authority on rare books, including Latin American manuscripts.
Frans Blom. Danish-born explorer and archaeologist.
Anita Brenner. Author of *Idols Behind Altars* and *The Wind that Swept Mexico*.
Ernesto (Butterlin). Expressionist artist, born in Mexico, admired Pollock, ran art schools in Ajijic.
Otto Butterlin. Ernesto's older brother, born in Germany. Chemist by profession. Prolific expressionist painter by choice.
Mortimer Carl. Soledad's stepfather. Left Mexico and found success with murals and sculptures.
Renate Horney. Author, wife of cinematographer Alfredo Bolongaro-Crevenna.
Herbert Johnson. First Englishman to build a home in Ajijic.
Tina Modotti. Italian model, activist and photographer.
Helen O'Gorman. Wrote and illustrated *Mexican Flowering Trees and Plants*.
Armando Quesada (Big Salvador). Studied in Paris. Showed monumental work in Mexico City. Wife Li was a portraitist.
Gustav Regler. German poet (*The Great Crusade* and *The Owl of Minerva*).
Louis E. Stephens. Industrialist, patron of the arts and artists. Called Stevie.
Annette Stephens Nancarrow. Painter.
John Upton. Soledad's tutor. Accomplished translator and Renaissance Man.
Alexander von Wutenau (Architect father of Maia). Author of *Unexpected Faces in Ancient America*.

Author

Katie Goodridge Ingram was born in Mexico and lived there for many years, first in Mexico City and then in Ajijic, a village and artist colony on the shores of Lake Chapala in Jalisco.

She wrote her first story when she was nine and has continued to write ever since. Much of her writing was influenced by the fact that, as a child of immigrants to Mexico, she felt neither completely Mexican nor fully foreign.

In her articles for *Mexico City News* she followed two of her many interests: art and the cultural variety of people and villages in her area. In her gallery she exhibited the works of resident artists, of visitors to the area, and of newly discovered talent. When her children were small she co-founded a bilingual school with other parents. Her children are also bilingual and multi-cultural.

Her poetry and short stories have appeared in a variety of anthologies, most recently in *Solo Novo: Psalms of Cinder and Silt*. She is currently working on a novel set in the state of Michoacán.

To contact the author: info@sombrerobooks.com

Also from this publisher

Geo-Mexico: the geography and dynamics of modern Mexico

Lake Chapala Through the Ages: an anthology of travelers' tales

Mexican Kaleidoscope: myths, mysteries and mystique

Mexico by Motorcycle: An adventure story and guide

Western Mexico: a Traveler's Treasury

Dilemma, a novel

*New Worlds for the Deaf: the story of the pioneering
Lakeside School for the Deaf in rural Mexico*

sombrerobooks.com

Sombrero Books, Box 4, Ladysmith B.C. V9G 1A1, Canada

Made in the USA
San Bernardino, CA
16 February 2020